EQBAL AHMAD

STUART SCHAAR

EQBAL AHMAD

Critical Outsider in a Turbulent Age

COLUMBIA UNIVERSITY PRESS   *New York*

♛

Columbia University Press
Publishers Since 1893
New York   Chichester, West Sussex
cup.columbia.edu

Library of Congress Cataloging-in-Publication Data
Schaar, Stuart.
Eqbal Ahmad : critical outsider in a turbulent age / Stuart Schaar.
pages cm
Includes bibliographical references and index.
ISBN 978-0-231-17156-4 (cloth)—ISBN 978-0-231-17157-1(pbk.)—
ISBN 978-0-231-53992-0 (e-book)
1. Ahmad, Eqbal.   2. Political activists—United States—Biography.
3. Political activists—Pakistan—Biography.   4. Journalists—Biography.
5. Political scientists—Biography.   6. Pacifists—Biography.
7. World politics—1945–1989.   8. World politics—1989–   9. Islam and politics—
History—20th century.   10. Social change—History—20th century.   I. Title.
JC273.A49S34 2015
320.092—dc23
2015003669

COVER DESIGN: CHANG JAE LEE
COVER IMAGE: EQBAL AHMAD AT CORNELL UNIVERSITY, 1996. (REPRODUCED BY PERMISSION OF
DOHRA AHMAD)

TO THE MEMORY OF MY SISTER, LEONA (1934–2005),

AND TO THE GOOD TIMES WE SHARED

CONTENTS

PREFACE

THE SOURCES FOR THIS BOOK INCLUDE MANY CONVERSATIONS with Eqbal Ahmad over forty years, starting with the time we spent together from 1958 to 1964 at Princeton University, in New York City, and in North Africa, where we both conducted research for our doctorates. Strangely but wonderfully, I kept our written correspondence from this period, including carbon copies of the letters I sent him. They supply not only chronology but also anecdotes of events in our lives.

I again became very close to him during 1970 to 1972 as a result of his being indicted in the Harrisburg 7 case. As the initial treasurer of the Harrisburg Defense Committee in New York City, I was privy to some of the decisions made by the defendants and got to know all of them except Phil Berrigan, who was imprisoned. I also paid legal expenses for the lawyers on the case and in this way got to know Leonard Boudin and Ramsey Clark. I used to love going down to Leonard's office on East

Forty-second Street in Manhattan and shooting the breeze with this very interesting man. I even did research for him and was impressed with his profound knowledge of where I would find the legal cases he was looking for. He was filled with anecdotes and wonderful stories about a storybook life. Ramsey and his wife, Georgia, also became friends, and I visited their Greenwich Village apartment often while the committee was in New York City.

My personal archive, especially hand-written minutes of strategy meetings with the defendants and notes on my private meetings with Eqbal, provides an excellent record of events that transpired. It was the first time in my life that I worked with and socialized with radical priests and nuns. I have cherished that fantastic experience throughout my life. I remember vividly the bigger-than-life Irish Jesuit priest Joe O'Rourke, the quiet, but profound Jim Forest, the energetic and very smart John Akagi, the wonderful nuns in blue jeans Judy Peluso and Lillian Shirley, the personable Kathy Jones, the intense Tom Davidson, and many others.

In the 1980s, Eqbal and I were neighbors for parts of each year on the Upper West Side of Manhattan. We saw each other often, organized together, wrote articles about North Africa together, and had great fun. I didn't keep many written records of those years, but I have vivid memories of conversations, meetings, visitors who poured through our lives, and especially the evenings spent over long dinners with scintillating people and fine food. We stayed in touch by letter and then email when we traveled abroad, remained close friends, and shared a great deal.

Through him I visited India and Pakistan in 1980 and returned to Pakistan in 2004, a few years after he died. I met his wonderful friends and relatives there and was astounded by the hospitality I received simply because I was Eqbal's good friend. I was overwhelmed by their friendship and cherish the memories of being with them. They told me much about Eqbal that is not written anywhere, providing me with oral sources that are precious. Writing this book was a wonderful experience because it brought back extraordinary memories of exceptional times.

ACKNOWLEDGMENTS

MANY PEOPLE HELPED ME TO DO THE RESEARCH FOR THIS book. First, Eqbal's family, especially his wife and daughter, Julie Diamond and Dohra Ahmad, shared a great deal with me besides their friendship over many years. They granted me permission to quote extensively from Eqbal's papers at Hampshire College's Johnson Library and to use photographs in that collection. His sister Sharfa Jahani Khanum in Canada gave me invaluable information about his birth date and childhood in India. The writer Radha Kumar, with whom Eqbal lived at the end of his life, provided insights into his activities in the United States, Pakistan, and India. Besides friendship, his nephews Zuli and Iftikhar gave me precious information about their uncle. So did his nieces and nephews Hajra Ahmad (Hajo), Pervez Hoodbhoy, Nasra Ahmad, Najeeb Omar, Kavita Ramdas, and Cindy Colter. His sister-in-law Husnara Ahmad was a witness to his early years and invaluable in contextualizing his early life in India and Pakistan. His nephew Kamran Asdar Ali was especially helpful.

His many friends in Lahore, Islamabad, and Karachi welcomed me into their homes and offices because they knew that Eqbal and I were close friends, and they treated me with great hospitality. They include Arshad Durrani, Imran Hamid, Mubashir Hassan, Asma Jahangir, Raza Kazim, Zia Mian, Jugnu Mohsin, Rani and Kemal Mumtaz, Abdul Hamid Nayyar, I. A. Rahman, Najam Sethi, Parveen and Zaur Zaidi, and Nasim Zehra.

Eqbal's friends Yogesh Chandrani, Richard Falk, Nadia Guessous, Amal and Nubar Hovsepian, Adam and Arlie Hochschild, Iqbal Riza, Adele Simmons, and Cora and Peter Weiss shared their knowledge of him with me. Marvin E. Gettleman and my friend in Morocco, Jim Miller, either suggested some changes in my text or discussed some of the sections of the book with me, helping to sharpen what I had written. Niels Hooper, editor at the University of California Press, pressed me to develop a thematic approach to the book and contributed greatly to clarifying points. Anne Routen, senior editor at Columbia University Press, backed the project and guided it through to its publication. I owe many thanks to Irene Pavitt of Columbia University Press and freelance copy editor Annie Barva, who did an excellent job of copyediting the text. Two anonymous readers for Columbia University Press made excellent suggestions to improve the manuscript. I am grateful for their advice, which I have followed closely. My literary agent, Edite Kroll, provided necessary encouragement, advice, and friendship.

Susan A. Dayall and Jim Jones, the archivists at Hampshire College's Johnson Library, where the Eqbal Ahmad Papers are stored, guided me through his voluminous papers. Many thanks to both of them.

Finally, I owe thanks to those close to me in Morocco, where I live, who encouraged me to persevere in this project: Dede and the late Mohammed Guessous, Fatema Mernissi, and my Tunisian friend Mahdi Sghair.

EQBAL AHMAD

INTRODUCTION

EQBAL AHMAD (1930?–1999),[1] A BRILLIANT PROFESSOR AND political analyst on the global left, saw trends developing in international relations that few others recognized. In the syndicated newspaper columns he wrote in the last decades of his life and some four million people read weekly, he offered his views on myriad subjects. He amazed his readers with predictions of future events that later transpired, making him into a guru for some and an uncanny analyst for others. Six examples suffice to illustrate his perspicacity, astuteness, and originality.

1. Years before it happened, he predicted the chaos that would follow if and when the U.S. military invaded Iraq and overthrew Saddam Hussein. An extract from a December 20, 1998, essay that he wrote for the Karachi newspaper *Dawn* demonstrates his special skill. In a prescient analysis, he wrote:

Dictators rarely leave behind them an alternative leadership or a viable mechanism for succession. Saddam Hussein is not an exception. Disarray and confusion shall certainly ensue if he is eliminated. Iraq is a greatly divided country, with the rebellious Kurds dominant in the north and Shias in the south. With the one linked to the Kurds in Turkey and the other to Shiite Iran, their ambitions in post-Saddam Iraq can cause upheavals in the entire region. It is not clear that the United States has either the will or the resources to undertake the remaking of Iraq. If it does not, the scramble over Iraq may ignite protracted warfare involving Turkey, Iran, Syria, Saudi Arabia, Israel, Kurd, Arab, Shia, Sunni, and, in one form or another, the United States.

The fundamentalist brand of Islamism may thrive in such an environment. Islamism will find at least two major sponsors in the struggle for Iraq: Iran borders on southern Iraq, which is home to the most sacred shrines of Shia Islam and is populated largely by Shia Muslims.

Iran's influence may easily fill the post-Saddam vacuum, a development Saudi Arabia, the sheikhdoms of the Gulf, and the US shall find intolerable. Since none of America's conservative Arab allies like Arab nationalism . . . they may counter Iran by promoting Sunni fundamentalism. Sectarian groups thrive in this brand of Islamism. Like Afghanistan today, Iraq may turn into a battleground of war parties backed by several states.[2]

Eqbal wrote this essay a year before his death and five years before the United States, joined by a handful of other states, attacked and conquered Iraq. An insurgency then ensued, which intensified and continued after Saddam Hussein's execution in 2006. As Eqbal predicted, Iraq faced civil war that its neighbors became involved in either directly or through internal proxies.

2. In Afghanistan, he saw the detrimental aftereffects of the U.S. organizing an international jihadist crusade there against the Soviet Union in the 1980s and predicted that blowback from those events would come to haunt the West in years to come. Before anyone else, he sensed that Osama bin Laden (1957–2011), the founder of al-Qaeda and initially

America's ally, would become its nemesis after the Russians withdrew from Afghanistan. In perhaps the best of his public lectures at the end of his life, before a packed house at the University of Colorado at Boulder on October 12, 1998, Eqbal analyzed the new U.S. foreign-policy paradigm of antiterrorism and predicted that bin Laden would turn against the United States. He did this well before al-Qaeda's attacks on the World Trade Center in downtown New York City and the Pentagon in Washington, D.C., on September 11, 2001. "Terrorists change," he argued.

> The terrorist of yesterday is the hero of today, and the hero of yesterday becomes the terrorist of today. In a constantly changing world of images, we have to keep our heads straight to know what terrorism is and what it is not. . . . Officials don't define terrorists because definitions involve a commitment to analysis, comprehension, and adherence to some norms of consistency. . . . The absence of definition does not prevent officials from being globalistic. They may not define terrorism, but they can call it a menace to good order, a menace to the moral values of Western civilization, a menace to humankind. Therefore, they can call for it to be stamped out worldwide. . . . The official approach to terrorism claims not only global reach, but also a certain omniscient knowledge. They claim to know where terrorists are, and therefore where to hit. . . . The official approach eschews causation. They don't look at why people resort to terrorism. . . . [There is] the need for the moral revulsion we feel against terror to be selective. We are to denounce the terror of those groups which are officially disapproved. But we are to applaud the terror of those groups of whom officials do approve. . . . The dominant approach also excludes from consideration the terrorism of friendly governments.[3]

Eqbal met bin Laden in 1986 at the moment that the Saudi was an American ally, recruiting jihadists to fight against the Soviet Union in Afghanistan. Bin Laden turned against the United States in 1990, Eqbal pointed out to his audience, when the United States, in its buildup to attack Iraq, sent troops into Saudi Arabia, the home of the Kaaba in Mecca, where non-Muslims are not welcome. Just as bin Laden fought to get the Russians out of Afghanistan, by 1991 he wanted to get the Americans out of Arabia. In another venue, Eqbal described why bin Laden became an enemy of the United States:

> [Bin Laden] was socialized by the CIA and trained by the Americans to believe deeply that when a foreigner comes into your land, you become violent. Bin Laden is merely carrying out the mission to which he committed with America earlier. Now he is carrying it out against America because now America, from his point of view, is occupying his land. That's all. He grew up seeing Saudi Arabia being robbed by Western corporations and Western powers. He watched these Saudi princes, this one-family state, handing over the oil resources of the Arab people to the West. Up until 1991, he had only one satisfaction that his country was not occupied. There were no American or French or British troops in Saudi Arabia. Then even that small pleasure was taken away from him during the Gulf War and its aftermath.[4]

Elsewhere Eqbal wrote that "for him [bin Laden], America has broken its word. The loyal friend has betrayed him. Now they're going to go get you. They're going to do a lot more. These are the chickens of the Afghanistan war coming home to roost."[5]

Eqbal described bin Laden as a tribal person who felt abandoned by the Americans after they had supported him and the jihadist movement in Afghanistan. Once the Russians withdrew, so did the Americans, losing interest in their once loyal allies. Working on the tribal principles of loyalty and revenge, bin Laden turned against the United States when it jettisoned the jihadists. Years before September 11, 2001, Eqbal explained the contradictions in the U.S. antiterrorist policies, educating as he spelled out how the new paradigm had developed and replaced the Cold War as the new integrating principle of U.S. foreign policy:

> American operatives went about the Muslim world recruiting for the *jihad* in Afghanistan. This whole phenomenon of *jihad* as an interna-

tional armed struggle did not exist in the Muslim world since the tenth century. It was brought back into being, enlivened, and pan-Islamized by the American effort. The United States saw in the war in Afghanistan an opportunity to mobilize the Muslim world against communism. So the United States recruited mujahideen from all over the Muslim world. I saw planeloads of them arriving from Algeria, the Sudan, Saudi Arabia, Egypt, Jordan, and Palestine. These people were brought in, given an ideology, told that the armed struggle is a virtuous thing to do, and the whole notion of *jihad* as an international, pan-Islamic terrorist movement was born.[6]

3. Participating in a delegation of peace activists to meet Iranian revolutionaries after they forced the shah to flee in early 1979, Eqbal used Persian, which he had perfected at Princeton University, to converse with the new leaders of the country and listen to their plans for the future. He hogged the conversation, and some members of the U.S. delegation were furious with him for doing so. But in the end he was the only one, based on what he heard, to predict that Iran would become a highly authoritarian state, with a centralized religious command backed by machine-gun-equipped revolutionary guards and a more pliant governmental structure without significant power.[7]

4. Eqbal devoted a great deal of energy to defending Palestinian rights and included references to their plight in much of his writing and public lectures. His family in India and Pakistan had sensitized him at an early age to the suffering of others. His older brother Zafar, who raised him, became a Buddhist and stopped eating meat at home in reaction to the ethnic cleansing of Jews and Gypsies in Europe starting in 1938. The Palestinians appreciated Eqbal's solidarity and invited him often to address their audiences. Because of his outspoken defense of the Palestinian cause, no major U.S. university would hire him for a permanent job.[8] He traveled to the Middle East to meet with Palestinian leaders on many occasions. In a memorandum he wrote for Palestinian leaders Yasser Arafat (1929–2004) and Abu Jihad (also known as Khalil al-Wazir, 1935–1988) in 1980 while visiting Beirut with Edward W. Said (1935–2003),

Eqbal "sadly forecast the quick defeat of PLO [Palestine Liberation Organization] forces in South Lebanon" by the Israeli armed forces.[9] Eqbal told the two PLO leaders that their people could never defeat Israel militarily and advocated the organization of massive campaigns of civil disobedience and large-scale nonviolent actions to shake Israel's legitimacy and fundamentally challenge its occupation of Palestinian territories.

5. Eqbal rejected analysis that placed the Cold War as the central feature of the world after 1945. He was one of the few political analysts to view the Cold War in terms of what it meant to its Third World victims. He derided the dominant viewpoint that it was a struggle between forces of freedom and democracy on the one side and totalitarianism on the other, and he raised questions about the validity of the notion that we should be grateful that the world was spared a third world war as a result of the threat of mutual nuclear annihilation between the two superpowers. Making an original contribution to international relations theory, he argued that a large part of Asia, Africa, and Latin America actually did experience a third world war as a result of the violence brought to bear on it during the Cold War. Eqbal lamented that frequent bloody regional and proxy wars took their toll wherein "an estimated 21 million people died, uncounted millions were wounded, and more than a hundred million were rendered refugees by what have been variously described as the limited, invisible, forgotten, and covert wars of the 1945–1990 period."[10] For Eqbal, the defining features of the post–World War II period consisted of national liberation struggles, revolutionary warfare, and counterinsurgency as people in the global South outside the United States and the Soviet Union faced constant assaults.

6. More than a decade before the outbreak of the Arab Spring at the end of 2010, Eqbal understood that young people would spearhead a revolt in the Middle East and North Africa that would challenge the old dictatorial order. In an interview he gave to David Barsamian that was published in the November 1998 issue of *Progressive* magazine, "Osama bin Laden Is a Sign of Things to Come," he saw the inevitability of a large-scale Arab uprising:

The Arabs are, at the moment, an extremely humiliated, frustrated, beaten, and insulted people. If you look at the situation from the standpoint of the Arab as a whole, this is a most beleaguered mass of 200 million people. What is actually uniting them at the moment is a sense of common loss, common humiliation.

This people has only two choices now, as its young people see it: It's either to become active, fight, die, and recover its lost dignity, lost sovereignties, lost lands, or to become slaves.[11]

This statement offers an explanation of why so many Arabs resorted to terrorism, but it also helps us fathom why so many people in the Arab world took to the streets to bring down their dictatorial regimes in the second decade of the twenty-first century.

This is only a sampling of Eqbal's insights, which gained him a reputation as an uncanny political analyst who saw trends emerging before any of his peers. Moreover, his mind was quirky, and you could never predict how he would react to issues, making interactions with him exciting events.

Eqbal's Wide Contacts

The combination of originality, intelligence, and fearlessness in confronting power drew to Eqbal some of the major intellectuals on the left and prominent figures in a variety of fields in the United States, western Europe, Africa, Latin America, and South Asia. He socialized with writers from around the world and learned from them. He was one of Edward Said's closest friends in New York City. He was also friends with Noam Chomsky (b. 1928), David Dellinger (1915–2004), Leonard Boudin (1912–1989), Howard Zinn (1922–2010), Richard Falk (b. 1930), Ibrahim Abu-Lughod (1929–2001), Janet Abu-Lughod (1928–2013), and many others. He corresponded with leaders of the international Left, and on the Indian–Pakistani subcontinent he knew and befriended the most gifted intellectuals, while political figures and military leaders courted him for advice.

He also simultaneously served as a coeditor of the British journal *Race & Class*, joined the editorial boards of the Paris monthly *L'Economiste du Tiers Monde* (1972–1983) and the mass-circulation French fortnightly *Afrique-Asie* (1968–1983) published in Paris, and helped establish *Pakistan Forum* (1969–1977) but broke with its editors over ideological and personal issues. In 1979, he was a guest columnist for the *New York Times*. He later contributed to the *Los Angeles Times*, the *Nation*, and the Parisian periodical *Le Monde Diplomatique*. At the end of his life, he wrote weekly columns for the Pakistani daily newspaper *Dawn* and was a contributor to the London-based newspaper *al-Hayat* and Cairo's *al-Ahram Weekly*.

Critical Outsider and Witness

As a Pakistani spending most of his adulthood after 1957 in the United States, Eqbal lived on the frontiers of several worlds, which allowed him to see issues from new vantage points.[12] Coming to the United States as a nationalist with left leanings, meaning that he had favored partition of India and the creation of Pakistan and had studied Marx and Lenin without becoming a Leninist, he gradually shed his nationalist identity and became a public intellectual with a global vision. Because he reached maturity outside the frameworks of Pakistan's social and political constraints, his place on the margins of different worlds freed him from the traps that surround those who work and live locally. He therefore approached the world with different assumptions than others. There lay his originality.

Much has been written about outsiders, exiles, strangers, and foreigners and their creativity or roles as gadflies. The sociologist George Simmel (1858–1918); the philosopher and writer Colin Wilson (1931–2013), a twenty-four-year-old British angry young man; the writers Richard Wright (1908–1960), James Baldwin (1924–1987), and Albert Camus (1913–1960); and the literary critic Edward W. Said (1935–2003), to name just a few, made the "otherness" inherent in alienation and exile a prototype for new insights, substantive change, and existential angst.[13] More than a decade ago Judith M. Brown (b. 1944) wrote about Mohandas Gandhi (1869–1948) in terms of his outsider status following his return to India from South Africa, where he had learned mass organizing and developed his oppositional strategies to colonial power.[14]

C. Wright Mills (1916–1962), the innovative and influential sociologist on the left, has been labeled a "radical nomad" because he moved tirelessly from one issue to another without settling down, which thereby helped him see reality in ways different from his scholarly peers.[15] Mills, like Eqbal, bore witness by speaking out against injustice, calling attention to wrongs, and revealing hard truth to power.[16] Eqbal went further than Mills in that he and a few others before him—such as the peace activist, labor organizer, and one of the initiators of the nonviolent civil rights movement A. J. Mustie (1885–1967) and members of both the Fellowship of Reconciliation, founded in 1916, and the War Resister's League, established in 1923—helped secularize the Christian concept of witness and shaped it into a powerful tool for social change.[17] Mustie, the tireless organizer, had tried a wide variety of ideologies, including Trotskyism, a fair sampling of Christian sects, pacificism, and so on, but even though early in his life he joined the clergy, he bore witness not to evangelize or to get people to become Christians but rather to obstruct the war machine and build an antiwar movement.[18] David T. Dellinger, the editor of *Liberation* magazine and, like Mustie, an indefatigable peace activist, likewise radicalized the nonviolent resistance movement and willingly went to jail to prove his antiwar convictions.

Although the nonevangelical direct-action civil disobedience movement began in the United States way before the 1960s, Eqbal brought a fresh view of Gandhi's strategy and tactics to the U.S. antiwar movement, mixed with a critique informed by the teachings of the 1913 Bengali Noble laureate Rabindranath Tagore (1861–1941), which I discuss in some detail later in this introduction. Eqbal promoted peaceful nonviolent actions (such as provoking mass arrests, staging sit-ins, disrupting the everyday order of things) to protest escalating wars and manifestations of gross injustice.

As Don Will (1949–2014), the Pakistani's late friend, explained, "Eqbal reversed the narrative of the Holocaust, by advocating marches and ship sailings of Palestinians to walk and sail back home and calling for them to organize a green, peaceful march from Jordan and .Lebanon into Palestine."[19] Eqbal argued that the Palestinians should claim that

> they are committed to peace. You are making war. We do not want to use violence against you. Peacefully we will march against you. We will sit in. We will clog the roads, start a full scale movement, and discipline the Palestinians not even to throw stones, *intifada* style, because Israelis will use and justify bullets against stones. They will use soldiers against children. Don't even give them that. . . . Israel will divide . . . as a society the way Americans divided [over Martin Luther King Jr.'s nonviolent movement]. I would keep it divided until it makes peace.[20]

As Cora Weiss (b. 1934), one of the founding members of Women's Strike for Peace as well as the president of the Hague Appeal for Peace and Eqbal's friend, wrote to me, "Eqbal's legacy is significant. His lectures and articles will be read by generations to come. Facing an impasse, we still ask, what would Eqbal have done?"[21]

Growing Up Surrounded by High-Muslim Culture

Eqbal's upbringing in homes filled with high-Muslim culture gave him special social skills and charm rarely found in North America. His family's progressive politics brought him out of the feudal age into modern times. His aristocratic bearing was reflected in his etched features, shock of black hair, piercing eyes, and special charisma and magnetism. But instead of exuding aristocratic aloofness, he was taught by his oldest brother's down-to-earth decency to be accessible and to greet friends and strangers alike with great warmth. His elite status as a descendant of a clan that allegedly participated in the conquest of northern India was reflected in the Persian miniatures that lined the walls of his homes, the fine carpets that he selected with great care to cover his floors, and the gourmet food that he prepared and served with just the right mix of spices.

Like the princes of old, he established a salon in New York City where intellectuals, journalists, novelists, poets, and political figures from around the world paid court. In this way, he kept up with events with a depth that few newspapers and books could provide. Besides being well informed and blessed with great analytical and synthetic skills, he would spellbind those hearing him talk about these events, whether around a dinner table, in a classroom, or in a rally of thousands of people.

These qualities only enhanced his position as an outsider because he was able to package his ideas in accessible form, which lessened the shock of their originality. He disarmed many of his critics through his sheer brilliance and charm. His quirkiness worked in his favor, for people who heard or read him came to expect the unexpected from him.

A Progressive Family

His mother and father, progressive landowners in Bihar, India, joined the Congress Party. In 1937, Mohandas Gandhi came to their home region after communal riots there threatened to turn into civil war. The bigger-than-life leader organized a children's march composed of Muslim and Hindu youth to demonstrate that the communities could live together in peace. Eqbal's mother convinced Gandhi to take her young son, then around seven years old, on the march, which brought Eqbal into close proximity with the Mahatma for several months. Eqbal told me years later that he hated Gandhi's asceticism and was not at all happy on the march because he himself had grown up surrounded by the trappings of wealth and culture, ate elaborately prepared meals, and ran free within his family's compound. My friend could not stand the invariably boiled vegetables served without spices or sauces, seasoned only with lemon, that Gandhi and the kids ate daily. Yet he confided to one of his closest Pakistani friends that even as a child he knew that he was in the presence of a great man, and later in his life that man's ideas helped shape his adherence to the ideals of nonviolence and civil disobedience as tools of the weak against the powerful. Rabindranath Tagore, the polymath antinationalist whom Eqbal as a child saw on his death bed in New Delhi in the 1940s, his gigantic white beard spread over his pillow, also had great influence in shaping Eqbal's choices as he matured and began to understand the limitations of narrow nationalism.

Eqbal had a deep moral sense that revolted against injustice wherever he saw it. He took up unpopular causes, such as defending Palestinian rights and saving Bosnians from ethnic cleansing, that others would not touch. If he felt that something was right, he championed the cause, wherever the chips fell. The search for justice rather than for personal rewards drew him to unpopular causes, even if it meant that he would suffer personally as a consequence of doing so.

His family in India and Pakistan where he was born and grew up shaped his moral sense. His father, a lawyer, was killed in 1937, while Eqbal cuddled next to him on the family's veranda, by peasants working for neighboring landlords who desired to punish him for defending exploited peasants in Bihar. His oldest brother became his surrogate father, and he too had a great moral force that also rubbed off on the young man. As the tax inspector of the newly created Pakistan, he was incorruptible and scrupulously honest in his dealings with tax dodges. Eqbal's mother, like Tagore, influenced his rejection of narrow nationalism in favor of an all-inclusive cosmopolitanism. As a young man, Eqbal was also inspired by his teachers at Foreman Christian College in Lahore. By his own admission, Princeton University's graduate school and the Firestone Library's remarkably rich collections fashioned him into the cosmopolitan intellectual that he became. "Princeton was intellectually . . . formative because it threw at me ideas and concepts that I had to confront and react to. I think intellectually my oppositional outlook . . . developed in Princeton. This [the late 1950s and early 1960s] was a time of conformity in America, and that conformity was very frightening."[22]

Eqbal's Notoriety

Eqbal became notorious beginning in January 1971 when President Richard Nixon's Justice Department indicted him and several U.S. Catholic priests, laymen, and nuns for plotting to kidnap National Security Adviser Henry Kissinger (b. 1923). They were also accused of conspiring to blow up heating ducts in tunnels underneath government buildings in Washington, D.C., and to raid U.S. army draft boards in several cities in order to ruin selective-service records. Over a period of fourteen months, Eqbal's and his indicted "co-conspirators'" names and photos appeared on television and on the front pages of major newspapers and magazines in the United States and overseas. To defend them, Eqbal, on the advice of Richard Falk, an international lawyer and then professor at Princeton University,[23] recruited one of the best lawyers in the United States, Leonard Boudin. Leonard, a renowned lawyer on the political left, had previously represented the great African American singer and actor Paul Robeson (1898–1976), and he would later defend Daniel Ellsberg (b. 1931), who leaked the Pentagon Papers. Former attorney general Ramsey Clark (b. 1927) led the legal team, seconded by the politician Paul O'Dwyer (1907–1998), who later became the president of the New York City Council. While out on bail, the defendants, initially known as the Harrisburg 8 and then as the Harrisburg 7 (see figure 7), after the conservative capital of Pennsylvania where their trial took place,[24] turned their case into an anti–Vietnam War indictment of the Nixon administration.

In a survey of the jury after the trial ended, the Harrisburg Defense Committee, which had been organized to raise funds and spread the defendants' antiwar sentiments,[25] discovered that the overwhelming majority of the dozen jurors were won over by the extraordinary clarity and expertise of Leonard Boudin, who, of all members of the legal team, had impressed them the most.[26] Leonard, with high drama, mesmerized the jurors, gained their sympathy, and demonized the Federal Bureau of Investigation (FBI) agents assigned to follow Eqbal when describing how two of those agents had sat smugly in their car and watched without intervening while Eqbal was mugged nearby.

The Defense Committee survey also discovered that one of the female jurors "would never have sent her favorite priest to jail." She had fallen in love with one of the clerical defendants during the trial, she responded, when asked why she felt that way.[27] The case ended on April 5, 1972, after ten of the jurors voted for acquittal on the main charges, with Father Phillip Berrigan (1923–2002) and Sister Elizabeth McAlister (b. 1940) found guilty of smuggling letters illegally into and out of Lewiston Prison, where the priest was already detained.[28]

Although Eqbal had previously lived in New York City, where his wife since 1969, writer and teacher Julie Diamond (b. 1944) had grown up,[29] at the time of the arrest and trial they resided in Chicago. He worked there as a research fellow for the liberal Adlai Stevenson Institute (1968–1972). On January 12, 1971, FBI agents arrested Eqbal in his office. Constance Perrin, an institute fellow, gave the following account to the press:

> Two men entered a row of three offices. . . . The two didn't identify themselves. They just asked, "Where is Mr. Ahmad's office?" I didn't ask them who they were. We're very trusting here. They came out of the office with him. He called to me, said, 'Would you call these people and tell them what has happened?' [Ahmad then gave the names of two people.] I asked the men where they were taking him. They said, "We'll be at the Federal Building." Eqbal said, "I don't know what the charges are." One of the men said, "The charge is conspiracy to commit kidnapping." When the men took him away, they had him in handcuffs.[30]

Eqbal spent the night in jail, had a hearing the next day, and was released after his close friends Prexy Nesbitt (b. 1944), later famous for being a principal leader of the Divest from South Africa campaign and other liberation struggles relating to the U.S. civil rights movement and southern Africa, and the Palestinian Northwestern University professor Ibrahim Abu-Lughod helped raise $6,000 toward a $60,000 bail, assuring his provisional liberty. Once free, Eqbal went on the offensive and spoke out before a barrage of reporters against the ongoing Vietnam War (see figure 6), calling the charges "ridiculous" and hoping that a court case would not distract from his and others' efforts in opposing the war "and bring[ing] the truth to the public."[31]

As soon as I heard of the indictment and his arrest, I called his and Julie's many New York friends to my Manhattan apartment. We formed a defense committee, which joined forces with some lay Catholics and other antiwar activists as well as radical priests and nuns in blue jeans who grouped around the famous Berrigan brothers. These clerics had become renowned for breaking into draft boards and pouring blood on selective-service records. Reverend Phil Berrigan, a Josephite whose order served the African American community, was the first North American Catholic priest to go to jail as a political prisoner.[32] He spent eleven years altogether in prison for actions he initiated in opposition to war. After he had served in the military during World War II, resistance to war and militarism had become an integral part of his life. Incarcerated since early May 1970, he remained imprisoned this time for three years. His older brother, Daniel (b. 1921), a prize-winning poet, Jesuit priest, and Eqbal's friend from Cornell University who had previously worked as the assistant director of the campus's United Religious Work organization, was on the run for four hectic months in order to avoid arrest. He was then one of the FBI's "ten most wanted fugitives," evading more than two hundred FBI agents who sought to incarcerate him for his participation in a draft board raid. Eqbal had worked behind the scenes with some well-known antiwar activists to hide Dan in middle-class homes,[33] moving the priest continuously to prevent the FBI from catching him.[34] As part of a wide network extending from the East Coast to the Midwest, Eqbal recruited me to hide Dan in a Manhattan apartment that I had borrowed. Eqbal and his associates had Dan appear at antiwar rallies, where FBI officers waited for the fugitive to show up so that they could take him into custody. On all occasions, just as the agents rose to accost Dan, the antiwar activists whisked the priest away and made him disappear. The director of the FBI, the all-powerful J. Edgar Hoover (1895–1972), had to be furious that a group of radical civilians continuously outwitted his seasoned officers. Putting an end to Dan Berrigan's freedom and cracking the organization that supported his life on the run must have become an obsession for the FBI director.

The occasion for Hoover to act presented itself when a paid FBI informant, Boyd Douglas Jr., a prisoner allowed to attend Bucknell University while serving time in Lewiston Prison, where Phil Berrigan was locked up, acted as a courier for the priest.[35] During those furloughs, Douglas carried letters to Phil from his secret love, Sister Elizabeth McAlister (b. 1940). Liz, as friends called her, had spent the night of

August 17, 1970, at Eqbal's in-laws' country house in Weston, Connecticut. There she joined for dinner Eqbal and Sister Jogues Egan (1919–1998), a college administrator, and Ann Davidon (1925–2004) and Bill Davidon (1927–2013)—both antiwar activists, she a playwright and he a professor of physics at Philadelphia's Haverford College.[36] This was six days after Dan had been arrested by FBI agents on Block Island, Rhode Island.[37] Despite Eqbal's objections that Dan not go there because he thought that the property on which Dan would be staying would be under FBI surveillance, the Jesuit priest, exhausted from being continuously on the run, wanted to escape to a wilderness sanctuary belonging to his close friends to breathe some fresh air and wander outdoors.

Unbeknownst to Eqbal, Liz had disclosed Dan's presence on Block Island in a letter she had written to Phil, which she gave to Boyd Douglas for delivery in the prison. J. Edgar Hoover saw the letter and immediately dispatched a Coast Guard cutter filled with FBI agents to the island to arrest the fugitive. After Eqbal learned about Phil and Liz's foolishness in writing all these details—including a conversation at his in-laws' house, Phil's reactions to the idea of a citizen's arrest of Henry Kissinger, his distrust of Eqbal, and now Dan's whereabouts (all to be discussed later)—he was furious over what they had done. He told his fellow defendants that the only thing that should be sent to anyone in jail were fresh oranges—no letters, nothing that could be traced and used against them. But the damage was already done.

By then Eqbal had reached the conclusion that draft board raids had become "ritualistic" and counterproductive and should be stopped. He argued with his codefendants that "they needed a moratorium on small group-based actions in which activists burst into selective service offices, destroy records, and have no lasting effect." Dan Berrigan agreed with him, telling the defendants that "both he and his brother Phil would not do such actions any more since they did not want to put their best people behind bars."[38] Eqbal proposed that they should organize large-scale acts of civil disobedience, such as May Day actions in Washington, D.C., in which hundreds, even thousands, might be arrested.[39] By early 1972, he publicly stated that draft board raids "had lost their political efficacy and

became means for 'personal salvation,' manifestations of 'American in-
dividualism and obsession with heroism.' "[40] Eqbal was interested in
building a mass movement of protest against the war in Vietnam and less
interested in creating or sustaining small resistance communities that
could not change quickly the way Americans viewed the war.

Each time more Catholic priests and nuns were caught raiding draft
boards and turned to the Defense Committee for funds to bail them out,
Eqbal became angry that scarce money needed for their trial had to be
diverted for what he now considered to be ego-fulfilling reasons. But
many priests and nuns who had joined the Catholic resistance community remained single-minded and thought that such raids were still necessary. The need to keep unity intact forced the defendants to refrain from
overtly criticizing draft board raids.

The So-Called Conspiracy

Liz McAlister and Jogues Egan had driven to Connecticut from New
York City on August 17, 1970, to discuss the consequences of Dan's cap-
ture. Eqbal proposed that they make a citizen's arrest of Henry Kissinger
and interrogate him, perhaps filming the whole event, and then release
him. As Jogues, the white-haired administrator, later confided, she heard
the idea with "shock and disbelief and treated the entire conversation . . .
as an exercise in fantasy, which she never took seriously."[41] Ann Davidon rejected the scheme out of hand on the grounds that "kidnapping"
could easily lead to violence, which she opposed as a pacifist. Yet Liz
wrote a letter to Phil Berrigan in which she recounted with grave seriousness the conversation two days earlier, and it was delivered to the prisoner on August 19 by way of Douglas.[42] This FBI informant forwarded a
copy of the letter to his handlers in the agency. J. Edgar Hoover had
earlier received a copy of another letter from Phil Berrigan to Liz relating that Phil and another priest had previously visited a seven-mile-long
system of steam tunnels that supplied heat to seventy-five government
buildings in the nation's capital to contemplate the feasibility of upping
the ante in the antiwar struggle by blowing up the steam tunnels to

disrupt the work of the nation's bureaucrats. During the Harrisburg trial, Douglas testified that Phil Berrigan had told him that he and another person had posed as underground electricians and entered the tunnels to determine whether such an action was possible.[43] Again, according to Douglas, Father Joseph Wenderoth (b. 1936), one of the alleged co-conspirators, had told him that they had chosen George Washington's birthday, February 22, 1971, as the target date for the explosions.[44] Hoover tied the two disparate events together and immediately saw the possibility of cracking open and putting an end to the radical Catholic opposition to the Indo-China War. By juxtaposing the threatened kidnapping and the so-called conspiracy to dynamite the steam tunnels, Hoover recommended putting the leaders of the Catholic Left on trial along with a Muslim foreigner, the Pakistani antiwar activist Eqbal Ahmad. In this way, the FBI director could tie them up in lengthy litigation. In November 1970, before the defendants were indicted, Hoover told a U.S. Senate subcommittee that the FBI had uncovered an "anarchist" plot to blow up heating tunnels in Washington and to kidnap President Nixon's national-security adviser. Even if the state lost its case, the significant expense of seeking justice and providing a legal defense would divert the attention of the Catholic Left and most likely put them out of business.[45]

The opposite happened. The Berrigans' followers continued to raid draft boards with greater frequency. Likewise, each of the defendants, especially Eqbal and Liz, became "movement heavies," taking to the road ceaselessly to give speeches castigating the war and thus capturing national media attention. Their notoriety gave them added luster and made them into heroes for many Americans.[46] They also brought in considerable amounts of money for their defense.

Revolutionaries and draft resisters abounded in America of the 1960s and early 1970s. Recall that in those heady days between fifty thousand and seventy thousand young men of draft age had refused to serve in the armed forces since 1964 and lived as exiles in Canada.[47] The Black Panthers and Latino Young Lords asserted their right to bear arms against their white dominators.[48] At the same time, radical whites organized as the Weather Underground advocated using and actually engaged in violence to try to bring down the American state.[49] In that environment, a besieged Nixon administration might convince a confused U.S. public that a small group of nuns and priests tied into a conspiracy with a Muslim expatriate was dangerous if left free. The charges against them initially were punishable by life in prison, but a second indictment reduced the penalty for conspiracy to five years. The defendants took the trial seriously.

The Question of Trust

However, a problem developed over trust between Eqbal and the imprisoned Phil Berrigan. In an August 22, 1970, letter from Phil to Liz, conveyed by Douglas and passed on to the informant's FBI handler, the imprisoned priest expressed his doubts about Eqbal, reflecting views of risk, class differences, the nature of activism, and educational disparities: "Just between you and me," he wrote to Liz,

> I have not been overmuch impressed with Eq. He's a dear friend; very helpful in the last months [allusion to Eqbal's organizing Dan Berrigan's underground life], lovely guy, and good ideologue, but still to produce ... (I have this terrible suspicion regarding academics). With few exceptions, the bastards will let others go to the gallows without a serious murmur. They did it in Germany, and they're doing it here. And, Eq is from that strain. . . . But there are more reservations. I'd be delighted to be wrong. Which is to say, no project can be more solid than its human foundation, and, with all respect, I don't trust Eq, though he's a nice guy.[50]

The priests and nuns who grouped around the Berrigans had formed communities of resistance to war and militarism. If you were within that community, you were expected to break the law, get arrested, and, if necessary, go to jail. Eqbal was too cerebral for Phil Berrigan. He had not accompanied the priests and nuns on draft board raids and did not risk getting arrested that way. As already pointed out, Eqbal even came to oppose such actions. The raids had become the test for trust for this segment of the Catholic Left. Because Eqbal had not participated in them and did not take the risk of imprisonment for what Phil considered significant illegal actions, he could not be fully trusted. As a by-product of that mistrust, Liz did not tell Eqbal that she was corresponding with Phil, speaking of sensitive matters, and using another prisoner, who turned out to be an FBI informer, as a courier. Moreover, as the journalist Garry Wills, who followed the trial in Harrisburg, wrote, "When they [Phil and Eqbal] did meet, it was with a tense formality that never, really, relaxed— Ahmad knew what Berrigan had called him in the letters."[51]

Jim Forest (b. 1941), who had gone to prison for a draft board raid in Milwaukee and who worked on the Defense Committee in New York, wrote a comprehensive account of events leading up to the trial and came to Eqbal's defense: "While the hard jabs at academics seem more than justified [in Phil's letter], one of the few academics who clearly doesn't warrant them is Eq, if for no other reason than his risky association with Dan's underground. It was no symbolic gesture."[52]

J. Edgar Hoover, having read Phil's most recent letter, including his distrust of Eqbal, surmised that placing Eqbal within the conspiracy would heighten divisions among the defendants and make their defense more difficult. Understanding that, Eqbal had to ignore Phil Berrigan's mistrust once the indictments came down and to bend over backward in his discussions with his codefendants to reach consensus, not allowing personal prejudices to stand in the way of a coherent defense. There was too much at stake to do otherwise. His training in the law as a political scientist proved decisive for the defense as they mapped out their strategy for facing government prosecutors.

Phil wanted to defend himself and not use lawyers at all. In this way, he would have been able to present his antiwar sentiments to a large public. The judge presiding over the case refused to allow him to do so. Four of the seven defendants voted not to present any defense. Phil, Liz, and Eqbal, the three "superstars" with extensive experience in speaking before large audiences, voted to present a public defense. The other four defendants, who lacked the same oratorical skills, decided they would not offer a defense and would instead take a chance that the jury would side with them.[53] Reverend Joe Wenderoth, one of the defendants who voted with the majority, summed it up best at a strategy session in New York City. After admitting that "some of the defendants disagree with the policy of draft board actions and that the government did a good job of bringing together seven different people, creating problems that at times became devastating, we are trying to be as open as we can and feel that we have a responsibility to the other defendants. Most of us are not superstars and do not want to be, since we are struggling to be ourselves."[54]

After the government prosecutors presented their evidence, the defendants announced that they would have nothing further to say and rested their case. Phil Berrigan disagreed with that decision because he wanted his day in court, but he had to go along with the majority.[55] The strategy worked, however: the jury voted ten to two not to convict them on the major charges.

In other tense moments during the preparation for the trial, Phil and Dan wanted on the legal team the famous lawyer on the left William Kunstler (1919–1995), who had defended the Chicago Seven.[56] Eqbal thought that activists on trial hired Kunstler if they were guilty, not innocent. Kunstler, a tireless defender of accused leftists, ran political trials and had not mastered conspiracy law the way that Boudin had. In discussions among the defendants about strategy, Eqbal purposefully suggested that Kunstler represent him, not Phil Berrigan. That suggestion sufficed for Kunstler to voluntarily withdraw from the case rather than have to deal on a daily basis with Eqbal, who would demand careful legal work in his defense.

The *Catholic Worker* owned Emmaus House on East 116th Street in Spanish Harlem, where Jim Forest lived. It became the Defense Committee's initial headquarters until the committee rented an office at 156 Fifth Avenue. While the committee was in New York City prior to the trial, it received some $300,000 in donations. As the trial date approached, the committee moved to Harrisburg. Through mass mailings, it had helped bring in needed money for the defense, garnering $1,000 contributions from figures such as Joseph Heller (1923–1999), the author of the famous novel *Catch-22*, and Caesar Chavez (1927–1993), the director of Farm Workers of America.[57] Marie M. Runyon (b. 1915), who is still alive and active in her late nineties, organized a fund-raising benefit on May 10, 1971, for the Defense Committee in the Central Park West apartment of Leonard Bernstein (1918–1990), the eminent composer and conductor. That event helped raise thousands more.

As already mentioned, Eqbal had become good friends with the poet-priest Dan Berrigan at Cornell University, where they both worked in the late 1960s. They had been drawn to each other because of their love of rhyming words and hatred of the war raging in Southeast Asia.[58] Eqbal had a rare poetic memory and could recite verses of great Urdu poets by heart for hours on end, simultaneously translating their magnificent images into English for anyone who cared to listen. Through Dan, Eqbal met and became friends with the Catholic nun Elizabeth McAlister.[59] Phil and Liz later suspended their vows of chastity, married, and raised three children. One of them, their daughter Frida (b. 1974), took a course on international politics with Eqbal at Hampshire College in Amherst, Massachusetts, in the 1990s.[60] Life had come full circle as Eqbal began getting as students the children of his friends from Harrisburg days.

An evaluation that Eqbal wrote about Frida's work, which I found in his Hampshire College archive, demonstrated the impact of her being a Berrigan and his ability to praise and at the same time criticize a friend's child in order to push her to excel:

Frida Berrigan attended class most regularly and participated in discussions most thoughtfully. The subject engaged her and she worked hard and with genuine interest. Her first paper, on the bombing of Hiroshima and Nagasaki, was excellent in that it was informed and reflective. She kept a log on Bosnia and wrote her final paper on it. This is an extremely well-written paper and Frida's own voice is both very clear and very moving. However, she does not move much beyond her personal belief in non-violence and the challenge that Bosnian genocide presents to it to explore either forces which underlie the outbreak of such evils or the ways in which the international system responds and should respond to them.

Frida is an extremely good writer. She is also a thoughtful and socially responsible person. What she needs is more grounding in meth-

odology, research, and readings both in social sciences and literature. I hope that in the remaining three years her advisors and
teachers will encourage her to focus on developing the discipline of
critical scholarship.[61]

By dint of his indictment in 1971 and trial in Harrisburg one year later,
Eqbal went from being just an academic who held a Pakistani passport—
although he was beginning to gain some renown in U.S. anti–Vietnam
War circles as a result of his writings on revolution and counterinsurgency
and his oratorical skills in mass teach-ins—to becoming an instant ce-
lebrity. How did he reach that point? What in his background prepared
him for his new notoriety?

1
Eqbal's Life

BIHAR, WHERE EQBAL WAS BORN, WAS NEVER A CENTER OF
Indian high culture. The region had some famous musicians, but no significant literary figures. The Mughal palaces and courts existed elsewhere, so the Biharis lacked rich and powerful patrons of high culture.[1]
Eqbal's ancestors nevertheless lived in a cultured environment filled with
poetry, music, dance, art, and fine manuscripts, all reminiscent of Sati-
yajat Ray's film *The Chess Players* (1977). Eqbal saw the film and left the
theater all abuzz, enthralled with the images of his high culture, which,
even in its decline, still had much refinement. Eqbal's grandfather had
purchased many manuscripts, putting together one of the finest collections in private hands in Bihar. His son, Eqbal's father, Atta al-Rahman,
was an atypical landlord, or *zamindar*, who relished high culture. Symp-
tomatic of his appreciation of the arts, according to both Eqbal and his
sister Sharfa, their father organized many evenings devoted to poetry

contests in which guests and members of their extended family invented verses and competed with each other for small prizes. Other evenings were devoted to classical Indian music and dances, with the best performers and musicians of the region invited onto their estate to perform.

Eqbal's family lived comfortably in a large house. They had some twenty servants, most of whom, Eqbal once explained, "were related to each other and not paid beyond the food, shelter, and clothing they got and the supplies and gifts they took to their extended families in festival times."[2] Arlie Russell Hochschild (b. 1940), Eqbal's friend since 1962, wrote to me about a conversation she had with him about his childhood:

> Eqbal lived a big life, and was bigger than his life. The son of well-to-do Muslim landowners in Hindu-dominated Bihar, he was fond of saying, "I was brought up in the Eastern middle ages." He loved Urdu poetry, and sang, he said, tunes with an Eastern seven-tone scale in the shower. He recalled the screech of peacocks from the family's back garden and his mother's complaints to a neighbor for not picking up flaps left on the road outside their home, behind the neighbor's sauntering elephant. He remembers being taken by the hand as a small boy from the woman's side of the house through a certain passageway to the men's side of the house. And the house kept "two kitchens," he would repeat, "*two* kitchens," so Hindus and Muslims could eat together at the family house.[3]

At the celebration for Eqbal's retirement from Hampshire College in 1997, Eqbal also reminisced about his childhood in the Bihari village of Irki:

> I was born, figuratively speaking, in the eighteenth century. . . . There was no electricity in the sprawling house in which resided—apart from my mother, three sisters, a baby brother . . . a dozen or so guests, and about a score of poor relatives, many of whom originally came as guests and then stayed on. There was no running water; the house was served by four wells; two inside the harem—*zanankhana*—and two outside. My earliest memory is of rows of lanterns and gas lights

cleaned to sparkle at dusk. I would join the servants to light them and follow, the gas lights especially, as they were hung in strategic places. Nights were always very dark in the village, so I remember our house as flooded with light. I did not see a light bulb, hear a radio, or ride a car until I was eight or nine and did not fly in an airplane until I was twenty-one years old.[4]

Eqbal also told me that the first time he saw an Englishman, when he was about eight or nine years old, he was so petrified that he jumped into a ditch to watch the man's movements from a safe distance.

His mother, Khartoon (d. 1972), like most upper-class women of the time, lived in purdah, apart from the men, and when she ventured out of her home, she traveled in a palanquin, or litter, carried by four men of the aboriginal *mushar* caste. The women had an abode behind the men's quarters, which they shared with the children and female servants. As most women of her class did, Khartoon wore a chador, which covered extremely beautiful saris that she sewed and embroidered by hand with delicate stitching that she had learned as a child (see figure 5).

All of Eqbal's paternal uncles lived along the same side of the road as his family in separate houses on their own land. In the evening, his father's brothers and male cousins would gather at Eqbal's house. Some of them would sleep over in individual rooms reserved for male guests. A dozen visitors regularly stayed in the house, and another score of poor relatives lingered as permanent retainers, rarely thinking about leaving.

Until his father's assassination, Eqbal had enjoyed a joyous childhood. His older sister remembers him as an intelligent and fun-loving kid. His command of English at the age of five, she recalled, equaled that of someone in the third grade. He would joke around and make up and recite his own poems, play the board games *Snakes and Ladders* and *Ludo* with other children and older relatives, dance around the women's quarters, and entertain the family with his pranks. Eqbal especially liked to make fun of the older women in the family and would bring them to tears with laughter. One of his poems, more akin to Japanese haiku, "A bibi Hasina, tum ko dekh kay ata hay paseena," translates as "Oh beautiful woman, when I look at you, I sweat at your sight"; all the older women in his family remembered and joked about it. Being so cute meant that he was smothered with love and many kisses from all those around him. Having so many relatives and retainers always surrounding him, Eqbal grew up an extrovert and developed exceptional social charms.

Eqbal's village, Irki, was one of a little more than a thousand small settlements in the densely populated Jahanabad district, which contained nearly four hundred thousand people at the turn of the twentieth century. By 1931, Bihar, the second-largest province in India, with a very high population density, had more than thirty-one million people. Several rivers cut across its flat, well-cultivated, and fertile countryside. The district town on which Irki depended, also known as Jahanabad, which was almost twenty-eight miles from Patna, Bihar's capital, had become famous in the eighteenth century for its weaving industry, but once the British arrived, the manufacture of cotton cloth gave way to trade in Manchester goods, food grains, oil seeds, and fancy imported articles of European origin. Jahanabad town, with a population of some seven thousand in the early twentieth century, served as the local government seat and even contained a jail for seventy prisoners. The jail must have been kept full because Bihar had a long history of protests and militant agitation, including the violent Naxalite movement against landlord exploitation and oppression.[5]

The Maliks

Eqbal belonged to a family with an illustrious lineage, whose ancestors, the Maliks, originally Turks from Central Asia and sayyids or Sufi (mystic) warriors, claimed to have participated in the conquest of India after sweeping down the Indus Valley from Persia and the Afghan highlands. Eqbal summarized this history in the talk he gave at the celebration for his retirement from Hampshire College in 1997:

The Maliks were a proud clan consisting of a few rich, many middle class, and mostly poor people—landlords, professionals, farmers and, increasingly, state employees high and low. All fervently believed that they were blue blood, and held tight to the legend that they had conquered Bihar in the 14th century for Jalaluddin Khilji. Their power and wealth was [sic] drastically reduced first by the Mughuls, then [by] the British. It was an ingrown clan. I may well be the first male to have married outside the clan, and am definitely the first to have wedded a Jewish woman. Maliks were about 100,000 in number. The children were taught the virtues of honor, audacity, loyalty, and dignity. Style in the world of the Maliks often triumphed over reality. "It's a shitty world," my mother told me once, "and a gentleman is sometimes reduced to eating shit in life. If you ever have to, do it with fork and knife."[6]

The clan slid down the feudal ladder, and its members became medium-size landowners retaining some regional renown in Bihar. They ultimately joined the middle class. Eqbal and his siblings became the first generation to be urbanized.

Unlike most of the Indian landed gentry, Eqbal's father, besides being cultured, also had a deep social conscience. During the height of colonial India, because of the significant amounts of land that his wife, Khartoon, brought into their marriage, this lawyer and *zamindar* received considerable income from rents and did not need to open an office and practice his vocation. So he instead defended poor peasants whenever Irki landlords illegally expropriated their holdings. When a case proved too weak, he gave them some of his own or his wife's land. As already mentioned, his benevolence provoked furious *zamindar*s, including a relative, into having him assassinated in 1937.

On the evening of the murder, Eqbal was sleeping on a settee on an uncovered veranda of their house next to his father when the assassins charged in. The young boy woke up at about 3:00 A.M. as the murderers struck his father with large machete-like swords. Recognizing the assailants, Eqbal frantically screamed for help. Frightened, the killers began slapping him. His father then threw himself over his son, shielding him from any further blows. The commotion woke up Eqbal's uncles, the women, and the servants, all of whom dashed to the veranda. The assassins fled. A family member drove his father to a dispensary in Jahanabad, but two hours later he died.

Eqbal's ordeal did not end there. The next day he had to appear before a local police inquiry in the district center. He named the murderers, and the family was amazed at the coherency of his testimony. However, when a fuller hearing took place months later to fix the blame for the murder, Eqbal froze up and could not identify the killers. Two years later the local authorities dropped his father's murder case. Eqbal's older sister Sharfa and other members of the family believe that their neighbors had used their influence and money to browbeat and bribe officials.

Before his last testimony, Eqbal had clammed up, refused to speak, regressed into a shell, and suffered from traumatic shock. Sharfa remembers him tuning out, becoming very quiet, and refusing to visit the homes of friends and relatives as he used to do. Psychiatrists examining him in the late 1930s tested his IQ, which then registered a scant 12, which meant that he was not supposed to have been able to use a spoon to feed himself.[7] It took him several years to overcome the trauma caused by his father's murder, and by then he had developed his originality and began seeing the world in his own quirky way. Sixty years later, while reflecting back on his father's assassination, he quipped, "From this point on politics and violence have shaped my life to a large extent."[8] He also began to understand "that class is more important than blood relationship and that property is more dear to people than friendship or loyalties."[9]

After his father's death, he had to move away from his mother with his siblings into the home of his oldest brother, Zafar, in Jahanabad because his mother feared that neighbors might kidnap her three daughters, Sharfa, Aziza, and Aba, or Eqbal and her youngest son, Saghir (for Saghir later in life, see figure 4). Along with her older sons, Ghaffar and Zafar, they were all that remained of the twelve children that she had brought into the world. In the 1930s, without a man to head the family, the household in an isolated Indian village became vulnerable.

Sharfa recalled Jahanabad as a reasonably large place. As a landlord's daughter, she did not go out much. While her father lived, he had brought in tutors for the children and invited bright peasant boys to join the sessions. Some of the brightest of these lads continued their education out-side the house on stipends provided by her father.

Eqbal's early schooling by Hindu and Muslim teachers, like his sisters', initially took place at home. He then entered the Ram Mohan Roy Hindu Seminary, a nationalist institution founded by a nineteenth-century Indian reformer. His early education combined Hindu, Muslim, and West-ern traditions and languages—Urdu, Hindi, English, and Persian.

Turmoil at Home

Life for Eqbal in his brother's house turned out to be frightful. Although his oldest brother loved him and demonstrated his affection when he was at home, the boy did not get along with his sister-in-law and even less with her mother, who treated Eqbal brutally. The older woman had be-come convinced that the child had been seized by evil spirits and did everything she could to exorcize them from his body. When his brother left on his frequent tax-inspection trips, she hanged Eqbal up by a rope for hours, expecting that the ordeal would cure him of Satan's curse.

Zafar had married Halima Khartoon when she was thirteen years old, he eighteen years her senior. She was uneducated and had absorbed little of Muslim high culture, but as many Maliks did, Zafar married into an important family. She brought with her large quantities of land and gold jewelry. According to Eqbal's sister-in-law Husnara Ahmad, Ghaffar's wife, Zafar had a nonconfrontational personality, refused to argue with his wife or her mother, rarely took sides, and made no attempt to improve the conditions for Eqbal at home. There was little affection between Halima and her husband and scarcely any conversation. Zafar often walked out of a room when his wife entered it. He took refuge in books, reading voraciously, and remained silent for long periods of time while at home.

When Eqbal's life worsened, Zafar began taking the boy with him on his tax-inspection trips in order to separate the victim from his torment-ers. In this way, Eqbal felt protected, blossomed once more, and became conversant with the law. A picture of Eqbal at nearly thirteen years shows him alert and bright-eyed, deeply in touch with the world (see figure 2). By then, he had completely shed his shell. But Zafar's vacillation in confronting personal problems seems to have rubbed off on his younger brother, for later in his life Eqbal often tried to avoid tough personal choices, but at the same time he remained fearless in confronting injustice and in speaking on controversial public issues.

A Strong Mother's Legacy

Even though Eqbal remained separated from his mother, Khartoon, while he lived with his elder brother, aspects of her personality and beliefs nevertheless influenced him. She had smothered her young son with love and gave him a nickname that stuck within the family, *munoo*, "little one." Thereafter, his nephews and nieces addressed him in Urdu as *munoo chacha*, "little uncle."

While reminiscing about his life, Eqbal explained at his retirement celebration in 1997 that his mother "was illiterate":

> But, like many women of her class, she was refined and self-possessed and gave the impression of being well educated, for she knew the great classics of Hindu and Islamic civilization from story telling and recitations. Since my elder brothers were away and also disinterested in matters of property, she had to take on the management of the family's small estate. She flowered in this role. My uncle tried to grab some land as uncles tend to do . . . as Muslim law entitles brothers to a significant share of their siblings' inheritance. She fought back, and in the process became addicted to litigation. . . . Yet, politically [she was] a product of Gandhi's *satyagraha*, she broke the law often, and always with great enthusiasm.[10]

Sectarian differences confounded Khartoon. She and her husband viewed the Indian Muslim League as a reactionary party of landlords and insufficiently anticolonial.[11] She argued, as Eqbal did years later, that Hindus and Muslims had lived together for centuries under the Mughals and should continue to remain united within India. She therefore opposed the partition of India and refused to migrate to the newly created Pakistan, following the lead of many other Indian Muslims who stayed behind. Her daughter Aba had fallen ill with typhoid fever and could not withstand a dangerous voyage, so Khartoon opted to stay in Irki and nurse her back to health in 1947. She remained in India until that child died in 1958, after which she turned the family's property over to a caretaker and moved into the home of her eldest daughter, Sharfa, in the Muslim state.

In Pakistan, Khartoon continued to curse partition, nationalism, and Islamic–Hindu animosity. She wanted nothing to do with building a homogeneous and artificial Muslim nation state. She could not long stay away from India, where she had grown up, and so she returned to Irki in 1961, where she lived surrounded by servants. When she fell ill in 1962, members of the family brought her back to Pakistan. With no one in Irki to protect the family's rights, her estate reverted to neighbors living in the village. After that, Khartoon rotated staying with relatives in Pakistan. Eqbal kept her alive by promising year after year to send her on a pilgrimage to Mecca "next year." He did so finally in early 1970, paying for the trip, arranging for friends to accompany her on the long voyage, and allowing her to return safely to Pakistan as a *hajjah*.[12] She passed away two years later.

In keeping with agreements worked out between political leaders of both countries, Pakistanis and Indians who possessed real estate and land among the millions of migrants moving east or west and who could prove that they had left holdings behind received property in their new states roughly equivalent to what they had previously owned. In this way, Zafar Ahmad was given land near Lahore, which the family later sold. As a result of this land and real estate exchange, both India and Pakistan maintained a large middle class of property owners, lending both states some semblance of stability despite the turmoil they experienced from separation and large-scale violence.[13]

Land dispossession had played a significant role in the Ahmad family's earlier history as well. At the very end of the nineteenth century, Eqbal's father, seeking adventure and wishing to reclaim family property that the British had confiscated after the Sepoy Mutiny in 1857, enlisted in the British army under a false name and shipped off to South Africa to fight in the Boer War (1898–1902). Using his real name would have precluded his serving because the Maliks had become notorious for their anti-imperialist positions. The ploy did not pay off. After the war, the British refused the young man's claim for restitution of the family patrimony, arguing that they had already distributed the confiscated lands to British loyalists. But Attar al-Rahman gained something else on the way back from South Africa. He had stopped in Arabia and performed the pilgrimage to Mecca, after which he sailed to Cairo. There he met and married his second wife, whom the family called "Misr" (Egypt in Arabic). Bringing her back to India, he set Misr up in a second household apart from the estate of Eqbal's mother, who disapproved of the marriage, refused to allow her husband's new wife to move into their compound, but could do nothing to end her husband's second marriage.

Partition and the Trek to Pakistan

Eqbal's childhood and teens coincided with the brutal Bihari intercommunal riots that both preceded and ushered in the partition of India. When the split occurred in 1947, Eqbal had to trek north part of the way on foot to the new Pakistan. This perilous journey represented the second turning point in his life after his father's assassination. He remembered the pitched battles between Hindus and Muslims, with thousands killed on both sides. Some of his oldest brother's family road toward the newly created Pakistan on a government-protected train reserved for top Muslim civil servants. Eqbal went part of the way with Zafar until they reached an airport. The plane to Pakistan was crowded, so Eqbal agreed to wait for the next one, while his brother went aboard and flew off. Eqbal then left the airport and joined people walking. He saved his own life by getting hold of a gun, which he used to ward off attackers. Many times during his life, Eqbal repeated the story about a drugged opium eater who started the trek to Pakistan on foot with him but gradually, as the drugs wore off, became the leader and hero of the small group he traveled with. The moral Eqbal drew from this experience was that even the most degraded person has it within herself or himself to reform and contribute to the community's well-being.[14]

Once in Lahore, Eqbal moved into Zafar's house in Model Town. Khwaja Habiballah, Eqbal's close friend in Lahore's Foreman Christian College (FCC), who later studied under Zafar in the tax academy, recalled his teacher warmly as a simple person, without airs, who remained honest and incorruptible.[15] Zafar's integrity led him to locate the former Hindu owner of the house that he and his family moved into after partition. The former owner turned out to be a textile merchant who had abandoned his property as the violence intensified. Zafar tracked him down in India and returned the cash and textiles that the man had left behind as he fled his house in panic.

Eqbal's Foray into Warring Kashmir

When Eqbal got to Lahore, he enrolled in the Talim-ul-Islam College, which had moved to that city after partition. Created by the Ahmadi sect, it had become one of the most prestigious colleges in India, only to be forced to relocate to Pakistan in 1947, moving first into an abandoned horse stable and then into an abandoned college. Once the new quarters were repaired, the college opened its doors as an educational establishment in the old city, where it remained until 1955. By the time it set up its classes in Pakistan, however, it had lost its luster and proved little challenge for Eqbal. He spent two years as a student there, which included a four-month stint fighting in Kashmir.

His daughter, Dohra, interviewed him about that episode of his life while they were in Pakistan in 1998. He told her:

> Muslim League workers arrived at the campus . . . to recruit boys who would go fight. The principal had notified the whole college to come to the talk on Kashmir; to give an idea of how disorderly things were in that institution, out of countless students, only thirty-five showed up, and not for lack of interest. The recruiters gave a big pep talk about how a war of liberation had started . . . and asked for volunteers. Five

of us raised our hands. We were taken to a Muslim League office, where there were lots of kids and a room filled with uniforms and shoes. They told us to find one of each that fit us. These were discarded uniforms of American GI's from the Burma front. Of course I couldn't find one that came close to fitting, since I was so small, an overly energetic and somewhat underfed boy of fifteen. We had four days of training, during which time they taught us essentially two things: how to stand at attention; and how to fire guns. From here [Lahore] they drove us for a few days until we reached near Muzaffaraband, and joined a raging crowd of four or five thousand people, mainly tribals from the northern areas armed with homemade . . . rifles.

We marched into Kashmir. There was no resistance; Indian troops had not yet invaded Kashmir. As the tribals advanced, I saw two occasions when the young *chapo*s from Yusufzai tribes, Pathans, burnt and pillaged Hindu villages, raping women and killing people. I heard stories of similar excesses—killings and lootings, but no rape—being committed on the Muslim villages as well. It's very difficult for a single unit to know what is happening in the war: your unit is the world.

In addition to the Pathans, there were three ideological groupings among those fighting. There were the Muslim Leaguers who had brought me there. Ahmedis had also joined, primarily in order to proselytize. Having no interest in either of these, I joined the single Communist Party unit led by Latif Afghani. . . . [His] cell was my introduction to the Left.

I did not see Srinigar [the summer capital of what became the Indian state Jammu and Kashmir], but I was eight miles away from there when rumors came that Srinigar was being taken. It was within those one or two days that the Maharaja signed the accession with India [in effect turning a large part of Kashmir over to India] and Indian troops began to arrive. About forty-eight hours later, I noticed that a lot of wounded were being transported back. In fact, fighting had broken out among the tribals. When they saw the opportunity to enter a big city, they began to fight with each other to see who would enter first and loot. . . .

It was in the retreat from Srinigar that I was shot: not in some martyrdom, but in the exchange between rival Pathans. I went home. As soon as the wound had slightly healed, Zafar Bhai beat . . . me. I had disappeared for four months, without telling anyone where I was going. But Zafar . . . also understood that I would not have gone off to Kashmir if I had any sort of challenge; I was getting no education at [Talim-ul-Islam] College. Soon the change was made to Foreman Christian College, which at ten rupees had initially been too expensive.[16]

Lahore's Foreman Christian College

Several people and places, including his oldest brother and FCC, shaped Eqbal in Pakistan. Zafar Ahmad was cosmopolitan, honest, hardworking, and humane. He continued to frame Eqbal's world and moral views and sent his younger brother to FCC, which had been founded by Presbyterians in 1864. After partition, it became part of Punjab University and recently gained independent chartered university status. One of Eqbal's teachers at FCC, Dr. Zaur H. Zaidi (d. 2009), the first director of the Jinnah Papers (the archives of the founder of Pakistan), with whom Eqbal studied South Asian history, recognized the young man's intellectual qualities and encouraged his ambitions. He thought that Eqbal was the brightest student he had ever taught.

While majoring in economics and history, Eqbal won a gold medal for scoring the highest on the English and history bachelor of arts exams in 1949. Staying at FCC in 1953, he earned his master's degree in modern history. In order to help pay his university fees, he enrolled in FCC's Officer Training Corps, which entailed drilling twice a week in the evenings, for which he received grades and a stipend. He was therefore obliged to serve as a lieutenant in the army when he graduated. He chose to lecture at Pakistan's Military Academy from 1954 to 1956 and taught at his alma mater, FCC, from 1956 to 1957.

While studying at FCC, Eqbal became close friends with Professor Randolph Clothier Sailer (1898–1981).[17] Dr. Sailer had been forced out of Yenchung University near Beijing, where he had taught from 1923 to 1950. He had graduated from Princeton University in 1919 and fondly recounted to Eqbal stories about the many good times he had there, in this way steering the young man to apply to his older friend's alma mater.

Dr. Sailer spoke in secular terms and never liked to preach, despite his missionary credentials. His strong moral values marked those who came in contact with him. A member of FCC's faculty from 1953 to 1963, Dr. Sailer had founded the Social Psychology Department there and recruited Eqbal to assist him in distributing questionnaires. Having little money, Eqbal also received a teaching assistantship from the FCC principal, Dr. E. R. Ewing, to pursue his master's degree and worked as a warden at one of the college's student hostels.

Professor Zaidi and his wife, Parveen, put me in touch with a few of Eqbal's former classmates at FCC. Khwaja Habiballah met Eqbal on the first day they arrived at the college. He told me that enrollment had dropped precipitously at FCC following partition, so their class had only ninety students. He remembered Eqbal as being very different from the other students, very frank and at times boisterous. Eqbal would speak his mind without hedging his thoughts. He also had a very good sense of humor, according to Khwaja, and was an excellent mimic, provoking great laughter as he imitated people they knew. In 1949–1950, he became president of the Bazm-i-Adab literary society, and in the next year he edited the college magazine. Khwaja thought that Eqbal never wanted glory for himself and never sought an office in student politics, although he played important roles behind the scenes in organizing political campaigns for other students.[18] The two friends maintained contact over the years, and Eqbal made it his business to see Khwaja whenever he visited Lahore. Another fellow student, Arshad Durrani, later an army officer and by 2004 a businessman, remembered that they were "raw youths who were groomed at FCC into becoming sophisticated human beings." He added that they respected their teachers as gurus.[19]

Syad Abid Hussein, another of Eqbal's fellow students at FCC, wrote to him from Dhaka, Bangladesh, late in 1983: "I vividly remember the happy time we spent together in the college. Your nice jokes and poetry are still fresh in my mind. Our indulgence and active involvement in the college politics was a good past-time. I can never forget your jolly company. You were a great fellow then and I am very pleased to know that you are *mash-allah* a great man today."[20]

As a young man in newly created Pakistan, Eqbal gravitated toward Marxism. His four-month experience with Communist guerrillas in Kashmir introduced him to the movement, but he never actually became a member of the Communist Party. In addition to his normal schoolwork, he did, however, attend special extracurricular schools established by Communist militants, where he sharpened his logic and analytic skills. Years later, when reflecting about Marxism's contribution to world thought, he acknowledged that

Marx focused our attention on the poor and the working class. . . . Marx and Frederick Engels rather brilliantly warned of and chalked out the exploitive oppressive patterns of capitalism development and the workings of the capitalist system. That capitalism has not been defeated or changed and continues to demonstrate a great deal of resiliency and dynamism are both true and were actually argued by Marx rather consistently; but it doesn't take away from the fact that capitalism is an exceptionally unjust system. We still have to figure out how to do away with it, or at least its worst features. . . . Finally the biggest achievement of Marx and Marxism may have been to offer the methodology of analyzing social and historical realities. I do not think that anyone has come up with a substitute for historical materialism as an explanation for the turns of history, the processes of history. Nor has anyone elaborated the idea of dialectics into a methodological system in the way that Marx and Marxism did. These are not mean achievements. . . . Marx and Marxism focused the intelligentsia's attention in a positive way on the other, the poor, the weak. And at least a section of the intellectual class, the intelligentsia as a whole . . . saw it as their moral and intellectual responsibility to comprehend reality in order to change it, to make the world better and not for themselves only. . . . This was the first time you saw secular intellect focus on issues of the common good.[21]

Even back then Eqbal was too independent to be wedded to one school of thought, intellectual fashion, or political party. The Communists may have helped form him intellectually, but they could not claim him as one of their own. Although he understood Lenin's historic importance, he came to dislike Leninism, in particular its centralization, its need to exact obedience, and its limited tolerance of dissent.[22] Stalin was the product of Leninism, and he produced Soviet communism, which Eqbal thought was "one of the most defective formations humanity has ever seen."[23] Eqbal was too much of a maverick, too independent a spirit, to cling to that or any party. If he followed any school of thought, he inclined toward the humanistic socialism of Antonio Gramsci (1891–1937), the Italian intellectual who wrote remarkable prison memoirs in the interwar period. "I still learn from him," he told David Barsamian in 1998. "He has a grasp of class struggle, of the effect that power has on weakness, that wealth has on poverty, and the state has on civil society. He is also the only one of the major theoreticians of our time who actually came from a poor background. He is also the only one who was deeply engaged in a day-to-day struggle of people, the only one who spent long years and disintegrated in the suffering of prison. Those details have given a texture to his insights that are in so many ways unique."[24]

According to Iqbal Riza (b. 1934), Eqbal, while at FCC in the early 1950s, organized a few of his classmates to travel north to Kalabar, a backward area near the Northwest Frontier, to set up a school for kids there.[25] He convinced his companions to take a bus with him for an all-day trip to the region. When they arrived in Kalabar toward evening, they announced that they were there to teach the population's children in a new school that they intended to set up. They generated a great deal of excitement among the local population, and the word spread rapidly of their arrival. By 2:00 P.M. on their first day there, they received an invitation from the ruler, or nawab, of Kalabar, to take tea with him at his home from 4:30 to 5:00 P.M. This official, who had studied at Oxford University, later became the governor of West Pakistan before being killed by one of his sons, probably over a property dispute and a future inheritance.

Of course, the nawab lived in a big house, probably owned the village, and was most likely the biggest property owner in the district. Speaking in English, he greeted the students and asked them why they had come there. Eqbal responded that they intended to bring education to a backward area and had planned to spend three months there teaching local kids. The nawab offered them tea and told them that they were right, there was no education there. He added that his family had ruled Kalabar for three hundred years. "We don't want education here," he told them. "If we did," he added, "it would not be you, but rather me, who would organize a school. There's a bus leaving town in the morning. You had better be on it. If you don't leave, you'll be skinned alive." Eqbal was an idealist but also a realist, so he and his friends, crestfallen, took that morning bus back to Lahore.

In a congratulatory letter Eqbal wrote to Arlie and Adam Hochschild's son, David, after David had graduated from college, he admitted that "the years immediately following [my graduation from FCC] were among the bad times in my life. There was fear of unemployment, uncertainty about what I wanted to do; anxiety that I might make a mistake and get stuck for life; and pressures from family and friends to do this and that. I did make wrong choices: army, then a tobacco company; had good luck—flunked the civil service examination in which my family, refugees from India, desperately wanted me to succeed because it promised stability and status."[26]

He then studied on a U.S. Rotary scholarship for a year (1957) at Occidental College in the Eagle Rock neighborhood of Los Angeles. He had come to the United States to learn what he could about its culture. At Occidental, he concentrated his research on Native Americans, their plight and resistance, examining the distorted Hollywood vision of American Indians as depicted in films. He returned to that subject constantly when confronting Americans' stereotyping views of Arabs or Muslims.

Eqbal also traveled to the southern United States to see firsthand the effects of Jim Crow. During one of his vacations from Occidental, he took a Greyhound bus trip on which a driver ordered him to step to the rear "and sit with the colored folks." African Americans on the bus screamed out for the driver to leave him alone: "Can't you see that he's a foreigner?" He told me he was totally confused and did not know what to do.

Princeton Years

Eqbal and I arrived in Princeton in September 1958, Eqbal on a university fellowship of $2,450 a year, $1,250 of which were earmarked for tuition.[27] I had grown up in a working-class family in the Bronx and had just received my bachelor's degree from the then free City College of New York. Our remarkably dissimilar backgrounds did not stop Eqbal and me from becoming and remaining close friends for more than forty years (see figure 3). When he arrived at Princeton's Graduate College, he wore a long brown winter coat, a wool scarf, and a Persian lamb cap (see figure 1). He looked undernourished, and his teeth were covered by red betel nut stain, which he promptly had a local New Jersey dentist remove.

The Ph.D. program in Near Eastern studies entailed spending more than half a decade learning Arabic and the field of Middle East studies. Disdaining Orientalism, we both decided to enroll in a joint program, he in the Politics Department and I in history, which gave us a broader grasp of disciplines beyond narrow area studies and philology. After the first year of intensive language training, Eqbal and I took a mix of courses in Near Eastern and North African studies as well as in our respective fields of politics and history.

Eqbal was poor by the standards of most Princeton students, and in his first year there he lived in a rented room some distance from the graduate college. He had to send home part of his fellowship money, which meant that he had to live frugally to make ends meet, but life then, unlike today, was affordable.

In those days, Princeton allowed into the Grad School a maximum of five hundred male students. It took another decade and a half before the university opened its doors to women and expanded the number of entering students ninefold. The undergraduate men lived apart in their own universe, and most of them joined Prospect Street eating clubs, the equivalent of fraternities without bearing the name. Their lives, when they were not studying, revolved around those clubs, which ranged from very upper-crust Ivy to slightly less class conscious. Their alienation from us graduate students was best expressed in the name the undergrads gave to the place where most grads lived and dined, "the goon castle."

After Eqbal excelled and proved his mettle, the university, following a pecking order based on achievement, rented him a spacious private room with a fireplace, which allowed him to live quite comfortably in the same place where he dined.

Causing Trouble

During our second year in graduate school, we became active in the university's affairs, and some of its officials saw us as troublemakers. We, with a small group of grad students, stirred up a hornet's nest when we attempted to unionize the kitchen and dining room staff, primarily African American women who worked for low wages and had few benefits. The university so intimidated these workers, threatening to fire them all, that the women ended up voting against unionization. Not to be stopped, we then forced the university to allow those grad students who wished to do so to skip high dinner, where we had to say grace and wear black gowns in a dining room with a gothic ceiling in imitation of elite British universities. As a result of our successful mobilization, those students who chose to do so thenceforth could eat in a separate dining room, with a normal low ceiling, skip grace if they so wished, and not wear black robes to dinner. We then organized the students over the issue of the new dorms being built in preparation for the university's expansion. The administration wanted to cut costs and put up modern buildings that had no relation to the generalized gothic architecture prevalent on campus. They attempted to do this without consulting the students. We wanted a voice in Princeton's decision-making process and hoped to open the way to implement democratic governance. We successfully organized the architecture students, who, on aesthetic grounds, convinced a majority of those studying at Princeton to oppose the university's project. The administration had to revise its plans after consulting with us. It could not do much to stop our activities because most of the students we worked with had the highest grades in the Grad College, and many of us had won outside grants and could not be intimidated by threats to cut or eliminate university stipends.

The Weight of Conformity

The late 1950s in America were repressive, and, as already mentioned, Eqbal felt the weight of conformity. So did I. We escaped from Princeton periodically to hang out in the cafes in Greenwich Village, where Beat Generation writers recited their poetry and created an alternate lifestyle that poked fun at the prim and proper "normal" life in the United States. Theater, too, was reaching new creative heights in pocket-size off-Broadway sites, and I took Eqbal with me to New York several times to escape small-town conformity and indulge in the counterculture developing on the fringes of Gotham. Small groups of creative artists were bursting out of their seams in rebellion and gave us a glimpse of an alternative lifestyle and ethnic communities very different from what surrounded us in Princeton. It was then that Eqbal began appreciating the lure of New York City.

Special Attributes and Skills

The refined and cultivated environment in which Eqbal grew up gave him special charm. In the United States, women adored his aristocratic manners, and as his body filled out from good living, he became extremely handsome. (See the cover of this book and figure 8, showing Eqbal in a Hollywood pose a few years later, in 1966.) The skinny Pakistani of 1958 had been transformed into a debonair, worldly intellectual.

Just as his body was transformed, so was his mind. Princeton's professors and the university's Firestone Library as well as the cultural resources of New York City nearby gave him the means to develop into an astute political analyst with the ability to predict the direction of events before they occurred. He was so good at what he did that he won the Graduate College's highest honor, the Proctor Scholarship (1960–1961), with a stipend of $3,250 (larger than his Near Eastern fellowship), from which he still had to pay $1,250 tuition.[28] He possessed uncanny gifts based on a profound comparative knowledge of political processes and systems.

The social sciences in the late 1950s and early 1960s were in transition. Scholars working in new fields, such as comparative and developmental politics, although completely mainstream, appeared radical to the old guard and challenged the old disciplines. Eqbal worked both sides of the divide, for the division gave him a unique opportunity not only to learn the traditional ways of political science, which emphasized reading the great thinkers of the past and the law, but also to master the newer fields of comparative and developmental politics. He took a wide menu of courses and always remained critical.

Eqbal mined the Islamic tradition and read many theological and legal texts. All the while, he spent a great deal of time in the Firestone Library, followed the Indo-Pakistani press, and read widely on the subcontinent's history and literature.

By 1964, he had developed into an organic intellectual with rare synthetic gifts and subtle analytical abilities. He was knowledgeable about Islamic lore; an expert on the Middle East, North Africa, and the Indian subcontinent; a master of Western political science; and profoundly humble about how much more he still had to learn. He also could read and speak Urdu, Arabic, and Persian.

During 1964, our last year in Princeton, we shared a spacious furnished apartment, and there began Eqbal's practice of inviting guests over for dinner, elaborately prepared and served with intense conversation and great warmth. People vied to dine at his table over gourmet meals that he cooked (see figure 9, showing him preparing a meal twenty years later). In this way, Eqbal established a salon that he continued to maintain throughout his life. He always invited over any Pakistani or Indian who wandered into Princeton. He drew the best out of them, made them feel important, and in turn gained friends and future allies. We also spent many weekend evenings at the home of Manfred Halpern (1924–2001), our teacher in Middle East politics, and his first wife, Betsy, a psychologist.

Roger Le Tourneau Enters Our Lives

A turning point came in Eqbal's and my lives when Roger Le Tourneau (1907–1971), one of the leading French North African experts with an encyclopaedic knowledge of North Africa from prehistoric times to the then present, came to teach at Princeton University in 1959 during alternate semesters. We studied with him, and both of us decided to write our doctoral dissertations on the area. Eqbal chose the topic of comparing Tunisian and Moroccan trade unions and went off in the autumn of 1961 to study French in Paris, and, with a fellowship from the Rockefeller Foundation, he began work on his thesis in Tunis in early 1962. I had already visited Algeria in September 1960 and spent the fall semester of that year studying at the University of Aix-en-Province.

That was the sixth year of the Algerian revolution against the French, and both Eqbal and I had from 1959 on constant and passionate disputes with Le Tourneau over the war. We took the Algerian nationalist side; Le Tourneau defended the French status quo. Our arguments often deteriorated into shouting matches. Yet Le Tourneau amazed us, for we found that the more we challenged him and the more we displayed our anger over the war, the more he encouraged us and the closer he drew to us. I learned only a few years ago from an article about Le Tourneau why he may have treated us so well despite what seemed like an ideological chasm between us.

Le Tourneau had served as French minister of education in the Tunisian Protectorate under the pro-Nazi Vichy regime during the early 1940s. When the Allied forces defeated the Germans and their French allies in North Africa, the victors jailed him. Through French military friendships and well-placed relatives, he rehabilitated himself, and between 1947 and 1957 he taught at the Faculty of Letters in Algiers and in 1958 established a center of North African studies at Aix-en-Provence.[29] His past collaboration with the Vichy government forced him in public to toe the official policy line of keeping Algeria French. He argued this public position in France and in Princeton and never wavered from it. His private correspondence, however, reveals that he never believed France could hold Algeria. He had concluded that the French would lose

Algeria and that doing so was necessary for the future healthy development of French society and politics. Because he felt that he could not reveal his true feelings about the issue, however, I think that he latched on
to Eqbal and me and made us his surrogates. He probably relished our
vociferous antiwar stances. Eqbal, itching to get to North Africa, skipped
a term studying with Le Tourneau at Aix and just visited the Le Tourneau family there. He stayed there for a short while before heading to
Tunis. Neither one of us had any idea that we were being manipulated.
Meanwhile, we absorbed all we could about French imperial history from
Le Tourneau, better to fight it.

Eqbal's Encounters in France and North Africa

Eqbal lived and studied French in Paris from October to November 1961.
In a letter to me dated December 19, 1961, he said that he had made "good
contacts" in Paris and saw some important people, including the socialist politician Guy Mollet (1905–1975), who had been prime minister of
France from February 1956 to May 1957. Mollet "harangued him for an
hour and ended up concluding that he was a very difficult Asian." Eqbal
recounted that he had landed a brief loading job between 3:00 and 6:00
A.M. in Les Halles market in Paris and spent his earnings with five Algerian co-workers. On the night of October 16, he was arrested with another
group of Algerians in a Parisian restaurant and spent eight hours in a Paris
police station. He wrote to me about this experience: "The most important
man escaped; it was a masterful act of courage and cunning on his part, of
admirable sense of unity and self-sacrifice on that of the others. I sustained some three strong butts of [a] rifle in the [police] van, one at the
prefecture—very kindly treatment considering the fate of the others."[30]

His relations with Algerians intensified in Tunisia, where he arrived
in early January 1962 after being laid up in Aix with pneumonia.[31] He
immediately began researching the Tunisian part of his dissertation. I
moved to Morocco.

In 1962, I visited him in Tunisia, and he spent August to October of
that year in my apartment in Rabat, Morocco, after having driven through

war-torn newly independent Algeria with an American graduate student, Clement Henry Moore (b. 1937, now Clement Henry, who teaches politics at Singapore University), and a German friend, Heide Wohlgemouth. Eqbal had hoped to do a comparative study of Moroccan and Tunisian trade unions, but the secretary-general of the Union marocain du travail (Moroccan Workers Union), Mahjoub Ben Seddik (1922–2010), found him too inquisitive and his questions too astute, so he gave orders to union officials to shut the researcher out of their headquarters. Ben Seddik also forbade union rank and file from talking to my friend.

In Tunis, Eqbal became a good friend of the general secretary of the Union générale tunisienne du travail (Tunisian General Labor Union), Ahmed Tlili (1916–1967), who fought to liberalize Tunisia's one-party state and paid for his principled stances with long spells of exile. The man confided in Eqbal and taught him a great deal about mass organizing and the need to create strong trade unions as a vital component of civil society.[32]

Eqbal studied the early stages of the Tunisian trade union movement of the 1920s as well as more recent developments. That research brought him in contact with pioneering historical figures who had laid the groundwork for the country's transformation into a modern society. Two important leaders of the period especially attracted Eqbal's attention: Tahar Haddad (1899–1935), who studied in Zaytuna's mosque university, and M'hamed ʿAli (1896–1927), an adventurer who returned to Tunisia after working for Enver Pasha (1881–1922), one of three Young Turk military leaders who controlled the Ottoman Empire during World War I for a powerless sultan. M'hamed ʿAli had followed his mentor to Germany after the Great War ended, got a job in a Berlin airplane factory, and attended night university classes in political economy. After his older patron died, M'hamed ʿAli returned to Tunis, where he and Haddad made an aborted attempt to set up a Tunisian workers' cooperative. They then helped found the first indigenous Tunisian trade union, the Confédération générale tunisienne du travail (Tunisian General Workers Confederation), the predecessor of the aforementioned Tunisian General Labor Union and the oldest labor union in Africa after that of South Africa.

Haddad wrote a book in Arabic about their experiences that was fifty years ahead of its time, filled with astute sociological observations of Tunisian daily life.[33] He also championed women's rights in another courageous book published in 1930.[34] Eqbal and I later coauthored articles about both of these men, and Eqbal's research into their lives made him understand how a small minority, all of whose projects had ultimately failed, could nevertheless decisively shape a country's future ideological options.[35] The lessons he learned there gave him added courage to champion causes that other people dared not touch.

As associate director of the newly founded Tunisian Cultural Center in Hammamet, Eqbal organized conferences and hosted prominent individuals. He also sponsored evening concerts and theatrical events in the wonderful white-washed beach-front former home of an eccentric Rumanian millionaire, which the Tunisian state had purchased. Eqbal had befriended the Lebanese diplomat Cecil Hourani, who served then as the personal adviser on international affairs for President Habib Bourguiba (1903–2000) of Tunisia. Bourguiba had appointed Hourani director of the new center, but given the heavy charges Hourani already had as presidential counselor, he recruited Eqbal to run its day-to-day operations. In response to an email I sent Hourani in February 2014, he recalled his friendship with Eqbal, whom he found charming. When taking the job, Eqbal renounced a second year as a Rockefeller fellow. He decided to do so in order to meet prominent Tunisians, visitors, and expatriates as well as to gain administrative experience, which he lacked.

Eqbal also began to comprehend firsthand in Tunis the power and influence of the press in shaping public opinion and popular consensus. The Algerian War attracted some of the world's best journalists to the neighboring country's capital and its suburbs. Because living in Algeria during the eight-year war was dangerous, most of the correspondents set up residences in the vicinity of Tunis and got much of their news from members of the Algerian government in exile residing there. Besides befriending several eminent French journalists, Eqbal saw regularly the *New York Times* correspondent in Tunis, Thomas F. Brady (d. 1972). Eqbal loved the talented people that Tunis then attracted. It also helped sensitize him to the necessity of befriending newspaper correspondents for political ends, and he invited many reporters over for meals. Later in his life, when he helped organize the U.S. anti–Vietnam War movement and especially when he faced his own trial after being arrested for those activities, he worked the press with great finesse and diligence, a process that he first mastered in Tunisia in the early 1960s.

The cosmopolitan mix of people in Tunis during the Algerian War had produced a very exciting environment in which to live and work, and Eqbal felt very much at home there. He made many Tunisian friends, and some people today still remember him fondly.

In the early 1970s, years after Eqbal had left the country, a group of Tunisian political activists contacted him in New York City to ask for his help in establishing the country's first independent human rights organization.[36] Eqbal formed a delegation of Americans to visit Tunisia and lend their support to this important endeavor under Jimmy Carter's presidency. We coauthored several articles about Tunisia's human rights crisis and campaigned in Congress to apply pressure on Habib Bourguiba's regime to ameliorate political conditions in the country.[37] In Tunis, Eqbal was happy to meet many old friends, including workers from the trade union movement, who welcomed him back.

In the early 1960s, Eqbal had a handful of close friends in Tunis. The daughter of the U.S. ambassador to Tunisia, Arlie Russell, was working on her doctoral dissertation there before going on to become the chair of the Sociology Department at the University of California in Berkeley. Clement Henry Moore, another American graduate student, also joined Eqbal's circle of friends. Clem later published his dissertation as *Tunisia Since Independence*, one of the best studies of the country's politics since 1956.[38] Clem had brought his British bride, Sue Alliston (d. 1969), to Tunis, and she too became part of Eqbal's coterie of friends. Bright with a caustic wit, Sue was an accomplished poet; she had an affair with British poet laureate Ted Hughes (1930–1993), the husband of the renowned U.S. poet Sylvia Plath (1932–1963), who later committed suicide. Eqbal adored Sue, who died in her prime from leukemia.

The brilliant Pakistani diplomat Imdad Hussein (b. ca. 1935) was stationed in Tunis during the early 1960s and also joined Eqbal's circle. Imdad played the violin and later gave up his diplomatic career to join the Sadler Wells Orchestra in London. He had studied at St. Anthony's College at Oxford University and was an intellectual match for Eqbal. He was also a gourmet chef and was able to create exotic meals out of whatever leftovers he found in Eqbal's refrigerator. He added to the top intellectual and culinary level of life in Tunis during the period of the Algerian conflict. Eqbal encouraged his friend's musical talents, and after Imdad left the foreign service, Eqbal invited him back to Tunisia to give concerts at the International Cultural Center. Imdad ultimately returned to live in Pakistan.

A Short Trip to Pakistan

Eqbal took a quick trip to Pakistan to see his family in August 1963. In a letter he wrote to me from Karachi, he spoke of the "tragedies and disappointments" that he met there:

I have never seen anything worse than Pakistan is today. The whole place smells of sickness. Corruption is rife—Ayub [Mohammad Ayub Khan (1907–1974), president of Pakistan from 1958 to 1969] has built himself and his family quite an empire—bureaucracy is at its worst, and acute frustration prevails among the masses. [A] majority of educated people are apolitical, more interested in getting a little more comfort in life and possibly a few luxuries. Nothing wrong with it. But to make this . . . the only pre-occupation, the only criteria of living is quite another thing. Political parties have multiplied but they are all torn by internecine warfare and even if two of them can claim some mass support in East Pakistan, none can boast of mass organization. The common man (my sampling of Karachi so far) has reached the end point. "Only blood can clean it now[,] Sahib. The country asks for sacrifice," is a sentence I am becoming used to.[39]

Return to the United States

While Eqbal worked in Tunisia, President Bourguiba attempted to recruit the budding scholar to write his official biography. Cecil Hourani had introduced them, and Eqbal toyed with the idea of working with the Tunisian president, but accepting the offer would have meant staying in North Africa for a few more years. Now that the Algerian War had ended and most expatriates had departed, Tunis reverted to its natural quiet status. Coming to the place for a few weeks as a tourist might give visitors the pleasures associated with a Mediterranean paradise, but living there on a permanent basis was another matter. It certainly could not match New York, Paris, Chicago, or Washington, D.C., nor did it have Algiers's dynamism. Eqbal also understood that if he accepted Bourguiba's offer, he would have to produce a laudatory paean, temper his criticisms, and bend the truth. After weighing the pros and cons of working directly with the president, he decided not to write the biography but rather to stay on track. He therefore returned to the United States to complete his dissertation while holding a teaching assistantship for 1963–1964 in the Politics Department at Princeton University.

Our Paths Diverge

At the end of 1964, Eqbal flew to the University of Illinois at Urbana/ Champaign to take up a year-long job as a substitute teacher for an absent professor in the Political Science Department,[40] a job that proved disappointing. As a foreigner uncertain about his career choices and an iconoclast, Eqbal frightened off potential employers. At that point in his life, he also wasn't sure if he wanted a permanent post in America; he still toyed with the idea of returning to Pakistan to get involved in politics. Most research universities sought young scholars who had figured out their career goals and had plans to write a multitude of books.

He explained his frustration in another letter:

Life in Urbana is distressingly dull and dreary. The air smells of cows, corn and color prejudice. The university, ten rungs lower than Princeton, invokes my sympathy but excitement is another world beyond the cornfields. . . . I am braced for the ghastliest year of my life and know that if I can't finish my thesis here, I might as well give up. . . . I could not find an efficiency apartment. Of the *ten* prospective places I visited after making 750 telephone calls during 12 long days and nights, seven rejected me due to my suspicious bachelorhood; three baldly disliked the color of my skin. PANICKED, I took the 11th and the first available place for which I am paying a fortune and getting a pittance worth.[41]

His despondency and alienation encouraged him to complete his dissertation quickly, and then gratefully he moved on.

He landed a job at the Institute for Labor and Industrial Relations at Cornell University from 1965 to 1968. Cornell in the 1960s had become one of the centers of the anti–Vietnam War movement, and Eqbal fell in with a committed group of activists. But he also alienated part of the Cornell faculty with his pro-Palestinian stances, especially after the Israelis defeated the combined Arab armies in the 1967 Arab-Israeli War (also known as the Six-Day War). Some of the teaching staff snubbed and ostracized him, so when he entered the school's cafeteria on days his antiwar buddies were not around, he had to eat alone. No one would join him even if all the other tables had filled up.

In 1966, the U.S. Immigration Services unsuccessfully attempted to deport him because he still held a renewable visa and his anti–Vietnam War activities had begun making him visible to U.S. authorities. He feared not being allowed back into the country each time he traveled abroad.

In February 1966, the Social Science Institute at Tougaloo College, which had been founded for the higher education of African Americans, invited him to participate in the first Vietnam teach-in held in Mississippi. Other speakers included Archibald Cox (1912–2004), who later became a special prosecutor and won notoriety after being fired by President

Richard M. Nixon, an act that contributed to the president's downfall; Dave MacReynolds (b. 1929) of the War Resister's League; and some nameless government official who defended the U.S. administration's position. Lewis Feldstein (b. 1941)[42] remembers Eqbal staying around late that night after the debate had ended, sitting on the floor in Feldstein's house and meeting with about a dozen black students and faculty. Margaret Burnham (b. 1944), a former municipal court associate justice and now a law professor at Northeastern University in Boston, was there and remembers this "giving young Indian man" close to the students' age who bonded immediately with them.[43] In a nonpedantic way, they discussed at length the relationship between Algerian history, the events in Vietnam, and their own civil rights movement. According to Margaret, he left behind a deep impression on those whom he met. In the three to four days he was there, they took him to visit with various civil rights activists in the Jackson area.

In a letter he wrote to the chair of Middle Eastern studies at Princeton University, Professor T. Cuyler Young (1900–1976), on April 29, 1969, Eqbal confided that his "several attempts to find a point of insertion in Pakistan have so far failed. Some eight months ago [in mid-1968] they offered me an Ambassadorial appointment. That was the first inclination I had of the desperate condition of Ayub [Khan's] regime. I gather the present junta will also welcome my participation in the government. But to collaborate with it at this time is tantamount to committing political suicide."[44] Not wanting to return home to work with a military dictatorship, he was left with little room to maneuver. By mid-1969, he was beginning to feel wary about both Pakistan and the United States. In a letter he wrote to Cornell colleague Dorothy Nelkin (1933–2003) at that time, a moment of temporary lull in the U.S. antiwar movement, he complained that "the atmosphere in the country [the United States] is very depressing. The anti-war sentiment has died out; the racial situation is becoming worse; the repressive edge of local, State and Federal governments have [sic] clearly sharpened. The élan and cockiness of the radicals has [sic] given way to deep pessimism and paranoia. I feel that things will remain this way, and the war will go on until at least 1972."[45] A year later, on May 4, 1970, the tragedy of Kent State, where the Ohio National Guard killed four antiwar demonstrators, gave activists within the movement a sober shock and transformed activism into pervasive caution. As Eqbal predicted, though, the war ended in 1972.

More Think Tank Work

After the Harrisburg trial ended, starting in the fall of 1972, as I already mentioned, Eqbal and his family moved to Washington, D.C., where he joined the Institute for Policy Studies (IPS). This left-of-center think tank was founded by two former members of John F. Kennedy's administration, Richard J. Barnet (1929–2004) and Marcus Raskin (b. 1934), both of whom had broken with the president over his foreign policy. IPS established an overseas affiliate known as the Transnational Institute (TNI), financed by the philanthropist Samuel Rubin (1901–1978). Eqbal became its first director in 1973 and remained in that position for two years. TNI was housed in an idyllic setting of Amsterdam within a limestone building on the elegant Paulus Potterstraat, directly across from the Van Gogh and Stedlyk Museums. Eqbal gathered there a wide range of Third World scholars and conducted seminars with them and other invited guests. As director, Eqbal helped TNI fellows publish their works. In some senses, TNI was a grand salon for Eqbal, broader in scale than his own dining or living room, a place to gather bright people and have continuous discussions about world problems. Even the food served at dinners was quite good, and the place, in one of the best sections of Amsterdam, could not have been better.

Fiona Dove (b. 1961), TNI's executive director since 1995, explained Eqbal's contribution to the institute in an email to me on January 9, 2011: "TNI was established by Eqbal as a loose, horizontal, internationally networked organization. This might seem very normal in these days of e-mail, internet and the global village, but back in the mid-70s this was a most unique structure. In this sense, Eqbal set TNI up as a pioneering type of network organisation, which has sustained itself as such for 35 years and served as a model for many others."

After directing TNI, Eqbal remained an IPS senior fellow, working for it six months a year at his own request. In his time off, he took a series of jobs as visiting professor at the Institute for Social Studies in The Hague (1975–1976); Sarah Lawrence College in Bronxville, New York (1976–1977); and Rutgers University, Newark campus (1982).

Many years later, in a retrospective moment, Eqbal wrote to his daughter, Dohra, from Islamabad, Pakistan, that he had "been reflecting on his life" as he tried "to cut down" on his "extravagant detours." He felt that he was quite "lucky to have survived and to have lived a rich life. There are few regrets though; they all concern relationships." He continued: "Edward [Said] said the last time I saw him that I truly deserved a distinguished chair at a distinguished university. I have really no such regret, in fact I think it would have been an inappropriate conclusion to my life, and conclusion it would have been had I ended up in a chair at Harvard or Princeton. But I do think that I was lucky to have drifted into academe. It gave me freedom, and led me to a life I might have entirely missed."[46]

Left but Not Doctrinaire

Eqbal understood that to improve conditions he had to work with the leftists he found in place. He did not always agree with them, though, and never hesitated to criticize U.S. antiwar movement leaders and foreign leftists when he thought they were wrong. When some activists on the left embraced dictators such as Fidel Castro and Saddam Hussein, he reminded them firmly that they should always set their sights on establishing democracies. As early as 1968, he took on Régis Debray (b. 1940), then a theoretician of revolution, and criticized his "foco theory," in which the Frenchman argued that a small group of dedicated people could foment armed uprisings without popular support. Eqbal contrarily argued that revolutionary movements could not succeed without mass popular support—and he said so with devastating effect.[47]

When leaders of the American Left paid little heed to the genocide taking place in Bosnia in the 1990s, Eqbal lost his patience and attacked them vociferously.[48] In a talk he gave at a small demonstration of some fifty people protesting U.S. policy on Bosnia in Springfield, Massachusetts, in December 1994, he complained about those who had spoken out for civil rights and against the Vietnam War but were now silent on Bosnia. "What happened to them?" he asked. "Where are they? Where are my friends right now? Where are they? Why are they letting this happen?"[49] People worldwide, Eqbal argued, had sworn not to let genocide happen again, but in Bosnia it *was* happening all over again.[50] The Holocaust had taught him the lesson that a people could be eliminated or totally dislocated while the world watched and did nothing. In the 1990s, most American leftists, in knee-jerk fashion, could not advocate U.S. involvement anywhere on the globe because they thought such action was a manifestation of imperialism. Eqbal contrarily advocated great-power intervention in Bosnia in the form of arms shipments to the besieged Muslim population in order to save the community. He saw the possibility that the Bosnian Muslims could be annihilated while the rest of the world stood silent. He toured the United States, speaking to any group that would listen, wrote columns about the situation,[51] and harangued liberal and leftist leaders, who turned deaf ears to his arguments.

In 1993, he told David Barsamian,

[T]he response to the Bosnian crisis has ranged from a very microscopic minority being concerned to a large number of people trying very hard to look the other way to the group of people whom I found and find the most nauseating trying to justify their silence. The World Council of Churches, the National Council of Churches, the major churches in the country [the United States] have sat through this Holocaust. They have not even raised a voice. Their answer is . . . that they do not wish to advocate intervention by the United States. . . . Intervention has never been the issue. The Bosnians never asked for American troops or bombers. All they asked for was that the arms embargo on the victims, on the aggressed, on the invaded, be lifted. . . . This to me is so incredible. I can't believe it.[52]

Near the end of his life in 1999, he likewise called for great-power intervention in Kosovo, a position that most U.S. leaders on the left opposed. He advocated sending in ground forces to separate the belligerents and ultimately save Kosovar lives. When U.S. and western European leaders chose the easy way, refusing to commit troops and thus absorb casualties but rather recklessly bombing the civilian population in Kosovo, Eqbal went on a rampage against the bombing.[53]

His was a rational voice, independent and humane. His positions often grated ideologues on the left who sometimes publicly broke with him because the most dogmatic among them expected him to toe a party line or the one in vogue at any given moment. Eqbal refused to do so, recognizing that each crisis had particular contours that led to varied solutions. At times, he ended contacts with former allies and friends over ideological issues or over strategy and tactics. He was never afraid to voice his opinions and did so with great conviction.

Intellectual Pursuits

After the Harrisburg trial ended and as the Vietnam War wound down in 1972 and 1973, Eqbal started traveling to Pakistan with some regularity. His friend Raza Kazim (b. 1930) thought that he was looking for a new agenda, "new battles to fight," after Vietnam.[54] Eqbal began paying increased attention to the Middle East as he came to realize its centrality in U.S. foreign policy. In 1970, he wrote three essays published in French for the Parisian weekly *AfricAsia* and one in Arabic for *al-Hurriya*, the newspaper of the Palestinian Democratic Front for the Liberation of Palestine, in which he argued that a major shift had occurred in U.S. Middle East policy, with Israel becoming central to its strategy. The argument was elaborated five years later in a special issue of *Race & Class* that he edited, "The US and the Arab World." There he criticized Henry Kissinger's policies and examined the reasons for U.S. intervention in the Middle East. He concluded that the United States needed to exert pressure on and control its old allies, western Europe and Japan, by dominating the oil markets in the region. Middle Eastern radical nationalists potentially challenged U.S. direct and indirect control of the conservative Arab leaders who sat on top of the oil there. These radicals therefore had to be contained, weakened, and even destroyed by allowing well-armed U.S. allies and recipients of large quantities of U.S. military aid, specifically Israel (after 1970) and Iran (prior to its 1979 revolution), to act as surrogate military powers that could rein in these U.S. adversaries. Finally, he castigated conservative Arab states, such as Saudi Arabia, for helping to finance the U.S. domination of the region. He despaired of the collaborative role, corruption, and dictatorial inclinations of many Arab rulers, whom he saw assisting American imperialism, and he condemned them.[55]

The Soviet invasion of Afghanistan in 1979 propelled Eqbal to tour the United States to educate audiences about Afghan realities. He astounded his friends with his knowledge of Afghanistan's history and politics and helped frame the debate within the American Left. He befriended Ashraf Ghani (b. 1949), who was later elected president of Afghanistan in 2014, when Ghani was a graduate student at Columbia University at the time. After paying several visits to Peshawar and the frontier zone on the Afghan border and a foray into Afghanistan, he wrote a detailed *New Yorker* feature article with Richard Barnet on Afghanistan and the U.S. connection.[56]

As explained in the introduction, Eqbal derided U.S. policy makers for bolstering the international radical Muslim movements in the 1980s by funding, arming, and training their members from all over the world, giving them invaluable experience in fighting Soviet troops with state-of-the-art weapons. He very quickly saw that these policies would have a spill-over effect and would boomerang to haunt the larger Muslim world—Algeria being a case in point, where an estimated two thousand so-called Afghanis (in truth Algerian radical Muslims who had been trained in Afghanistan and returned home after 1991 to join the civil war in their country) contributed to the escalating levels of violence there. Russia, the United States, and western Europe would pay the price as former Afghan fighters from the jihadi international radical Muslim brigades dispersed after the war and returned to their home countries and other bases of operation, in some cases carrying a great deal of money and arms and new notions of jihad promulgated by their former U.S. trainers.[57] He condemned Pakistan's military secret services for acting as surrogates for the United States by funding, arming, and training first the mujahideen and later the Taliban, who ultimately conquered Afghanistan from Pakistani bases using captured sophisticated U.S. weapons. The initial U.S. backing of the jihadists stemmed not only from America's desire to contribute to the defeat of the Soviet Union but also from its desire to create more malleable allies in Kabul, who would control a strategic area close to Russia and China as well as to neighboring Central Asia, where large deposits of oil and natural gas abounded, perhaps one day necessitating new pipelines through Afghanistan to evacuate that fuel.[58]

Hampshire College

In 1981, Hampshire College in Amherst, Massachusetts, hired Eqbal to a half-time position one semester a year, by his own choice. He needed to earn enough money to help support a widened circle of dependants. They included his New York City household and in Rawalpindi, Pakistan, the widow and six children of his older brother Ghaffar, who had died in 1969. He wanted to return to Pakistan, but he also desired and needed to spend time with his family in New York City. They all had visited Pakistan in 1986–1987, where Julie undertook a study of Pakistani schools and wrote a two-part article, which she published there. His need for sufficient funds to keep all of his dependents afloat and his obligation to stay in the United States while his daughter went to school did not allow him to return to Pakistan full time. In addition, he told Dr. Mubashir Hassan (b. 1922) of Lahore, a former finance minister in the government of Zulfikar Ali Bhutto, that he would have to stay at his job in the United States at least until Dohra graduated from New York's Hunter High School and went to college. That happened in 1989, after which she went to Yale University. He then began spending a good portion of each year in Pakistan. The end of military rule and the restoration of Pakistan's parliamentary government made it ever more feasible for him to get involved then.

Eqbal also earned extra income from frequently lecturing at colleges and universities throughout the United States and from the many newspaper and magazine articles he placed in multiple venues. Acquiring that income entailed his writing constantly and traveling continuously in the United States and abroad to gather material, give lectures, and widen his contacts. Julie had gotten a master's degree at the Bank Street College of Education, had taught young children in the New York City public schools for many years, and then worked briefly in private schools before returning to the public-school system.

When Hampshire College president Adele Smith Simmons (b. 1941), whose father had presided over the Adlai Stevenson Institute Board of Directors in Chicago at the moment that Eqbal was arrested, decided to bring Eqbal to the college in 1982, Cora Weiss supported that decision. Cora sat on the Hampshire College Board of Trustees and had worked with Eqbal during the anti–Vietnam War struggle. Her father, Samuel Rubin, the head of the Rubin Foundation, had funded the TNI in Amsterdam, which Eqbal had directed.

By that point in his life, Eqbal seemed ready for the move away from New York City even though he continued to visit the city and his family on a regular basis. Its attractions were just too powerful for him not to come back frequently. Reflecting later on what he felt as he embarked on his new post at Hampshire, he wrote to his daughter:

Somehow '81–'82 stands out as an important time. When I started teaching at Hampshire, I knew there was no future for me in New York. I had stopped trying to find and define a life in the city. What kept me there was family and friends. After 1982, I had also become alienated from the "peace movement" which largely sat through the invasion of Lebanon as it now sits through the holocaust in Bosnia. There was in fact no peace movement; what did emerge was an anti–Vietnam War movement which fizzled out after the war was over. . . . Yet, strangely I miss New York. After all, my primary relationships are . . . there.[59]

Words are so powerful that someone not knowing Eqbal might take away from this statement the conclusion that he ceased being an activist and only spent time with his family and friends when in New York. Nothing could be further from the truth. Throughout the 1980s, he continued going to New York and stayed there for months when not teaching at Hampshire or heading to Pakistan. The excitement of the city energized him, and his and Edward Said's salons continued there, a parade of Americans and foreigners coming to their Upper Westside Manhattan apartments to meet with them and bring them fresh news and insights. Dinners at Eqbal and Julie's place continued to attract interesting people. Someone such as he, working on and studying countries controlled by dictators, needed to speak with opposition leaders, human rights activists, as well as the best novelists, poets, journalists, and other intellectuals from those places to discover what the world's media did not report. Eqbal did just that with gusto and accumulated a great deal of firsthand knowledge about global hot spots. He also pressed his friends on the U.S. left to get involved in a multitude of issues, attended meetings galore in New York City, and spoke frequently on local radio programs and in other fora. Wherever he appeared, he energized people and sparked activity.

At Hampshire College, he very quickly became a popular teacher and drew to his courses many Five College students in the Pioneer Valley, who traveled to Hampshire from their own nearby colleges to study with him. Edward Said often pointed out that Eqbal's classes, unlike those of many in his profession, overflowed and grew larger instead of emptying as the semester proceeded. In a document I found in the Eqbal Ahmad Papers at Hampshire College, an evaluation dated November 14, 1989, in favor of his second ten-year appointment at the college, one of Eqbal's colleagues and friends, Professor Carollee Bengelsdorf (b. 1946), wrote exuberantly in favor of keeping him on the staff:

> In the work I have done with him . . . Eqbal has been simply extraordinary. With a blend of gentleness and careful insight, he has consistently managed to critique students' work, in both form and content, and to guide them in the process of developing skills in thinking, analyzing, writing and editing which has, as a consequence, put them on

planes which seemed inconceivable, both to the students and to other committee members, at the beginning of the committees' work. In so doing, he has literally reshaped the lives and the self expectations of students, in the manner in which Hampshire, at its very best, sees itself as capable of doing.[60]

Eqbal believed that education consisted of having students understand complexities, and he never accepted facile explanations.

He also wanted to inculcate in his students a sense of morality that he had absorbed in India and Pakistan from his family and teachers. He argued in 1992 that morality invests knowledge and learning with its social significance. Two aspects of morality are the educator's concern: integrity and responsibility. A person who lacks integrity has missed the essence of education. In the academic world, there is no sin greater than plagiarism; in life generally, this translates into a taboo against all forms of misappropriation and misrepresentation. Similarly, an educated person without an active moral outlook is at best an isolated consumer, albeit of ideas and information: "The educational purpose is truly served when students are helped to develop a moral outlook; when they internalize the idea that the educated person is distinguished by his/her ability to relate abstract moral principles to individual and collective behavior; when they know that a primary purpose of learning is to elevate the quality not merely of one's personal and family life but of the social environment."[61]

Teaching with passion and conviction, he changed the lives of many who studied with him. A few of them, such as Yogesh Chandrani (b. 1959), or Yogi, as his close friends call him, had a conversion experience after encountering Eqbal. The young Hampshire student from India met Eqbal while he, Yogi, was hitchhiking from one campus to another in the Pioneer Valley (which is normal for students there, whatever their family income), and Eqbal gave him a ride. He told me that his first contact with Eqbal changed his life. Yogesh watched in fear as the hopelessly unmechanical professor drove hesitantly back to their campus. He decided right then and there that he would henceforth chauffer Eqbal wherever he needed to go rather than risk having a heart attack as the professor's passenger or hearing later about the Pakistani scholar who ended up crushed in a major accident. Yogi was brought up with a silver spoon in his mouth, the son of a wealthy Hindu family that had three hundred servants. He never learned something as elementary as tying his own shoelaces. He had a couple of young retainers who followed him everywhere and did everything for him. Meeting Eqbal, a Muslim Pakistani born in India who was knowledgeable about its high culture but who was able to cook his own meals, wash his own dishes, make his own bed, and clean his own house and liked doing so, changed Yogi's priorities and worldview. He became Eqbal's teaching assistant, absorbed his mentor's knowledge like a sponge, and made life choices that he never would have contemplated making before that fateful day that he hitchhiked. Yogi eventually married our friends Mohammed and Dede Guessous's daughter, Nadia, also one of Eqbal's students.

Adele Simmons recently summed up Eqbal's contribution to the college:

> Hampshire attracted students who were challenging the status quo, asking tough questions about the direction of U.S. foreign policy, and willing to think outside of the box. It is easy to speak out, to stage a rally, and occupy the president's office. What makes these actions effective is if they are grounded in careful and thorough analysis, based on fact and an understanding of the complexity of the issues at hand. And what is even more effective is a critique that has solutions, that includes a vision of a better way forward.
>
> Eqbal never let his students settle for easy answers. He forced them to go beyond the slogans to understand why U.S. policy in Afghanistan was setting the country up for trouble, why our failure to respect Palestine and Palestinians would be the source for more conflict, and more. His students had to do more than criticize dictators (or their college president). They had to understand what needed to be done to strengthen a nation—or the college. The quick superficial answer was not sufficient. With Eqbal as their mentor and professor, students grounded their activism in careful analysis that enabled so many of them to leave Hampshire and become effective advocates for a more just and peaceful world.[62]

Eqbal often invited me to lecture to his classes at Hampshire. On one occasion, I joined his class on the Arab world. He immediately asked me to describe any misconception that Westerners had of Arabs. The subject, of course, is vast, and he had no idea how I would respond. I blurted out that they had a total misunderstanding of the Arab concept of hospitality. That set off a half-hour discussion, which intrigued the students. The rule adhered to often in the Arab world is that a guest is welcomed for three days without complaint. After that, reciprocity comes into play. Hosts thereafter expect their guests to contribute to their own maintenance by buying food, which the family will share. If not understood, heads of families often become irritable, and guests will be made to feel uncomfortable. Eqbal ran with the concept and tied it into other customs that are likewise misunderstood. The discussion spiraled into a fascinating class.

In 1997, Eqbal retired from Hampshire College. After his daughter entered graduate school, he left his American family in the United States and moved to Pakistan. As already noted, he attempted to found a new liberal arts college in Pakistan, but lack of government support and private funding and personal illness forced him to abort the project. Both in the United States and on the Indian subcontinent, he will be remembered as a peacemaker. In South Asia, he worked tirelessly against nuclear proliferation and, in the face of official opposition, for intensifying exchanges between Indians and Pakistanis in order to normalize relations between the two states.

There in Pakistan and on frequent trips to India, after Julie and he separated in 1990, he afterward shared his life with the well-known Indian intellectual Radha Kamar (b. 1955). The two loved each other, and they contemplated a future marriage. Although he and Radha traveled to India, where they lived for short spells, he lived in Pakistan, where he discovered he had colon cancer. He died at around age sixty-nine in Islamabad on May 11, 1999, from a heart attack after undergoing surgery for colon cancer.

2

Reflections on Eqbal's Life

YOU COULD NEVER PREDICT HOW EQBAL WOULD REACT TO A given crisis, which meant that speaking to him about current events was always an adventure. Sometimes he would shock people whom he barely knew by defending positions diametrically opposed to what he surmised was their received knowledge. He did so not to provoke but to force those listening to rethink their positions and see events in a new light. This approach, combined with significant rhetorical skills, meant that once you heard him, you never forgot him. And he did it all with such charm that even though his arguments may have appeared outrageous to some, they listened and paid attention. Others on his wavelength appreciated the clarity with which he presented his arguments, for he had the habit of packaging his talks in numerical order, three or four points, which followed from one to another. His humor, the force of his logic, and his clarity sometimes helped win over his opponents.

Eqbal and Edward Said

Eqbal met Edward Said for the first time in 1968. The U.S. war in Vietnam and the protests against it defined in those days America's intellectual and political environment on the political left. Eqbal, as a leader of the antiwar movement, had become a prominent figure. He surmised that Edward already knew about him even before they met and that the critic would favor an outspoken dissenter who lived in the United States without becoming a citizen. Their friendship grew continuously and never broke. Eqbal wrote on December 7, 1992, about the circumstances of their meeting in a letter to Tim May and Frank Hanly, BBC producers working on a program about Edward's life:

> [O]ur meeting and, later, . . . our friendship . . . had to do perhaps with the fact that we were both exiles. . . . We shared the exiles' experience . . . as it induces a certain relationship of alienation and intimacy with one's chosen environment, and of constant often secret negotiations between one's colonial past and contemporary metropolitan life. I and Edward never talked about this. I should, nevertheless, note that he mentions in *Culture & Imperialism* the experience of exile with feeling and insight. . . .
>
> I first came to know of Edward from an article—"Portrait of an Arab"—which I read in *The Arab World*, a magazine which used to be published by the Arab League. . . . It was an unusual piece to be printed in an official Arab organ. At the time when Israel was routinely referred to [in the Arab media] as . . . the Zionist entity, Edward wrote of the Palestinian Arab as a shadow of the Jew— tormented, persecuted, and devalued. More important, it was a seminal essay. [Its] themes . . . later [re]appeared full bloom in *Orientalism*— of representational forms and narratives as defining the moral epistemology of imperialism, instruments in the creation of imperial ethos, legitimacy, and identity. I was deeply moved and impressed by the essay and asked Ibrahim Abu-Lughod, a mutual friend, to introduce me to Said. He did a few months later.[1]

Eqbal recalled to the TV producers that only a few dissenters spoke out in the United States after the 1967 Arab-Israeli War. "Those around us, including the 'peace people,' considered Zionism and Israel to be blameless and [the] heroic survivor of wanton Arab aggression. The media was closed to us . . . there was no mainstream magazine open to our viewpoint on the Middle East." Among those who "advocated the restitution of Palestinian rights Edward stood out for his open and critical posture not only towards the Arab governments, but also towards the PLO. . . . It was rare at the time to find pro-Palestinian critics of the PLO's strategy and politics."

Eqbal then recounted to May and Hanly the negative reactions to a talk he had given after the 1967 war at the second convention of the Organization of Arab Students. In it, he criticized the tactics used by the Arab states and argued that they could never defeat Israel militarily. Eqbal thought that his talk was "fool hardy [sic]" and "given at the wrong time to the wrong audience." When Eqbal and Edward first met, Edward asked him about this speech. He seemed quite curious, and he surprisingly agreed with Eqbal's conclusions. Eqbal therefore appreciated Edward's "consistently critical solidarity" with the PLO and its leaders.

Imperialism took many forms, and Eqbal reflected on that issue in his letter to May and Hanly. He explained his and Edward's affinities—especially their similar views on imperialism—and summarized the reasons why they had become close friends:

[The year] 1967 had a lasting effect on Edward intellectually and politically. During the weeks that the Arab-Israeli conflict occupied center stage in the American discourse, an astounding system of beliefs, images, myths, and anxieties about Arabs and Islam unfolded before us. Layer after layer of libel were heaped daily by certified experts, columnists, and politicians. The simple minded [sic] Arab could dismiss it as the work of an influential lobby. But to a discerning intellect, it was obvious that on display was a historically rooted and complex culture of imperialism.

Edward proceeded to excavate and expose its roots. His skills and methods as a critic were great assets, but what invested power and originality to his work in the next two decades was a seminal insight regarding the relationship of knowledge to imperial power. *Orientalism* was a milestone in this regard. What makes his current work extremely interesting is that he also elaborates on another set of relationships—between imperialism and the novel, poetry, and music, and the relationship between culture and resistance.

Edward wrote *Orientalism* to demonstrate the depths of imperial ideology within Western culture. He applied the lessons he learned from Michel Foucault, who demonstrated the importance of substructures of knowledge, which at first sight were not apparent but had to be excavated and extracted from cultural forms and constructs, the whole constituting patterns that assumed the power of institutions. Edward also mined Antonio Gramsci, the secret head of the Italian Communist Party whom Mussolini imprisoned, because Gramsci recognized the power of hegemonic knowledge and advocated creating alternate institutions in order to foment and spread new knowledge, the better to replace old dominant structures of thought and practice.[2] As Eqbal told May and Hanly, he recognized that "a common anti-imperialist outlook went into the making of [his and Edward's] friendship more . . . than the shared experience of exile."

Both men had cosmopolitan views, and by the time they met, they had seen a considerable part of the world. Their status as refugees had made them into critical outsiders. Both of them could see the societies in which they lived from without, and they had developed sufficient yardsticks with which to gauge with some detachment and discernment what they experienced and saw. Eqbal recognized this when he observed to May and Hanly that although Edward was a "Tory in life style [*sic*], and to some extent in taste," he also was a "critical democrat, which explains, at least partially, the absence of third worldism, and the antipathy he feels to authoritarian minorities which rule the Arab world, their addiction to arms, narrow vision, and indifference towards the future":

The colonial encounter left a permanent mark on us as it did on the colonized lands. Fortunately, its impact has been more even on individuals like me and Edward than on our societies as a whole. To different degrees both of us have shared a consciously dual relationship to the West and to our native environment. We are, to paraphrase Nehru, at home in both civilizations, at ease in neither. Anti-imperialism has been a defining sentiment with us, but it has never degenerated into anti-westernism. In differing ways we both love and appreciate much about western civilization at the same time as we are appalled by the imperious patterns of sectarian prejudices, informed ignorance, callousness, and hypocrisy. . . .

As his latest book shows, Edward is a universalist despite or because of the anguish which sectarian ambitions inflicted upon him and his people. This may be yet another factor which explains the durability of our friendship.

And they certainly grew to depend on one another. They adored and admired each other and fed off of each other's intelligence and wit. The fact that Edward's and Eqbal's own family and friends lived in New York was one of the main reasons why Eqbal returned to the city with regularity. Edward rarely let anyone read his completed manuscripts but published them mostly as they were written, so confident was he about the validity of his views. He made some exceptions to his policy of immediate publication without review in the 1990s, when he began showing his finished work to Eqbal and a few other close friends before sending manuscripts off for publication. Edward dedicated his book *Culture and Imperialism* to Eqbal, and that act was a tribute to the ongoing creative dialogue they had over the decades.

It was a delight to see them together, for they joked around, and each brought out the best in the other. Their letters and email exchanges over the years would make a remarkable book. Their correspondence, for fun, overflowed with imitations of the flowery language of medieval Muslim royalty, whose missives would begin with adoring words, comparing the other to a rose in bloom or the sun rising to majestic heights, but then

announce abruptly that the wielder of such compliments had just conquered "his dear brother's" prize city. Forgive the indiscretion, the bearer
of bad tidings would then beg, but he knew that the receiver of the news
would understand why the aggressive prince had to act the way he did.
Eqbal and Edward, in jest, incorporated these sorts of protocols into
their letters and emails with hilarious effect. One salutation at the end
of a letter Eqbal wrote to Edward on September 25, 1997, gives an idea
of what went on in their voluminous correspondence: "With much
humble affection and prayers that I stay a particle of dust under you[r]
vigorous feet," Eqbal rhapsodized, "I remain: Forever your homage paying *chamcha* ['spoon,' implying that he was a mere utensil in relation to his
superior]."[3] The humor had no bounds, and they reveled in thinking up
such adornments to their correspondence, which gave them enormous
pleasure.

The humor extended to gentle criticism Eqbal gave Edward on a subject as ponderous as the Kosovo crisis. In response to an article Edward
had written on the subject for the Karachi newspaper *Dawn*, Eqbal sent
his friend the following letter, which Edward read at the celebration of
Eqbal's life at Hampshire College on September 18, 1999, four months
after he died:

> Son of Palestine, Moon over Jerusalem, Light of the Semites, Refuge
> of the World, Shadow of the Lord on Earth . . . a humble particle of
> dust offers salutations from down under your expensively dressed
> and glorious feet . . . and welcomes you back to the land of bombs and
> missiles, cold milk, and caned honey. With deep interest and in humble
> submission, I read your stirring thoughts in *Dawn* . . . on the plight of
> Kosovo and the nefarious imperial intervention therein to advance its
> own purposes. Since in your wisdom and forbearance you have for-
> saken your abject bat man, this august essay is the one august sign I
> have of your return to the not-so-glorious belly of the beast. I enclose
> an abject effort on the subject, which unfortunately was written and
> dispatched before I could enlighten my dusty self and decorate my
> humble effort with a quotation from your brilliant observations.[4]

Edward thought the world of Eqbal, and it was fortuitous that they had found each other and become good friends. Edward expressed his admiration for Eqbal in a letter of recommendation he wrote for his friend when the latter applied for a job at Hampshire College in 1983, beginning it by calling him "a truly remarkable man":

> Knowing him has been an education. He is . . . the finest, most astute and brilliant analyst of contemporary politics from a non-European and non-Western point of view that I have ever encountered. Deeply learned and humane, he is a man of great, genuine learning . . . he commands history, politics, society, culture and everyday life, and as a consequence his analyses are regularly enlivened by the insight and generosity that eludes most other people in his field. . . . He is also . . . a man of reason and dispassionate fairness, never more than when his own sympathies are engaged . . . no one has the command and learning that he has. . . . I cannot think of anyone more distinguished as man and as scholar than Dr. Ahmad.[5]

Eqbal was probably the most loyal friend anyone could ever have. Friends could do no wrong, or if they did something he disapproved of, he would have it out with them privately but never in public. He defended friends beyond the call of duty, sometimes refusing to see shortcomings or the value of external criticism. That attribute solidified his friendships and created close bonds between him and many people. But such blind loyalty also had its drawbacks. He broke with several people with whom he had collaborated for decades when they criticized his closest friends publicly in print. Others broke with him. For example, he went on offensives on behalf of Edward time and again as Edward's detractors mounted concerted campaigns to discredit the critic. Eqbal had no tolerance for anyone who joined the frenzy of attacks against Edward, one of his closest friends.

Eqbal's Attributes and Interactions with Friends and Students

There were many things about Eqbal that his writings do not reveal. He had the extraordinary ability to cut through chaff and get to the heart of matters in his own distinctive way. His ironic and mischievous sense of humor mitigated the seriousness with which he confronted life's problems.

He was also a remarkable teacher who practiced his trade full time, not just in the classroom. Conversations with him offered new analysis. He tailored his many newspaper and magazine columns to teach about the complexities of society and politics without ever talking down to readers. He rarely wrote for the powerful but rather aimed his analysis at those who might enhance civil society and ameliorate the conditions that he described. He taught in order to motivate people to try to improve the world. In the classroom, he wanted to stamp on his students a sense of morality and also to empower them.

He summarized best what he stood for in a commencement speech he delivered at Hampshire College on May 17, 1997, just as he was about to retire from teaching. After entertaining the students and their parents with a witty oration, he concluded his talk by telling them what he thought the term *third world* really meant, while echoing the epithet on Karl Marx's tombstone, "Philosophers have only interpreted the world; the point, however is to change it":

> Power is more or less unequally distributed in nearly all spheres of life—internationally, nationally, and even in the family, and this inequality—be it racial or sexual, of classes, or of nations—stands [as] a major obstacle to human liberation. To ameliorate it is an enlightened, educated project. Viewed thus, the third world is a metaphor for unequal exchange. The "expectation" then is that the educated person would discern its patterns, within and without, and work at obviating it. The function of knowledge, after all, should be to comprehend reality in order to change it.[6]

Teaching with passion and conviction, he changed the lives of many who studied with him. He grouped around him a large number of loyal students who venerated him as he aged and as he exuded an air of determined wisdom. He cultivated such adulation, sometimes to his detriment. Some young people in his entourage have complained that as he aged, he accepted less and less criticism from them, making it difficult for those who disagreed with him to voice their opinions. A few became estranged, and others had to go through elaborate dialogues with him to reestablish relationships. But, to his credit, he never let his students become complaisant and continuously challenged them when they least expected it.

Outsider Status and Rapport with Those in Power

Problems also sometimes arose from Eqbal's being an outsider. For example, his distance from Pakistan on occasion bred misunderstandings and, worse yet, at times fantasies. Some accused him of chasing pipe dreams and applying yardsticks to Pakistan that were sometimes irrelevant to realities on the ground. For example, beginning one month after Prime Minister Benazir Bhutto (1953–2007) came to power, in his newspaper columns Eqbal attacked her policies and the corruption of her husband, Asif Ali Zardari (b. 1955). He continued these attacks at the same time that he expected the couple to endorse and underwrite plans he had to establish a new university in Pakistan. In fact, he heard that the prime minister, in a fit of megalomania, had told people a far-fetched story that Eqbal was responsible for the death of President Zulfiqar Ali Bhutto (1928–1979) by attacking him openly and bitterly in the press before General Zia al-Haq (1924–1988) overthrew his regime.

Zia Mian (b. 1961), who shared a house in Islamabad with Eqbal in the mid-1990s, remembered a "bad encounter" Eqbal had with Prime Minister Bhutto in 1995 at an event concerning the creation of Bangladesh, organized at the Pakistan national library in the capital and attended by about four hundred people. After Eqbal criticized Zulfikar Ali Bhutto in his turn at the podium, Bhutto's daughter took the stage and defended her father's policies without referring to what Eqbal had previously said. After the session, when Eqbal extended his hand to shake hers, she ignored him and afterward avoided him.[7] In a letter to Dr. Saidar

Mahmoud, the secretary of the Ministry of Education, on January 6, 1998, Eqbal wrote that between August 1994 and October 1996 the university he hoped to found faced "undue delays by officials who felt that the Prime Minister [Bhutto] was not keen on the project." In fact, Bhutto's husband, while she was alive, confiscated the 200 acres in Islamabad that the cabinet of Prime Minister Nawaz Sharif (b. 1949) had promised to Eqbal in January 1993 for the construction of the projected university; Zardari supposedly intended to use that land for a country club and golf course. After a great deal of organizing, in July 1994 Eqbal was promised a reduced land grant of 70 acres that was much less desirable than the first.[8] Another 130 acres were reserved for future acquisition by the university but not assigned to it at the time. Eqbal's nephew Najeeb Omar, an architect who worked closely with Eqbal on the project, had inspected the smaller parcel located "in a remote area near Lake Rawal in the vicinity of Islamabad. Unlike the first allotment, it had no road frontage and the cost of building new roads and infrastructure to make the place accessible to students and teachers would have been too prohibitive to use." Eqbal could have taken the 70 acres, but he had no charter to set up a university on it. Without one, he did not want to assume title to the land.[9] By placing himself in the impossible situation of needing a corrupt regime to supply him with state land for his new venture, he made the realization of his dream that more difficult to achieve.[10] He had also hoped to raise substantial funds for the new university from U.S. foundations. Adele Simmons, the president of the John D. and Catherine T. MacArthur Foundation at the time, concluded that the most her foundation could do for him was to give him some seed money, but no more. She did not think that any U.S. foundation would help him underwrite the establishment and running of a foreign university. He had found some rich Pakistani backers for the scheme, but they would not or could not put up enough money to launch and sustain a full-fledged university. Before Eqbal died, he and his Pakistani friends had raised more than $3 million of the $30 million needed to open the new school.[11] He found it difficult to raise these funds and confided in a letter to his daughter on August 17, 1993, "Nothing sickens like fund raising; I must find someone else to do it."[12]

Most educational institutions set up with private funds in the Third World concentrate on business education, not on the humanities with a large Islamic component and the pure and social sciences, as Eqbal had hoped to do. Rich parents in many countries are willing to invest in business education for their children, expecting them to be able to get well-paying jobs in international corporations upon graduation. Few of the same parents would invest in high tuition for degrees in low-paying fields such as philosophy, sociology, history, and political science. As a result, most students in the Third World study the humanities and social sciences in state universities rather than in private ones. With all good intentions, Eqbal was bucking trends that went against his inclinations. Moreover, a government's opponent cannot expect that same government to underwrite a venture for him. Because of such contradictions, Khaldunia, Eqbal's university, therefore faced insurmountable hurdles. Near the end of his life, he admitted to close friends that the project had failed.

Unlike others in a similar position, Eqbal did not have major financial inducements to prod Pakistan's business elites to support his university project in a grandiose manner. Gandhi in his loincloth, by contrast, had shored up his position as leader of a nonviolent, anti-imperialist struggle by getting the support of significant Indian businesspeople, who underwrote his campaigns. By advocating the boycott of British products and substituting local handmade goods, such as homespun cloth, Gandhi guaranteed that rich industrialists would back his movement. In fact, Gandhi became the darling of the very rich Indian industrialists within the Congress Party, who found his anti-British campaigns useful for their businesses' expansion at British expense. Eqbal needed such backers to launch his university scheme. Few Pakistani entrepreneurs, however, saw long-term benefits in Eqbal's Khaldunia like those that Gandhi provided to Indian businesses for the expansion of their own enterprises.

Eqbal's Algerian Interests

Eqbal visited newly independent Algeria on July 10, 1962, and witnessed the first flush of euphoria of the victorious population. He and his party celebrated independence with the Algerians whom they met, and the experience affected Eqbal profoundly. Any voyage into Algeria at that point in time had to transform anyone coming in contact with the exuberant population. He took away an important lesson that stayed with him throughout his life. Even though the Algerian National Liberation Front had ultimately lost the war militarily to the French, they had won the hearts and minds of the Algerian population and therefore gained their independence.

Eqbal followed postindependence Algerian events closely from his Tunisian base and quickly saw the dangers of a military takeover there, a civil war, which would eliminate those who fought and won the revolution inside Algeria. The National Liberation Front army of Colonel Houari Boumediene (1932–1978), whose troops had been stationed throughout the war in Morocco and Tunisia, marched in and took over the country in a coup immediately after independence. The Algerian population, exhausted from the eight-year war, did not oppose the military then. The army leader allied himself with Ahmed Ben Bella (1916–2012), the first president after independence.

When I visited Eqbal in Tunis just before New Year's Day in 1963, we spoke at length of the Algerian tragedy. He already had premonitions of doom, which became stronger when both of us returned to Algeria to attend the first congress of the Algerian trade union. We watched incredulously as the new Algerian president, Ben Bella, had the delegates whom the workers had selected democratically as their representatives arrested and replaced by bussed-in peasants, who were instructed to vote for the government's program. Eqbal fumed and ranted and at the podium had the audacity to confront Ben Bella, whom he had never before met. Taking a great risk of being arrested, he screamed at Ben Bella that he had betrayed the revolution. Many years later, in another context, he called Ben Bella a "mindless opportunist."[13] At that point in 1963, he concluded that Algeria's destiny would be bleak.[14] While residing in Tunis, he had developed close friendships with Algerian revolutionaries living in exile there. The most important of them was the Kabylie Berber Belkacem Krim (born in 1922 and assassinated in Frankfurt, Germany, in 1970), who was also one of the original founders of the revolution.

Eqbal saw Krim and other Algerian leaders quite frequently and learned a great deal from them about how they organized the uprising and the complications of keeping the revolt alive. As an astute political analyst, Eqbal used that information—from the source—to begin to develop his theories of revolutionary warfare.

3

Polemics

THROUGHOUT HIS ADULT LIFE, EQBAL STIRRED UP OR
entered into controversies over intellectual positions that he disagreed
with. I dealt in chapter 1 with his critique of Régis Debray's "foco
theory" of revolution, one of many polemics he engaged in early in his
academic career. His friend Edward Said joined him in criticizing their
detractors and responding to fierce attacks, which they sometimes provoked because they disagreed with the paradigms of thought at vogue at
any given moment. Both especially disliked Third World dictators, ratio-
nalizers of U.S. foreign policy, and the purveyors of new forms of global
imperialism. Edward made his mark on a variety of fields and became
globally famous by dissecting the imperial roots of Western culture. Eqbal
did the same in his political and foreign-policy analysis. This chapter
presents a small sample of the polemics Eqbal launched against his

intellectual opponents, some of whom, such as Ernest Gellner, were internationally famous.

Ernest Gellner, over Frantz Fanon

By the late 1950s, Frantz Fanon (1925–1961) had already written in French a series of books about the psychological dimensions of the Algerian revolution and the pitfalls of Third World transformations. While Eqbal was at Princeton, Fanon's publications provided fodder for the budding political scientist's critical analysis of revolution. Fanon, a trained psychiatrist, was one of the best propagandists of revolution ever to write about the phenomenon. He had been a newspaper editor and had honed his skills in that arena.

As a psychiatrist at the Blida clinic, he had systematically collected data about psychological reactions to revolutionary warfare and torture that no one had ever done before. He also secretly worked with revolutionary cadres to prepare them for the horrors of torture, which the French army regularly applied to imprisoned militants, both Muslim and French. His writing reflected both the propagandist and the psychiatrist. He often exaggerated; at times he twisted reality because his public job as he saw it was to win over liberal French people to the Algerian cause, widen fissures in French society, and lead the French to support Algerian independence. Bending truth became a tool of struggle, and he excelled at it. Privately, he was a valued militant of the Front de libération nationale (FLN, Algerian National Liberation Front).

Eqbal learned from Fanon's writings and activism the importance of organizing and provoking divisions in civil society in the metropolis in order to defeat imperial ambitions. He also absorbed Fanon's teachings on the significance of self-management for transforming workers' lives and establishing a more equitable society. Though Fanon may have glorified violence as a cleansing force in revolution, he understood a battered population's deep urges for closure and revenge for enduring more than a century of profound dislocation and deep class and racial cleavages that followed mostly ethnic and religious lines. As Abderrahmane Moussaoui has shown in his brilliant book on Algerian violence, and as the historian Mohammed Harbi (b. 1933) increasingly realized as he worked through hundreds of documents chronicling that violence through more than a century, somehow the heritage of strife and confrontation that marked Algerian colonization, perhaps the worst experience endured by a people in the Middle East and North Africa, had to be expiated or surface instead of being pent up and sublimated.[1] Because of his in-depth psychoanalysis of victims, Fanon understood this better than most.

Eqbal also appreciated Fanon's contributions to postcolonial theory. Fanon correctly predicted that many Third World nations would fall prey to a predatory local ruling class, whose members would step into the shoes of their former colonial masters, leaving conditions unchanged.[2] Faiz Ahmad Faiz (1911–1984), the celebrated Pakistani poet and Eqbal's friend, echoed this notion when he described decolonization as a "false light."[3] "I know of no third world poet other than Faiz who was so prescient in catching the mood of disillusionment with the decolonized post-colonial states," Eqbal told David Barsamian in 1998.[4] Fanon's appeal was echoed in Eqbal's favorite poet.

In an April 2, 1993, *Times Literary Supplement* letter criticizing the British Czech philosopher and social anthropologist Ernest Gellner (1925–1995),[5] Eqbal took the polymath scholar to task for not understanding Fanon's legacy. This criticism was part of a much wider polemic between Gellner and Edward Said in the *Times Literary Supplement* letters pages that lasted from February to June 1993. Eqbal wrote this letter in response to a negative review that Gellner had written of Edward's book *Culture and Imperialism*, which he had dedicated to Eqbal.[6] In this book, Edward continued to explore the permeation of imperialism in Western culture that he had begun in his groundbreaking work *Orientalism*. Using Jane Austen's *Mansfield Park*, Giuseppe Verdi's opera *Aida*, and works by Joseph Conrad, Albert Camus, and Charles Dickens in the first part of the book, and delving into the output of Frantz Fanon, among others, in the second, Edward wrote a clearer and more forceful book than his previous classic. Gellner's review was nevertheless blatantly hostile.

As part of his solidarity with Edward, Eqbal systematically defended his friend as he increasingly and simultaneously came under attack from

Zionists and mainstream scholars who did not approve of his method of deconstructing the Western canon. Some leftists, such as the Pakistani Indian Marxist scholar Aijaz Ahmad (b. 1941), also erroneously lumped him with postcolonial theorists such as Harvard University professor Homi Bhabha (b. 1949) and Columbia University professor Gayatri Spivak (b. 1942) and attacked his work as part of a ploy to dismiss Marxist analysis and to replace it with what Ahmad considered to be unintelligible gibberish. Edward felt under siege.

I met and was friends with Gellner in Morocco in the early 1960s, where the latter conducted anthropological research after establishing himself as a major British philosopher, having taken on and criticized Ludwig Wittgenstein (1889–1951), the central figure in the linguistic philosophical movement.[7] During the late 1960s, I lectured to Gellner's anthropology seminar at the London School of Economics, where he taught before moving to Cambridge University and finally in 1993 to the Central European University in Prague.

At the time of my talk, I spent an evening with him in his very old and beautiful thatched-roofed cottage in a region outside of London. His daughter, Sarah Gellner, reminiscing about her father in 2011, said that he loved living there and that these times were the happiest of his life.[8] He took me to a local cocktail party filled with the most conservative British intellectuals I had ever met, which took me to what I imagined the 1930s to be like. Clearly, his references were in the distant past. Sarah Gellner also said that he had adored Margaret Thatcher and that his closest friends were Conservatives.[9] Yet putting him into any box would be difficult because he believed that poverty could be eliminated by the application of science and thought that all states should do so.[10] This position was not in any sense conservative. But by virtue of who Gellner was, he was not going to like the iconoclast Edward Said.

In the same review of Edward's book, Gellner praised the astuteness of the French anthropologist Robert Montagne (1893–1954), leaving out the all-important fact that Montagne's ethnographic studies of rural and urban Moroccans disclosed the secrets of the segmentary system of clans living in the mountains of Morocco. Early in his career, Montagne had worked for Marshall Hubert Lyautey (1854–1934), the first *resident gé-*

néral of Morocco, as an adviser on Berber affairs. Using the information supplied by Montagne and by the scholars working with him, the French military allied itself with dominant clan segments to facilitate the conquest of the dissident parts of the country. This type of collaboration by a scholar, who admittedly was quite good at what he did, did not at all concern or upset Gellner. All he could say was that Montagne was right. The moral implications of Montagne's research and its application by the military carried no weight with the British anthropologist.[11]

In his *Times Literary Supplement* review of Edward's book, Gellner complimented the very people whom Edward and Eqbal abhorred: Bernard Lewis (b. 1916), professor emeritus at Princeton University, and Lewis's friends and allies Patricia Crone (b. 1945), Andrew Mellon Professor of Historical Studies at the Princeton Institute for Advanced Studies, and Michael A. Cook (b. 1940),[12] Lewis's former student and Class of 1943 University Professor of Near Eastern Studies at Princeton University—well trained and extensively published scholars with deep language skills. Early in their careers they had sought out the Jewish roots of Islam and debunked Marxist interpretations of the prophet Muhammad's life and early Islam, approaches with which Gellner would have concurred.[13] Chris Hann, who knew Gellner, pointed out in his obituary for Gellner in the *Independent* (London) on November 8, 1995, that Gellner's "scorn for western Marxism was unswerving."[14]

Bernard Lewis and Edward Said were enemies, and Edward had attacked the old gentleman continuously for his pro-Israel biases and for being the epitome of what was wrong with Orientalists.[15] The two had debated at the Middle East Studies Association meeting on November 22, 1986, a standing-room only event, which Edward felt that he had won. Edward's young followers took over the association, and by 2007 Lewis and his conservative allies left it to set up the smaller and fringe Association for the Study of the Middle East and Africa, with Lewis as the chair of its Academic Council and Fouad Ajami (1945–2014) of the Hoover Institution in Stanford, California, as its vice chair.

As John Hall demonstrates in his biography of Gellner, the latter thrived on combative exchanges. Eqbal knew that when he wrote his critique of Gellner's review of Edward Said's book *Culture and Imperialism*.

Respectful of Gellner's intellect, Eqbal, always the gentleman, wrote the scholar a personal letter telling him that he planned to react to Gellner's unfavorable review of Edward's book. He wrote that he had always held him "in high regard," adding that he promised "not to feel hurt by a harsh response from you."[16] That did not stop Eqbal from attacking Gellner on his most vulnerable point, his knowledge of Frantz Fanon.

Gellner, among other issues, had criticized Said for concentrating on Fanon rather than on the Algerian religious scholar Abdelhamid Ben Badis (1889–1940). Gellner argued that Fanon "was for export only," meant nothing to the Algerians, and "made no contribution to the content of Algerian life and thought," whereas Ben Badis, little known internationally, was far more important for the Algerians and contributed to the Arabization movement and the later emergence of Islamism. Taking exception to Gellner's assertion that Fanon had little effect on Algerians, Eqbal summarized Fanon's contributions to the Algerian revolution and his long-lasting contribution to Algerian working-class culture and the field of psychiatry. Beginning with this last point, Eqbal pointed out that as the director of the psychiatric ward at Blida hospital, Fanon had taught FLN paramedics and cadres how to train revolutionaries to withstand French torture, which was widespread. He himself treated many torture victims, and his records of those cases formed the basis of his book *A Dying Colonialism*.[17] Eqbal concluded that "[t]his was risky clandestine work; it did not involve winning international support." In Tunis, Eqbal continued, Fanon taught and practiced psychiatry while editing the FLN newspaper, read by Algerians, not by foreigners.[18]

Eqbal maintained that Fanon's influence was greater in Algeria than Gellner imagined. During the chaotic period immediately before and after independence in 1962–1963, nearly a million Algerian workers followed the teachings of Fanon on the importance of self-management and saved the newly independent state and economy by taking over major industries and keeping them running through a period of political turmoil. Based on his firsthand encounter with Algeria immediately after its independence and on research he conducted for comparative analysis of the worker's movement in Algeria, Morocco, and Tunisia, which he later published,[19] Eqbal argued:

As France withdrew [from the war-torn country], Algerian leaders and army commanders jockeyed for power, threatening civil war. Meanwhile the French settlers, who controlled Algeria's economy, embarked on a countrywide program of lock-out sabotage, and terror, hoping to scuttle [the] Franco-Algerian Treaty. Fortunately, the cadres and workers who were influenced by Fanon's ideas of decentralization, worker's control, and community governance saved Algeria from chaos.

Thus Algeria produced a most promising movement in history of "self-management" and participatory democracy. By 1963, when central government became organized, nearly a million workers in the "auto-gestion" movement had comprised all the key industries and a third of the labor force; production approached Algeria's pre-war level. The military-bureaucratic elite, which took power with mindless opportunists like Ahmed Ben Bella, paid verbal tribute to Fanon but systematically undermined the remarkable legacy of his ideas.[20]

Kanan Makiya

Eqbal and Edward also had a major falling out with Kanan Makiya (b. 1949), an Iraqi exile who became a British citizen in 1982 and then taught in the Department of Near Eastern and Judaic Studies at Brandeis University, where he is now the Sylvia K. Hassenfeld Professor of Islamic and Middle East Studies. In the 1960s and 1970s, he was a Trotskyist and then in the early 1980s switched sides. His father, an architect like his son, owned a Baghdad construction company, which worked for Saddam Hussein's state. In 1989, Makiya wrote a book about Saddam's Iraq, *The Republic of Fear*, and published it in 1990 under the pseudonym "Samir al-Khalil." The book took off after Iraq invaded Kuwait on August 2, 1990. It was well received in the United States and became a best seller, probably because it enumerated all the faults of the Iraqi dictatorship but left out any details of U.S. aid to that regime during the ten-year war between Iran and Iraq beginning in 1979.[21] When the book appeared, Eqbal and Edward thought that Makiya was dishonest.

Another book Makiya wrote, published in 1993 again to rave reviews in the U.S. liberal press, *Cruelty and Silence: War, Tyranny, Uprising, and the Arab World*, condemned Arab intellectuals for their silence in the face of Saddam Hussein's tyranny in Iraq.[22] He included Edward W. Said in his blanket condemnation. With hyperbole, the New York press waxed eloquent: Geraldine Brooks in the *Wall Street Journal* called *Cruelty and Silence* "one of the most important books ever written on the state of the modern Middle East." Mixed with some skepticism, Michael Massing wrote in the *New Yorker*, "What Emile Zola did for French Anti-Semitism and Arthur Koestler did for Soviet totalitarianism, Kennan Makiya now intends to do for Arab nationalism."[23]

In a May 1993 interview by *LOOT* reporter Nabeel Abraham, Edward attributed Makiya's success in *Cruelty and Silence* to

> a widespread ignorance and hostility toward Arab culture[,which] already exists. Then somebody [Makiya] who seems knowledgeable comes along and writes as if from within, and trashes it, such a work is going to be very popular. . . . What is particularly scurrilous about the book and about Makiya himself . . . is that all the intellectuals he attacks [including] the Palestinian poet Mohammed Darwish, the Syrian Adonis, the Lebanese Ilyas [Elias] Khouri, North Western University Professor Ibrahim Abu-Lughod, and exiled Saudi novelist Abd al-Rahman Munif, are in fact the most vocal in opposition to the current regimes in the Middle East. Why? Principally because all of them opposed the [U.S. and British-led] Gulf War at the same time they all opposed the Iraqi invasion of Kuwait. . . . With a few exceptions, all the intellectuals he attacks have been imprisoned, and/or exiled for speaking out.[24]

Eqbal reviewed the book in the *Nation* on June 28, 1993, under the title "Cruelties Compounded." After highlighting the positive reception the book had received, Eqbal commented that it fed "anti-Arab and anti-Muslim hatemongers in ways that are unfair, and unhelpful to Makiya's stated mission of bringing a democratic order in the Arab world." A significant portion of the book, he said, indicted Arab intellectuals, who, according to Makiya, sustained tyrants such as Saddam Hussein and, worse, nurtured cruelty. Eqbal then criticized the author's lack of scholarly discernment in accepting tales by eyewitnesses without attempting to verify them and gave concrete examples of this shortcoming. He checked out this criticism among human rights experts covering Iraq, who claimed that Makiya had led his interviewees, putting words in their mouths and pushing them to reach conclusions that they resisted.[25]

At a more profound level, Eqbal was saddened by Makiya's lack of appreciation of anything positive in the besieged Arab people's values and traditions, whether they be "tribal, communal, spiritual, or aesthetic," those elements that gave them meaning and created solidarity in the face of tyranny. The picture Makiya painted of conditions was so drab that the only salvation lay in foreign invasion by Americans. Makiya blamed Edward Said and Noam Chomsky, not "the regimes that wield the guns," for facilitating tyranny, Eqbal complained. "No thinking person," he argued,

> least of all the intellectuals Makiya attacks, would question the need for drastic changes in the Middle East toward a democratic and sovereign future. For, this is the worst of times in Middle Eastern history. Never before had it experienced such tragic convergences of wealth and weakness, material resources and moral bankruptcy, imperialism and obscurantism. The region is afflicted with extremes of disorganic growth, expensive machines abound here but there is no technology. Tyranny has subsisted for decades on populist rhetoric no less than imperial support. Governments have grown enormously like malignant tumors on civil society, and national sovereignty has been mortgaged to personal ambition and dynastic interests. In the era of decolonization, Arabs alone have been subject to conquests and colonization.

Intellectuals have been forced to choose between prison, collaboration, exile, silence, or death, he added as a challenge to Makiya's principal thesis.

Both Makiya and his father, before the son's books began appearing, took the easy way out, Eqbal added. The family business collaborated with Saddam's regime and garnered lucrative contracts to build state projects in Baghdad. But Makiya, Eqbal quipped, "is a stranger to integrity" and would have no problem doing that. A book like his in the post-Communist era, Eqbal concluded, feeds into the new paradigm being developed that posited Islam as the new menace and the Arabs as the demons.

After the article was published, Eqbal learned from friends in Cambridge, Massachusetts, that the *Nation* editors had sent a prepublication copy of Eqbal's review to Makiya. Makiya claimed to find an error in the text after publication. When the *Nation* published a retraction of what Makiya claimed was a factual error in Eqbal's piece without consulting Eqbal, the latter complained bitterly. Why didn't Makiya complain when he read the review before it was published? Eqbal asked *Nation* publisher Victor Navasky in a letter dated August 5, 1993.[26] He claimed that the charge of an error was false and asked Navasky to issue a retraction of the retraction. It never happened. The *Nation* apparently was fearful of being sued, and the editors caved in rather than face legal challenges from Makiya.[27]

Makiya later allied himself with the Iraqi exile Ahmad Chelabi (b. 1944), who had established a close rapport with neoconservative figures in the U.S. Republican Party and was a major force behind the U.S. invasion of Iraq in 2003. Makiya hired the services of the conservative publicist organization Benader Associates, which arranged his media appearances. As a consequence, he showed up with Iraq War hawk Richard Perle (b. 1941) on many programs. Makiya was also one of a group of Iraqi exiles who pushed the United States to invade Iraq and overthrow its dictator in 2003. This was at a time when three thousand protests against the war marshaled some estimated thirty-eight million marchers around the world. When appearing with Perle before the National Press Club in Washington, D.C., on March 17, 2003, two days before U.S. and British troops attacked Iraq, Makiya told the assembled journalists that on January 10, 2003, he had seen President George H. W. Bush and had mentioned that the allied troops "will be greeted with sweets and flowers" by the exuberant Iraqi population. As one of his close friends, Christopher Lydon of *Open Source Radio*, wrote on November 7, 2007, "Makiya's scripts and interviews, which informed much mainstream war-mongering, read now like the full catalog of illusion, self-delusion, and folly."[28] And this from a friend!

Ambalavaner Sivanandan

In the 1970s, Eqbal worked to revitalize the British journal *Race*, which soon became *Race & Class*. He joined its editorial board and coedited it from 1983 to 1996, when he had a falling out with his coeditor, Ambalavaner Sivanandan ("Siva," b. 1923), over an article that Marxist Pakistani Indian scholar Aijaz Ahmad wrote in which he attacked three prominent critics, Gayatri Spivak, Homi Bhabha, and Edward W. Said.[29]

Edward had lent his famous name to *Race & Class* and had agreed to be on its editorial committee, so Eqbal was furious that Siva approved the publication of what he considered a spurious attack against his friend. In the correspondence that followed, it became clear that Siva and the journal's assistant editor, Hazel Waters, published Aijaz Ahmad's article because they believed that the premises of the new criticism should be attacked forcefully. Eqbal thought that the critique was without merit and felt that its publication was an act of disloyalty against a major supporter of the journal and one of his closest friends.

As a loyal friend, Eqbal would never publicly attack or sanction attacks against someone who was close to him. Both Siva and Hazel thought that anyone who put friendship before principle was not serious. Moreover, Edward in the mid-1990s was besieged by multiple foes, and, as previously explained, Eqbal did not think that *Race & Class* should join the fray at Edward's expense. Siva and Hazel seemed not to care about such loyalties and saw the issue as one of theoretical and ideological importance. The three argued at cross purposes, with each approaching the issue from totally different premises. Siva and Hazel also had expected Eqbal to devote more time to the journal than he possibly could.[30] The break remained permanent, and I believe that Eqbal had no further contact with the journal's staff after this dispute.

The examples provided here of the polemics in which Eqbal and Edward engaged over the years are only a few among many. They took on opponents from both the left and right of the political spectrum with whom they disagreed, attacking them sharply without mincing words. They thought that was the duty of public intellectuals who had positions to defend, especially when those who disagreed with them intensified their attacks on them or the positions they held.

4

Islam and Islamic History

DESPITE BEING AN OUTSIDER, EQBAL WAS DEEPLY ROOTED in Muslim culture. His attachment to Islam, more cultural than religious, kept him grounded during his long years abroad. He had studied the Islamic corpus and knew it well.

In response to the juxtaposition of terrorism and Islam in the media and dramatic news events of our day as well as to the focus on the extremes in the popular Western imagination, which knows little about how most Muslims act and what they believe and how many of them abhor Muslim ultra-radicals, Eqbal argued on many occasions that the best antidote to Islamic extremism lay in freely organized elections emanating from a vibrant civil society. He also pointed out that Islamic radicals such as the Taliban in Afghanistan and Pakistan could not win majorities in fair elections because most Muslims rejected the strictures placed on them by such an alternative. Islam allowed for great diversity and celebrated differences, he argued.

At Princeton University, Eqbal examined alternative models of change and had doubts about those models that renowned scholars, such as Bernard Lewis, touted as successful. For example, he questioned the achievements of Mustapha Kemal (Atatürk, 1881–1938) in Turkey, a controversial position because scholarly consensus in the late 1950s and early 1960s touted Atatürk's model for change as a great success.[1] Eqbal viewed this Turkish leader as just another dictator who imposed a foreign ideology on the Turks, disestablished Islam, and robbed his people of their rich cultural heritage. He also fretted over those Muslim leaders who abhorred Islam, disparaged the Islamic tradition, and disestablished it under the guise of secular reforms. Likewise, he saw no room for mullahs in politics.

As a graduate student, Eqbal argued endlessly about models of change: Was Atatürk an appropriate example to follow? How could the Islamic tradition be harnessed to facilitate change? Eqbal believed that any major social and political transformation involving Muslim society had to include an important Islamic component, for the soul of the people lay within it. He also saw Islam as the link that tied communities together.

He believed strongly in a progressive Islam, a little understood concept in the West and equally misunderstood in the Muslim world. Most left-leaning Muslims with whom he dealt had cut themselves off from their culture and had no idea that a progressive tradition existed at all within Islam. As secularists, most of them distrusted anything having to do with religion. Having studied Islamic history, Eqbal could stand on his own in debates on the subject.

At the end of his life, when he attempted to establish Khaldunia, a private liberal arts college in Islamabad, he faced criticism not only from the right but also from his allies on the left. Some Islamists argued that he was attempting to open "a school of Greek revival" in the country, a code phrase that evoked foreign philosophical influences within early Islam that Muslim scholars had rejected during the high Middle Ages. Leftists and liberals were upset because they thought he was catering to Islamic sensibilities, positioning himself, as one critic put it, "between theocracy and secularism."[2] They wanted a totally secular curriculum, whereas Eqbal argued that Islamic studies had to be taught in order to provide students with roots. He did not want them to grow up estranged from their own culture.

Eqbal and I discussed the notion of progressive Islam endlessly, and later in life we coauthored essays that incorporated the ideas of progressive Muslims from North Africa and Muslim India, such as the Tunisian Tahar Haddad and the Indian Ubayd Allah al-Sindhi (d. 1944).[3] Eqbal's vision of forward-looking Islam came from those sources and others, including Abd al-Rahman Ibn Khaldun, the brilliant polymath fourteenth-century North African statesman and scholar after whom he named his projected university.

In support of his views, Eqbal argued in an essay on Islamic history that already by the mid–tenth century, when the Buyids began ruling over parts of the Abbasid Empire, there existed a separation between religious and worldly power.[4] This position ran counter to the views of most modern-day Islamic radicals, who wanted states ruled by Islamic law (sharia) and rationalized this choice by arguing that worldly power and religion had always remained combined in the Muslim world.

Eqbal likewise opposed the dictatorial model developed by Habib Bourguiba in Tunisia. He pointed out that Bourguiba, like Atatürk before him, had forced change and robbed the Tunisian people of their souls, and so Eqbal expected a backlash, which ultimately came. This approach marked his work during the rest of his life, for he always sought the means to foster change using the best of a people's traditions, opposing always the imposition of foreign ideologies and methodologies in transforming society. Following in the footsteps of scholars in Princeton and Chicago at the turn of the twentieth century, he stressed the need to harness social change to inherited traditions, preferably progressive ones where they existed, and he abhorred those leaders who imported ready-made notions and ideologies of change from abroad.[5]

Eqbal had a great appreciation for Muhammad Ali Jinnah (1876–1948), the founder of Pakistan. Despite his aristocratic airs and deep secularism, Jinnah understood the rich traditions that Islam offered on which to build a modern state. Eqbal pointed out "that the Ulema in their overwhelming majority opposed him [Jinnah] and he made scant effort to placate them. . . . [He] also remained uncompromisingly opposed to theocracy." Religion, Jinnah argued, "was dear to us. All the worldly goods are nothing when we talk of religion. But there are other things which are very vital—our social . . . and economic life, and without political power how can you defend your faith and your economic life[?]" Jinnah was likewise progressive regarding women: "it is a crime against humanity, the founder of Pakistan argued, that our women are confined with the four walls of their home like prisoners. Women are our companions and you should take them out to work shoulder to shoulder in all spheres of life."[6]

Eqbal opposed political leaders' manipulation of Islam for their own political ends and criticized Pakistani leaders Zia ul-Haq and Nawaz Sharif (b. 1949) for doing so. He went further and claimed that "Islam has been, in Pakistan and also in other Muslim countries, a refuge for weak and scoundrel regimes in modern times. Whenever they feel threatened and isolated—and are losing their grip, losing popularity, and losing the consensus of the people—they bring out Islam from the closet and use it as a political weapon."[7]

Eqbal also criticized the modern madrassas (madaris, Islamic religious schools), which bear little resemblance to the great mosque universities in the wider Muslim world in medieval times. Subjects such as mathematics, chemistry, botany, astronomy, and philosophy were taught then, but not today, which makes it impossible for them to produce great philosophers, mathematicians, and legists like the ones in the past. In a fierce condemnation, Eqbal concluded: "Their curriculum reduces Islam to a penal code, a ritual of ablutions and prayers[,] and a litany of crimes and those harsh here-and-now punishments. Thousands of energetic and motivated youth who graduate from these institutions are men abandoned in the middle of the ford, cut off from their real past, totally unprepared to meet the challenges of the future and fevered by the dreams of a theocratic state in which they shall be assigned their merited roles." He estimated that between ten thousand and fifteen thousand of these young men had by that time fought with the Taliban, one-quarter of the forty thousand to fifty thousand armed militants living in Pakistan, mostly products of the modern-day madrassa.[8]

As pointed out in the introduction, Eqbal foresaw something like the Arab Spring developing among Muslims, for he located a powerful insurrectionary strain within Islamic political culture, rooted in doctrine and historical examples. He observed that among Sufis (mystics), the most renowned were the ones who challenged those in power. In fact, one could not become a great Islamic saint without having done so, he argued. While the traditional ulema rationalized power, insurrectionists invoked the Qur'an and prophetic tradition to struggle (jihad) against oppressors. Islam spread as part of a social revolt, and, Eqbal argued, in fact Islam "is a religion of the oppressed." It still appealed to the poor and disinherited throughout the world, becoming the fastest-growing religion in Africa and the East Indies and having great appeal among African Americans and prisoners in the United States.[9]

Likewise, Eqbal had an original view of the movement mistakenly called "fundamentalism" in Islam. He saw the Islamists as a "modern phenomenon, a response to the crisis of modernity and identity" as societies moved from the agrarian/pastoral mode of production to the industrial. Such a massive transformation affected all aspects of life and forced people to adapt to new ways of existence, challenging the old givens, values, mores, as well as class and gender relations. It produced a rupture in the social order, putting old values into question, with the world seeming as if turned on its head. Capitalism and industrialism have produced total revolutions, threatening old ways of life and values: "Complexity and pluralism threaten most . . . contemporary Islamists because they seek an Islamic order, stripped of its humanism, aesthetics, intellectual quests, and spiritual devotion. Their agenda is simple, therefore very reassuring to the men and women who are stranded between the deep waters of tradition and modernity."[10]

Eqbal was one of the first analysts to see the connections between Muslim and other forms of "fundamentalism," such as the Christian evangelical movement in the United States, Hindu extremism, and Israeli right-wing settlers:

The resurgence of right-wing religious movements in the eighties and nineties was world wide. They have a particularly violent role in Is-

rael where the state-armed Zionist zealots became [e]specially oppressive toward the Arabs of Palestine. In India, the Hindu movement
launched a campaign against the Babri mosque as part of its effort at
mobilizing mass support. It ended in the destruction of the 16th century mosque, widespread communal violence, and the rise of the BJP
[Bharatiya Janata Party] to national power. After the Russians withdrew, the victorious and faction-ridden Mujahideen of Afghanistan
tore the country apart. In Sudan, an Islamic government imposed a
reign of terror. . . . Christian "fundamentalism" linked with Serbian
nationalism and Milosevic's diabolic opportunism has aided . . . ethnic
cleansing in Bosnia-Herzogovina and now it battles on in Kosovo.[11]

Eqbal lamented that to a varying degree all of these movements "frown
on joy and pleasurable pastimes. They have few positive links to culture
and knowledge and regard these as dangerous sources of corruption.
Hence the control of educational institutions and regulation of society's
cultural life become the primary objectives of these movements."[12] For
the same reasons, he abhorred the Taliban in Afghanistan, who denuded
Islam of the joys of life that he knew as a child growing up in a Muslim
household in the Indian countryside. He wrote one of his most poignant
columns about their madness in denying Muslims joys such as music,
games, women's work, and schooling outside of the home.[13] In the column "The Taliban's Unlikely Story," which he published in the Egyp-
tian newspaper *al-Ahram Weekly* on October 17, 1996, he called the Taliban "unreconstructed misogynists." "Girls of all ages are banned from
school. Women are forbidden to work outside their homes, and ordered
to cover themselves from head to foot. Kabul's schools have lost 80 per
cent of their teachers, all government offices have 50 per cent less female
employees and hospitals have but few male nurses. An inch of exposed
female body causes her to be beaten in public by gun-toting Taliban."
Eqbal knew a more gentle Islam, which provided enjoyment and culture
for all who participated in the Islamicate.

When on February 14, 1989, Ayatollah Ruhollah Khomeini (1902–
1989) issued his fatwa against novelist Salman Rushdie (b. 1947) and
established a bounty for his death, forcing the writer into hiding for

several years, Eqbal and Edward Said mobilized some intellectuals to sign a letter to the *New York Review of Books* condemning the action.[14] Rushdie had become famous after writing *Midnight's Children* when it won the 1981 Booker Prize, the most prestigious award given to British novelists. The title of his controversial novel *Satanic Verses* (1988) refers to verses that the prophet Muhammad supposedly added to the Qur'an, accepting as divine three goddesses who were worshipped in Mecca. According to legend, the Prophet later relented and removed those verses, saying that the devil had tempted him.

Eqbal's nephew Iftikhar was Rushdie's friend and before Rushdie published the controversial book had invited him to a party in Manhattan when the well-known author visited the city for a PEN meeting of famous international novelists. Eqbal was also present at the party. Rushdie had just heard the Peruvian writer/politician Mario Vargas Llosa (b. 1936), who in 2010 won the Nobel Prize in Literature, speak to the assembled authors, and he entertained us for a half an hour doing an imitation of Llosa's talk. His accent was perfect and had all of us enthralled with his talent as a mimic, giving us a clue to his gifts in capturing the voices of his characters as he heard them.

Eqbal, Edward, and their friends deplored the death threat against Rushdie and labeled the action "antithetical to the Islamic tradition of learning and tolerance."[15] At the same time, Eqbal thought that Rushdie was wrong to hand himself over to the British police for protection, therefore fortifying the state's role in antiterrorism. Given his own experience hiding Dan Berrigan from the FBI in the early 1970s, he thought that the marked man would have been better off having friends organize a network of civilians to shelter him while he was hunted by the ayatollah's followers and other radical Islamists. Rushdie clearly didn't want to take any chances and felt that his life was on the line after the ayatollah issued his fatwa. At any rate, the author hid under official protection and felt free to travel and make public appearances only after the threat was partially, but not fully, rescinded.

As mentioned in the introduction, Eqbal became concerned about the manipulation of Islam by Western powers as well as radical Islamists for their own ends. For example, he blamed the United States for resurrecting the medieval concept of jihad as holy war and arming and funding Islamic radicals recruited from all over the Muslim world to fight the Soviet Union in Afghanistan after 1979. He pointed out that there are two forms of jihad: the first is "striving for the faith" and can take the form of redoubling individual efforts to be a good Muslim, trying to convince fellow Muslims to follow Qur'anic commandments, and the like. The "lesser jihad" included holy war. For Eqbal, "[c]ontemporary 'fundamentalism' reduce[s] complex religious systems and civilizations to one or another version of modern fascism. They are concerned with power not with the soul, with the mobilization of people for political purposes rather than with 'sharing' or alleviating their sufferings and aspirations. Theirs is a very limited and time-bound political agenda."[16]

For Eqbal, Islam was wondrous, more than a religion, for it represented a way of life, progressive and varied, ever changing, and adaptable to a variety of cultures and peoples. It was not the religion's fault that its adherents distorted it and made it into something that it was not. The Islamicate had produced great civilizations, brilliant minds, spectacular art and poetry, priceless carpets, miniature paintings, and mosaics, all of which Eqbal knew and celebrated and had grown up with and collected throughout his life. He was a Muslim and felt totally at home in its traditions.

FIGURE 1. Eqbal sporting a Persian lamb cap, ca. 1956. (Reproduced by permission of Dohra Ahmad)

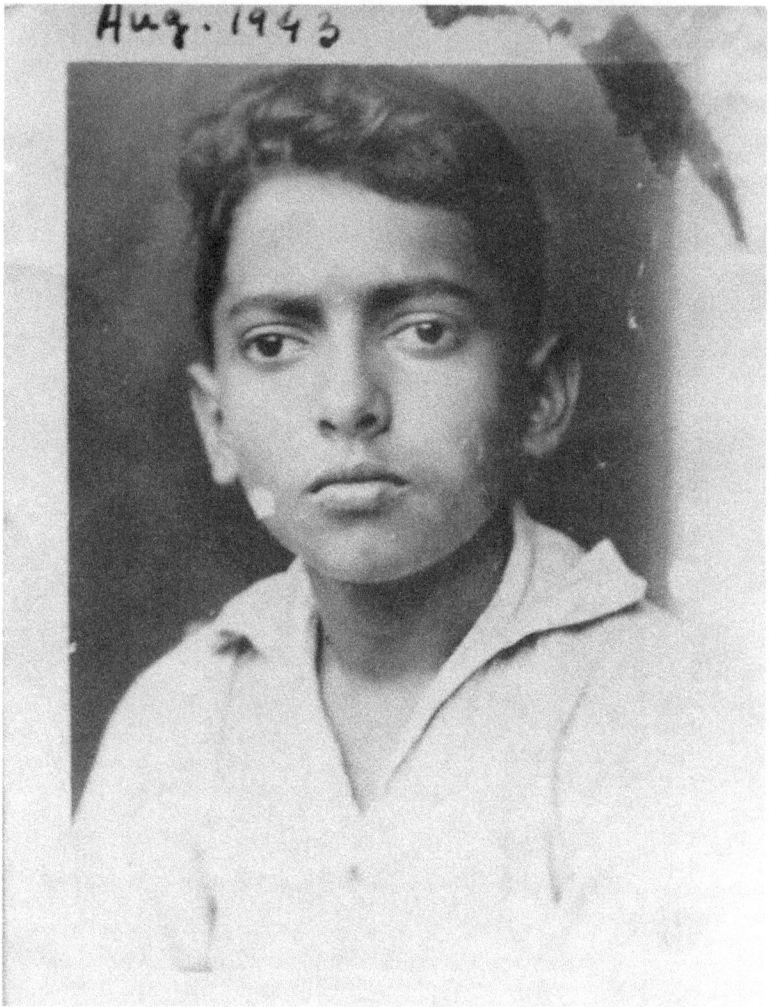

FIGURE 2. Eqbal at about age thirteen. (Reproduced by permission of Dohra Ahmad)

FIGURE 3. Eqbal and I in the Princeton snow, 1958, holding our Arabic textbook by Ferhat Ziadeh and R. Bayley Winder. (Author's personal archive)

FIGURE 4. Eqbal (*right*) with his younger brother Saghir, who died in an accident in Canada in July 1971. (Reproduced by permission of Dohra Ahmad)

FIGURE 5. Eqbal's mother, Khartoon, c. 1970. (Reproduced by permission of Dohra Ahmad)

FIGURE 6. Eqbal at a press conference after being indicted by the U.S. Justice Department, 1971. (Reproduced by permission of Dohra Ahmad)

FIGURE 7. Harrisburg defendants Father Joe Wenderoth, Eqbal Ahmad, Father Neil McLaughlin, Ted Glick (whose case was severed from that of the other defendants), Mary Skoblick, Anthony Skoblick, and Sister Elizabeth McAllister in front of the Harrisburg courthouse, 1971. Father Phil Berrigan is not in the photograph because he was imprisoned at the time. (Reproduced by permission of Dohra Ahmad)

FIGURE 8. Eqbal in a Hollywoodesque pose at Cornell University, 1966. (Reproduced by permission of Dohra Ahmad)

FIGURE 9. Eqbal in his Manhattan kitchen about to prepare a meal, 1984. (Photograph by Jean Mohr, reproduced by permission)

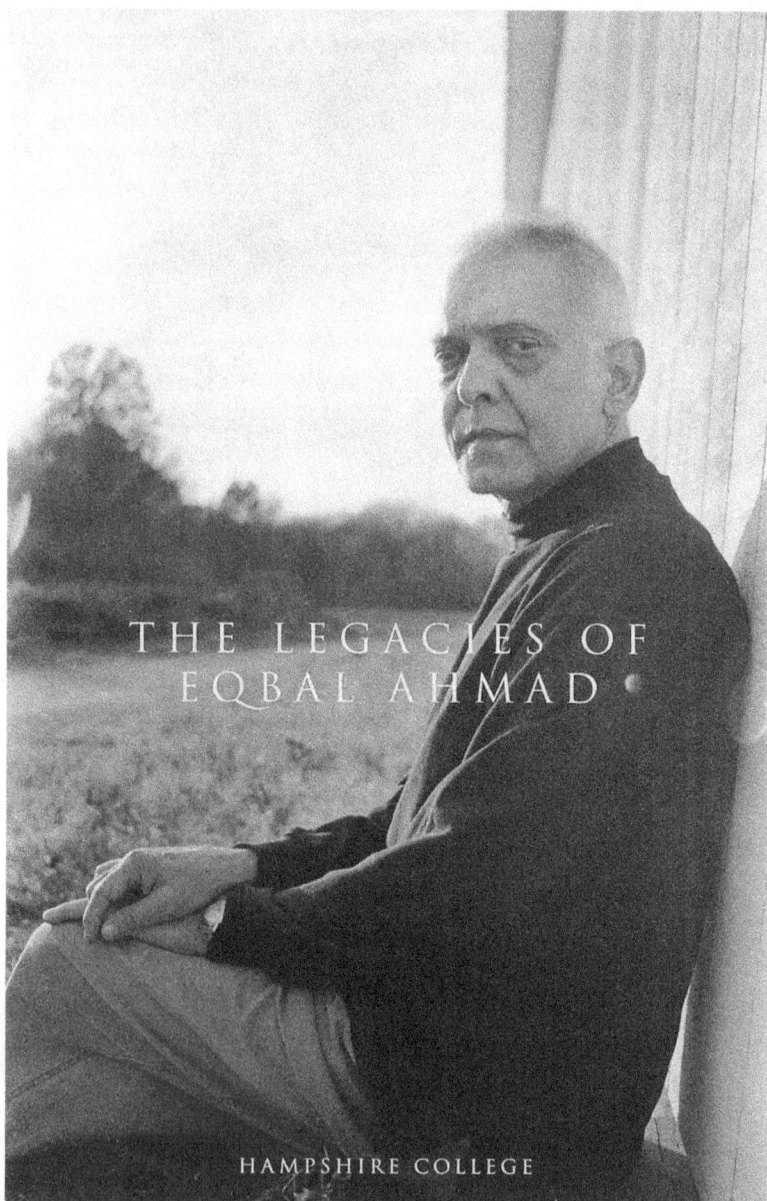

THE LEGACIES OF
EQBAL AHMAD

HAMPSHIRE COLLEGE

FIGURE 10. Eqbal near the end of his life in the late 1990s at Hampshire College. (Reproduced by permission of Dohra Ahmad)

5

Imperialism, Nationalism, Revolutionary Warfare, Insurgency, and the Need for Democracy

EQBAL CAME OF AGE AT THE MOMENT THAT LIBERATION movements spread rapidly through the Third World. As part of wider trends in the late 1940s and through most of the 1950s, he became a nationalist activist. In high school and college, he supported Kashmir's annexation to Pakistan and taught in Pakistan's war college as part of his UOTC (the Pakistani equivalent of ROTC) obligations. His move to the United States and his advanced academic training transformed him from an avid nationalist into a critical outsider and a public intellectual whose opinions could not be pigeonholed.

Eqbal abhorred imperialism as much as he hated dictatorships and believed that all imperial powers and dictators would crumble with time. He never, however, believed in destiny and advocated hard work by radicals to speed the decline of these adversaries. For him, the Algerian, Vietnamese, and other colonial wars, the struggle for civil rights in the

United States, and the global campaign to end apartheid in South Africa were the final stages of long processes that had begun in the fifteenth century. Western Europe's expansion into Africa, Asia, and the Americas had opened the modern imperial age. The old imperialism, already under assault he was convinced, was going to end, but he watched as the United States replaced the former imperial powers and established an informal system of control that was global in scope. He called it "the Latin Americanization of the world," the extension around the world of earlier U.S. policies of control over Latin America. In effect, he described the process of globalization before the term became fashionable. As a convinced and well-informed anti-imperialist, he dedicated his life to elucidating this new phenomenon and opposing its worst aspects.

Echoing Lenin's writings on imperialism, Eqbal believed that global corporations based in the First World shaped the world's economies. They recruited states and their coercive forces to rearrange the world in favor of corporations, creating over time an advanced center and a backward periphery.

Eqbal celebrated resistance to empire and the creativity that resistance engendered. In his own case, the Algerian revolution against France and the Vietnam wars against France and the United States galvanized his anti-imperialist instincts. He had learned important lessons about revolutionary warfare and counterinsurgency in graduate school. What he had learned from Algerian revolutionary leaders in Tunis he later shared with an American audience and then finally a global audience. He did so as a superb intellectual who through rigorous training and exceptional intelligence could examine history, the present, and comparative movements to project what might happen in the future. He startled those who knew him best with the accuracy of his predictions.

This gift was not crystal-ball gazing. It was a product of working extremely hard, reading prodigiously, and having an encyclopedic memory for facts and figures, which peppered his arguments. He also took notes and tucked them away for when he needed them. He kept up with his fields of interest by buying the best books available as they were published. The first thing he read in the *New York Times* Sunday edition, for example, was the book review section. He also read regularly the *New*

York Review of Books, the *Boston Review of Books,* the *London Review of Books,* and the *Times Literary Supplement* (London), looking for the best new works. This intellectual curiosity fed his analysis, and what was wonderful about it was that he followed new publications so effortlessly, so naturally. And he read widely.

Interest in the Iranian Revolution

Anti-imperialism was later to play itself out in Iran, leading to its mass revolution in 1979. Eqbal viewed the Iranian Revolution as a major event in world history, arguing that it was the first significant urban revolution in the post–World War II period and a portent for the future. In the journal *Race & Class,* he pointed out that all previous mass revolutions had taken place in the countryside and had mobilized peasants. Demography had changed in the Middle East by the late 1970s, making the urban populations a majority. Iran reflected that transformation, and the political upheaval there took place in urban centers where the majority lived, ushering in a sea change whereby future revolts would henceforth begin in urban areas. In response, Eqbal edited a special issue of *Race & Class* on the upheaval, which he later published separately as a book in Pakistan.[1]

In preparation for that issue, he flew to Paris and, using his ability to speak Persian, interviewed Ayatollah Ruhollah Khomeini and other Iranian exiles who supported the revolution. Raza Kazim, his Pakistani friend, told me that when Eqbal asked Khomeini a question about the ayatollah's intentions, the old man looked at Eqbal with venom in his eyes, as if to say, Why question my motives?[2]

In a well-informed essay in *Christianity & Crisis* entitled "Iran and the West: A Century of Subjugation," Eqbal explored the history of domination of Iran and its oil by the British and the United States over one hundred years, placing the 1979 uprising in perspective. He pointed out that the revolution represented the seventh or eighth time in one hundred years that Iranian national forces had fought the Iranian monarchy, which foreign corporations and states had supported. He outlined what every expert on the Middle East had learned about Iranian history but escaped most Americans.

In this article, he concentrated on analyzing U.S. policies in shoring up the shah's regime. Crisis after crisis pitted the Iranians against their rulers because the rulers caved in to imperial pressures, with the most egregious intervention being the joint overthrow in 1953 by the U.S. Central Intelligence Agency (CIA) and British Military Intelligence (MI-6) of the democratically elected prime minister, Mohammed Mossedegh (1882–1967), who had nationalized British Petroleum holdings in Iran. Eqbal argued that if the U.S. public knew the history of how the Iranians had suffered through so many traumas at the hands of foreigners, they would be much less likely to dismiss Iranian revolutionaries as just another band of "emotional fanatics."[3]

The Algerian Counterinsurgency Model Applied to Vietnam

Eqbal's earliest publications criticized U.S. policies in the Vietnam War. With his knowledge of the Algerian revolution and other colonial wars, he brought a comparative and global perspective to his writing. Since the French had fought and lost in both Vietnam and Algeria, there was much to learn from their flawed approaches and mistakes. For example, the Americans in Vietnam, as the French had done in Algeria, regrouped the Vietnamese peasantry into new towns surrounded by barbed wire in order to separate the rural fighters from the population. In both places, though, the insurgents infiltrated the new settlements at nightfall and took them over. Despite France's failure in Algeria, the United States introduced the same system in Vietnam, with the same disastrous results. Eqbal saw this flawed policy and many others developing in Vietnam and said so. He read widely about insurgency and counterinsurgency throughout the Third World, and using the data culled from Algeria and other cases, he revealed the weaknesses of U.S. policy in Vietnam and elsewhere.

One of Eqbal's acquaintances from Princeton University, Frank Wisner Jr. (b. 1938),[4] while working as a U.S. State Department official stationed in Algeria at the end of the war there, had observed closely the French organization of the strategic hamlet program. He was later assigned to Vietnam to help set up a similar calamitous system there.

Revolutionary Warfare

In an article in the *Nation* in August 1965, Eqbal held that the conditions promoting revolutionary warfare evolved out of dislocations and upheavals caused by rapid social change and did not have conspiratorial roots, as most French and U.S. policy makers then argued.[5] For Eqbal, conspiracy lay at the root of imperial policies regarding insurgencies. Counterinsurgency theorists and U.S. experts, he argued, could not acknowledge their adversaries' political legitimacy, so they focused on outside agitators and conspirators as the main agents behind revolutionary warfare. They saw guerilla warfare as a technical and military problem, so, for them, throwing in more ordinance and troops sufficed to win the day. There were also attempts at ideological warfare and social reforms, which did not work either. Eqbal argued contrarily that revolutionaries viewed their warfare as a moral and political problem and saw as their main task the draining of their enemy's legitimacy. Because of that priority, they stressed the primacy of politics and played down the importance of military victories. In order to win, insurgents had to begin guerilla warfare built on popular support; they had to outadminister their adversaries and create parallel institutions in regions that they controlled even before gaining full power. By concentrating on outside support for revolutionaries instead of on the issue of revolutionary legitimacy, Eqbal argued, counterinsurgents became misguided and their responses irrelevant.

Gandhi and Tagore: Divergent Views on Nationalism

A BBC dramatization of Eqbal taking a bus trip over the grand trunk road from Calcutta to Karachi shows him returning to Irki, his family's village in Bihar, and staring at the veranda where assassins killed his father while he held Eqbal in his arms.[6] He also reminisces about a trip he took with his family to Calcutta in 1940 to visit relatives who had been imprisoned by the British for alleged subversive acts. While there, as noted in the introduction, he went on a family pilgrimage to the home of Rabindranath Tagore. Eqbal recollects that Tagore hated nationalism and in his poetry and novels constantly reiterated that India was heterogeneous and should remain that way. Nationalists despised the old man, but Eqbal found in Tagore a model of humanism, someone who dismissed ideologies of difference in favor of a universal inclusiveness. Eqbal quips at the end of this segment, "Tagore was right."

Tagore, "the Poet," and Gandhi, the mass activist, met in 1915, and thereafter these two bigger-than-life figures of twentieth-century India maintained a life-long correspondence, visited each other's ashrams, and needed each other's approval and support for their individual projects and causes. Despite the fact that they had profound philosophical and political differences, which they aired in print, they maintained their friendship solidly until Tagore died in 1941 at the age of eighty-one.[7] All of India followed the debates of these two great men, and Eqbal, as he matured, sided with Tagore but paid great attention to Gandhi's achievements.

Tagore deeply influenced Eqbal as the latter came to abhor the worst aspects of nationalism. The poet's universalism and humanism initially tempered Eqbal's own nationalism, which in the context of violent partition, could not be jettisoned completely—at least not yet. Tagore succeeded in sensitizing Eqbal to the evils of nationalism when carried to extremes. Eqbal explained to David Barsamian, "In 1920 Tagore argued that nationalism tends to create emotions of exclusion and separation based on differences and not commonality."[8] Later in life Eqbal adopted Tagore's and his own mother's skepticism of nationalism altogether.

The poet contributed to Eqbal's larger worldview. He provided a model of fearless criticism even though his doing so cost him his popularity. Eqbal learned to speak his mind, and Tagore's example convinced him of the validity of doing so. Finally, he learned from Tagore the importance of fashioning change to traditional values and cultures in order to allow for smooth transitions and profound popular acceptance of necessary transformations.

Eqbal had a romantic streak, which attracted him to Tagore. His friend Raza Kazim thought, in a pithy style all his own, that "Eqbal was a sentimentalist first and a logician afterwards. For a sentimentalist, encountering Tagore was like eating oysters and caviar. Tagore gave the Bengalis their language and stood for the Indian spirit soaring and bypassing earthly issues and quarrels," Raza told me in 2004. Tagore had adopted the Upanishad's notion that God can be found through personal purity and service to others. He wanted a new-world order based on transnational values. Tagore befriended and supported Gandhi morally when he could, even sent him telegrams (which Gandhi sometimes requested) encouraging the Mahatma's fasts and other nonviolent actions, but he remained wary of Gandhi's unswerving nationalism. All of these views appealed to Eqbal, who rejected Gandhi's asceticism and some of the Mahatma's political choices and opted to follow instead the bigger-than-life, all-embracing, and inclusive figure of Tagore. At the same time, Eqbal recognized Gandhi's significance for India, and he, like Tagore, stood in awe of the frail man's ability to mobilize millions of Indians against the British. Eqbal's nephew Zulfikar Ahmad remembers vividly Eqbal praising Gandhi's ability to organize and keep alive a mass movement so effectively.[9]

Tagore believed in the perfectibility of humanity and wanted to harness science and universal knowledge, regardless of its source, to improve people's conditions. He abhorred superstition and thought that poor people should not sacrifice themselves so that Indian elites could achieve their nationalist goals. Although he thought that Mohandas Gandhi, his very close friend, possessed extraordinary moral force and represented a gift to India, he gradually found himself isolated and detested when he dared to criticize the Mahatma's strategy and tactics in confronting British domination on the subcontinent. But the more he spoke his mind, the more Gandhi drew near to him because the Poet was one of the few genuine friends the political activist admired who dared take him to task.

Tagore openly disapproved of Gandhi's noncooperation campaigns, in which students were asked to drop out of British schools and other Indians were told to spin their own clothes and burn all British textiles. Young people would in this way, Gandhi thought, escape the temptations of collaboration with the colonizers and not subject themselves to Western influences. Home spinning, if generalized, would deprive the colonialists of their markets. Tagore, however, refused to sanction students dropping out of school when no other decent educational institutions existed to prepare them for their lives. He could not allow India to sacrifice a generation of young people for nationalism.

He viewed knowledge as universal and thought that people should take it from any source available. Information's provenance mattered little to him. For the poet, British, French, German, Russian culture all had elements to offer Indians. He could not bring himself to boycott any knowledge because of its British origin. Likewise, he preferred that rural folks improve their farming methods and their crop yields by applying scientific and proven methods of agronomy rather than spin cloth. Tagore viewed that pastime as an inefficient use of peasants' energies and talents.

In 1934, Gandhi, as part of his campaign to improve the lot of the untouchables in India (ironically within the framework of strengthening the Hindu caste system and keeping caste distinctions), claimed that God had caused an earthquake in Bihar as vengeance on the population for treating the untouchables miserably. Tagore called that reasoning "unscientific" and refused to admit that catastrophes somehow had something to do with people's morals. If changes came about, Tagore argued, they had to grow out of India's own "social mentality." That meant that change had to be rooted in a people's social heritage and culture. Eqbal absorbed those teachings and made them into a central theme of his own life's work.

The Need for Democracy

Eqbal viewed the unreasonableness of many leaders in the Third World in the 1970s and 1980s in terms of the "pathology of power." He explained what he meant by this term to David Barsamian in 1998:

> Saddam Hussein of Iraq requiring typewriters to be licensed is pathological. Saudi Arabia opening universities, which is a good thing, but fearing that the students shouldn't get together—because they might

talk politics or revolt—and therefore doing everything to prevent the students from discussing matters, from meeting together, and from collaborating—this is the exact reverse of what universities should be.

Third world writers are among the most endangered species in the world. Nearly all Arab writers today are living in exile. . . . The only great novelist that Saudi Arabia has ever produced in its entire history is Abdelrahman Munif. He has been divested of his citizenship. . . . Munif lives in exile in Damascus. Adonis, another important writer, is a Syrian. He lives in exile in Paris or sometimes in Beirut. In Pakistan, since independence, I think there has not been a major literary figure who has not served time in prison. To me these are all examples of sickening behaviour on the part of the state which expresses an illness, a pathology. These are not natural ways of behaving.[10]

In 1979, Eqbal went to a conference at Brooklyn College on Third World transformations, and there he argued that the minimum requisites included the following: radical revolutionary leadership; a coherent, consistent, and functioning ideology; an operative commitment to the principal of democracy and accountability; institutions and mechanisms to ensure the practice of democracy; congruence of new institutions with the historical inheritance and local culture; self-reliance and endogenous development as a basis for planning and organization. These principles guided him in his own lifetime, and he fought for their implementation every chance he could.[11]

In the early 1980s, Eqbal wrote a series of three articles on postcolonial societies in which he further examined the contemporary crisis in the Third World. In the first article, using the formulations that he was working on, he attempted to establish "a set of criteria for judging the extent to which the crisis is being faced in a manner which contributes toward the development of an even, equitable and democratic society; and . . . [to] identify . . . the attributes which best equips a government, party or a political movement to meet this unprecedented challenge." He repeated his arguments for the "primacy of democracy and accountability; institutions and mechanisms to ensure the practice of democracy."[12]

Personal power, the favored mode of governance for many dictators, had major drawbacks, he argued elsewhere. "The person in power becomes the focus of all discontent. . . . [S]hort-circuiting the rule of law is a temporary and, in the long run, harmful expedient. Only a reformed, competent and independent judiciary is the ultimate guarantee of justice, an attribute without which a system and a government shall lack legitimacy. A last lesson is that governments and leaders who drag religion into politics distort politics, society, and religion itself, but fail to draw political gains from doing so."[13]

His attraction to Antonio Gramsci was in part based on the Italian's preference for democratic governance despite his Communist affiliation. His writings contain the seeds for the later development of Eurocommunism, which transformed the dictatorial party into a more participatory one. Gramsci stressed the need to develop a mass base and alternate institutions to loosen the hold by hegemonic ideologies and power. Eqbal wrote in 1995,

> The contrast was drawn again in our century by Antonio Gramsci. . . . He distinguished the state and civil society as distinct entities. Gramsci draws three fundamental conclusions: (i) When civil society (which includes professional, literary and artistic institutions and associations) conforms uncritically or is coerced by the state into silence, totalitarianism prevails. (ii) When civil society enjoys a lively network of institutions and associations, and these maintain critical links with state institutions, then democracy prevails. (iii) When state and society are structurally and culturally antagonistic to each other, then conditions of civil war and anarchy obtain, and a society evades either fate only when its intelligentsia forges and popularizes a program for reform or revolution. In all these situations the choices artists and intellectuals make effect not only their own but their society's destiny.[14]

In response to David Barsamian's question "How would you define your own politics?" Eqbal responded, "Socialist and democratic. Those have been my two lasting commitments. By democratic, I mean genuine commitment to equality, freedom of association, critical thought, and the accountability of rulers to citizens. By socialism, I mean control of the wealth by people rather than by the state or corporations."[15]

Eqbal believed that in Pakistan and throughout the Third World the Mughal and British colonial heritage of strong state structures, especially bureaucracies and armies, coupled with the weakness of most indigenous commercial and industrial bourgeoisies, forced all social classes, with the exception of the feudal elite, to be highly dependent on the state. Because power ultimately derived from proximity to state institutions and state-controlled or licensed enterprises, he concluded that all classes were subjected to state pressures. In most newly liberated countries, populations initially supported radical nationalist ideologies calling for state control and nationalization of foreign enterprises. Such processes, however, speeded up the centralization of power and often paved the way for dictatorship. Eqbal also pointed out that modern states in former colonies were vestiges of imperial institutions, so that the strengthening of states had the nefarious effect of buttressing those elements of society tied to imperialism.

Yet he viewed Muhammad Ali Jinnah, the founder of modern Pakistan and thus a follower of a nationalist ideology, as a staunch defender of democracy and therefore admired the man. According to Eqbal, Jinnah emphasized "the congruence of democracy, social justice, and rule of law to Islamic values and believed that Islam and its ideals have taught us democracy. It has taught equality of man, justice and fair play to everybody. In any case Pakistan is not going to be a theocratic state, to be ruled by priests with a divine mission. We have many non-Muslims—Hindus, Christians, and Parsis—but they are all Pakistanis. They will enjoy the same rights as any other citizens."[16]

Eqbal also understood that many people in Pakistan rallied to the nation because they longed "for a society free of oppression, injustice[,] and inequality." For most Pakistanis "the appeal of an Islamic state . . . was their way of saying that they wanted a good state and just government."[17] "At the heart of the Pakistan Movement lay the aspiration for economic and social justice, political democracy[,] and cultural freedom," he told a friend in 1980.[18] In the mind of Pakistanis, a Muslim state meant a "just" state. But nearly all governments of Muslim countries that Eqbal observed and studied in the Middle East, North Africa, and South Asia at the end of the twentieth century were "composed of corrupt and callous elites more adept at repressing the populace than protecting natural resources or national sovereignty."[19]

Eqbal gradually came to believe that social democracy provided the best way to reorganize Third World societies. He reached this conclusion even though he understood the theoretical and practical shortcomings of this option. He especially did not think that Muslim countries such as Pakistan could or would embrace any form of radical socialism or communism. He argued that progressive Islam, coupled with social democracy, would help bring about a transition to a humane mixture of capitalism and socialism that would allow for greater social justice and open the way to a democratic polity.[20]

But Eqbal's advocacy of social democracy constituted a double-edged sword. Any ideology advocating social justice countered reality on the ground as the superpowers fought their Cold War battles in the Third World and armed allied military dictatorships to unprecedented degrees. Weapons pouring into countries served more to put down internal opposition and consolidate dictatorships than to open up new horizons. Many leftists also disdained social democracy as the worst of poisons because both Marx and Lenin had devastatingly attacked this ideological alternative. By embracing this option, Eqbal opened himself to attack from his doctrinaire friends within the left.

6

The Middle East and the
Palestinian-Israeli Conflict

THE MIDDLE EAST WAS A SIGNIFICANT POINT OF "CONVERGENCE"
on the globe, Eqbal explained to David Barsamian in 1993:

> Areas of convergence are always so strategic that no one leaves them
> in peace. . . . A lot of things related to world politics come together in
> the Middle East. . . . This is the center of energy for the Western world.
> For the West, economic and strategic interests converge in the
> Middle East. . . . Geographically, it's in the middle of everywhere.
> Africa and Europe and Asia, Central Asia and South Asia and West
> Asia converge here. This has been known since Roman times as the
> crossroads of civilization. . . . Here the worst conflicts of our time are
> converging. Israeli Zionism and Arab nationalism. Secularism and
> fundamentalism. Nationalism and internationalism. The result is that
> it has remained in a state of total crisis. . . . [F]inally . . . [t]his is the

last of the great non-Western civilizations to decline. . . . [It] held out as the powerful center of the world right up to the nineteenth century. . . . Its kind of a violent situation, a situation of great confusion, uncertainty, not knowing which way this boat may turn. Hence the current crisis. Who knows how long it will last?[1]

As I explained earlier, Eqbal began paying especially attention to the Middle East in the 1970s as he realized its growing centrality in U.S. foreign policy. When most people rejoiced over President Bill Clinton's brokering of the 1993 Oslo Accords between Israelis and Palestinians, Eqbal joined Edward Said in objecting to the agreement on the grounds that if it succeeded, it would create a series of Bantustans like the apartheid-driven black homelands in South Africa and would never work. In keeping with his opposition to partitions of states, he advocated instead a binational single state, a position that at the time challenged the unique Jewish nature of Israel but that some contemporary critics of Israeli and U.S. policy are now advocating. In keeping with his disdain for partitions anywhere and long-standing opposition to narrow nationalisms based on ethnicity or religious beliefs, including the ones in India and Pakistan, he envisaged the possibility of Palestinians and Jewish people living in peace side by side within one state.

Edward, like Eqbal, opposed the proposed Oslo and Wye settlements for the Israeli-Palestinian conflict. Eqbal argued that

[t]he Oslo agreement . . . is extremely unjust, because it does not respond to any of the fundamental issues in this conflict. It offers no compensation, no restitution, no return to the half of Palestine's population who are now refugees. It offers no settlement of the issue of water rights in the occupied territories. It offers the Palestinians no right to self-determination. It offers Palestinians no protections against expanding Israel settlements. It offers Palestinians no solution or Arabs generally of the problem of Jerusalem, which is as holy to Muslims and Christians as it is to Jews. So in a very genuine sense, Oslo leaves open all the fundamental questions that have defined the Arab Israeli conflict.[2]

Continuing to concentrate on the escalating violence in the Middle East, Eqbal stressed the need to study both Palestinian and Jewish history. He understood that the two peoples had suffered terribly, and in discussing the issue with his Palestinian friends, as Edward later remarked, he sensitized them to the weight of the Holocaust on the creation of the State of Israel. At the same time, he never wavered for a moment from his support of Palestinian rights and never feared appearing in synagogues to argue the Palestinian case with firmness and conviction. For Eqbal,

August 1947 marked the beginning of decolonization, when British rule in India ended with a last spasmodic human carnage. In January 1948 Burma became independent, and in February Ceylon; and October 1948 witnessed the exhilarating final liberation of China. It was in those days of hopes and fulfillment that the colonization of Palestine occurred. It was formalized in 1948 by the establishment of Israel—co-sponsored by the post-war super-powers, consecrated by the United Nations and conceded by the abject failure of the Arab governments. Thus, at the dawn of decolonization, we were returned to the earliest, most intense form of colonial menace—the exclusivist settler colonialism which had dealt genocidal blows to the great civilizations and peoples of the Americas. As if to compel our historical memory, Israel's sectarian, racialist character was ensured by the expulsion of the native Palestinians from their homeland. The tragedy occurred as a counterpoint to contemporary history, a reminder that all was not well with the era of decolonization.[3]

In the same way, Eqbal approached the sensitive issue of the future of Jerusalem with Palestinian intellectuals in September 1994 as part of a series of discussions sponsored by the Palestinian Academic Society for the Study of International Affairs and held in Jerusalem.[4] Here was an example of Eqbal being willing to tread where even angels feared to go, for he dropped a bombshell when he advocated internationalizing Jerusalem and sharing sovereignty between Christians, Jews, and Muslims. He began his proposal by calling on the Palestinians and Israelis to renounce "their intention to make Jerusalem a capital of a nation's state." That would mean that Israelis would keep their capital in Tel Aviv and the Palestinians would set up theirs in Ramallah or elsewhere on their territory. Second, he argued, the world community should support the renunciation of sectarian claims to the city. Third, the international community should push for Israel to withdraw from Jerusalem, which it "occupies . . . in violation of the United Nations charter." Fourth, Jerusalem should remain united and be governed by a denominational council made up of the three religions that have interests in the place.[5] Of course, the Palestinians on the panel shot down his proposal, citing fourteen centuries of Muslim control versus twenty-seven years of occupation by Israel, making the asymmetry ludicrous. Nevertheless, Eqbal thought that his effort at dealing with the subject worthwhile in order to shake up Palestinian smugness about their rights and have them begin to think about the issue outside of the box. It didn't work because his audience could not digest his proposals, which appeared to them outrageous. All that Eqbal was trying to do was to show that there could be many different ways to proceed on the thorny Jerusalem issue and that creative thinking was needed to break the deadlock of this issue and many others between Palestinians and Israelis. The thinking on these conflicts had become routinized, and Eqbal wanted to explore new creative solutions to old problems. Clearly, his approach did not work for others.

Eqbal reviewed Edward Said's book *The Question of Palestine* in 1980, calling it a "most impassioned and morally compelling book,"[6] and he edited a special double issue of *Race & Class* on the 1982 Israeli invasion of Lebanon and another on Israel and the Palestinians.[7] After he and Edward developed a strong friendship, the two traveled to meet Yasser Arafat and other Palestinian leaders in the 1970s. Eqbal wrote reports for them, advocating a massive march on Israel by unarmed Palestinians, carrying banners that said "we want to go home," as an act of mass passive resistance in order to dramatize the Palestinian's plight in exile.

Edward recollected years later, "I remember the look on their faces, when I patiently explained Eqbal's proposal, of disbelief and mild panic, especially when I emphasized the need for peaceful means and disciplined organization. This was a time when Eqbal was mercilessly critical of the cult of the gun, the misuse of slogans like 'armed struggle,' and the creeping, ultimately debilitating militarism of Palestinian thinking and organization."[8]

Edward also recalled Eqbal embarrassing PLO leaders at a seminar organized especially for him in Beirut in which he urged the Palestinians to create in the United States a lobbying organization similar to that of the American Israel Public Affairs Committee, an Israeli organization. Doing so would have entailed gathering information "on every congressional district" in the United States and analyzing the "workings of important civil institutions such as churches, college, and labor unions," all of which appeared too daunting a task for the PLO leadership. Edward pointed out that such an endeavour would have cost "one-tenth of the resources that were squandered on first-class air tickets, an expanding bureaucracy, and bottles of Black Label whiskey."[9] In the 1980s, Eqbal repeated a similar but more detailed analysis of what the PLO should be doing in America to the Palestinian leadership in Tunis—again a fruitless effort on his part. Arafat told Edward at that time that the PLO was planning to set up "an American committee at the highest levels" to conduct research and formulate strategy. When Edward checked this out later, he discovered that "the committee was something straight out of *Gulliver's Travels* . . . composed entirely of people who knew no English. They never met," he continued, "and they managed to appoint only one full-time researcher[,] . . . [who] had persuaded her superiors to allow her to buy a subscription to *Time* magazine and occasionally to buy the *International Herald Tribune*."[10]

As mentioned earlier in this chapter, Eqbal also toured the Palestinian camps in Lebanon and told the Palestinian leadership that Israel would quickly defeat the Arab forces two years before war broke out in 1982. He saw that despite all the rhetoric about armed struggle in the Palestinian ranks, they were poorly prepared to battle an enemy armed with U.S. state-of-the-art F-16s, missiles, and advanced high technology. He had formulated these ideas more than a decade earlier, as revealed in a letter he wrote on December 7, 1992, to Tim May and Frank Hanly, BBC producers working on a film on Edward Said's life, mentioned in chapter 2. He told them, "At the annual convention of the Organization of Arab

Students [after the June 1967 Arab-Israeli War] I had shocked the audience with dire warnings that if it were to stay its present course, the PLO was destined to fail as a liberation movement. I had argued that *Al-Fatah* and other armed Palestinian parties were 'radical but wrong,' that armed struggle was ill-suited to the Palestinian-Israeli environment, and that the PLO had better chances of success if it were to launch a sustained and militant non-violent agitation."[11] Here he was repeating a theme he had expressed many years earlier in a letter to the Israeli peace activist Israel Shahak (1933–2001): "I am not a pacifist, but I do believe that the Arab-Israeli problem cannot be settled by military means. I am, therefore, convinced that we must put an accent on the political aspects of the struggle[,] which is the only way to bring into full relief the basic contradictions of Israel before the Israeli people and the world. Needless to say, I whole-heartedly support any effort that is likely to contribute to a human and workable solution."[12]

Eqbal thought that the violence that the PLO practiced was that of the oppressed, but it was not revolutionary violence. It had no mobilizing content. It represented a feeling rather than a program. The PLO was not a revolutionary organization in Eqbal's estimation. It was "an organization of the oppressed, carrying on nonrevolutionary tactics with a nonrevolutionary program by a nonrevolutionary organization."[13] He also noted that in the Palestinian struggle there was "a certain absence of learning from the past."[14]

He never feared speaking frankly to friend and foe alike, and because he always lived simply, his arguments carried great moral authority. He could not be corrupted by money or promises of fame. The Palestinians chose not to listen, primarily because they could not in the 1980s master either the logistics of a mass march, were carried away by their own rhetoric, did not have a strong tradition of passive resistance, and could not gather the resources needed to build an infrastructure reserved for states.

His position grated on partisans of a two-state solution to the Israeli-Palestinian crisis. But he thought that if the Palestinians created a separate independent state alongside Israel, it would become another "Zionist" state, exclusive and racist, with a large role for religion needed to help define its identity. He thought that one Zionist state in the Middle East was enough. Instead he envisioned the Israelis and Palestinians sitting down and negotiating a solution based not on the principle of land for peace, but rather on respect of differences. He really thought that a binational state could work there.

Edward and Eqbal came to realize, without seemingly ever talking about it, that Arafat was preoccupied with working out a deal with the Americans that would allow him and his followers to stay in power in return for collaborating with the Israeli occupation of Palestinian lands. As Edward and Eqbal increased their attacks on the Oslo peace process, Arafat froze them out and increasingly ignored their advice. In 1994, when Eqbal intended to attend a human rights conference on the West Bank, he said that Arafat gave orders to the hotel where the meeting was scheduled to prohibit the gathering.

Two other issues preoccupied Eqbal relating to the Israeli–Palestinian conflict. Because he viewed Zionism and the creation of Israel as manifestations of a larger trend of establishing settler colonies that had been in existence from at least the fifteenth century, he expected either dispossession of the Palestinians, as happened when more than seven hundred thousand of them fled into neighboring Arab countries in 1948, or else the proletarianization of the remaining population, who did initially serve as workers for the dominant Israelis. His global education taught him how imperialism had dealt with vulnerable populations such as Algerians assaulted and displaced by the French, the native peoples in North America and the Aborigines in Australia either eradicated or removed to distant reservations, and Muslims in the Caucuses as czarist Russia moved in and chased out the populations living there. Eqbal fit the Israeli-Palestinian conflict within a much larger grid that took it out of the normal ethnic and religious framework that most analysts used when dealing with the problem.

The second preoccupation he had with Palestine was the replacement of the native Arab population with outsiders, Jews who lived elsewhere but were gathered into Israel to fill the homes and lands belonging to the fleeing Palestinians. Beyond the displaced Jewish victims of the Holocaust who ended up in displaced-persons camps after World War II and who flocked into Israel after 1948, two other immigration waves added significantly to the population of Israel: first, the migration of Sephardic Jews from North Africa and the Middle East, whose flight to Israel, Eqbal argued, had been facilitated by Arab leaders, sometimes in return for monetary payments; and the second, after the fall of the Soviet Union, the mass migration of a million highly educated and technically gifted Soviet Jews to Israel, arriving to offset the growing numbers of Arab Palestinians living on the Israel side of the Green Line. Both of these migrations hardened Israeli attitudes against Arabs and moved Israeli society to the right.[15]

Eqbal watched closely the events transpiring in the Persian Gulf, where the world's major oil resources lay, which the United States protected and some of the largest American corporations dominated. In one his most eloquent pieces of writing, he wrote in the aftermath of the Gulf War in 1991 about the low point reached by the Arabs and Muslims:

We live in scoundrel times. This is the dark age of Muslim history, the age of surrender and collaboration, punctuated by madness. The decline of our civilization began in the eighteenth century when, in the intellectual embrace of orthodoxy, we skipped the age of enlightenment and the scientific revolution. In the second half of the twentieth century, it has fallen.

I have been a lifelong witness to surrender, and imagined so many times—as a boy in 1948, a young man in 1967 . . . and approaching middle age in 1982—that finally we have hit rock bottom, that the next time even if we go down we would manage to do so with a modicum of dignity. Fortunately, I did not entertain even so modest an illusion from Saddam Hussein's loudly proclaimed "mother of battles."[16]

He also devoted a special issue of *Race & Class* to the Lebanese civil war,[17] where he saw sectarian divisions underlying the conflict deeply rooted in class inequalities. The Shia were poor and underserved, while the other Lebanese communities lived relatively comfortable lives. Civil war ensued as the Shia claimed a greater political role in order to equalize their situation in the society. The same drama is playing out in Lebanon today, with the Hezbollah representing Shia claims for equality. Of course, there were other internal factors at play in Lebanon, which Eqbal recognized, such as sectarian Muslim, Maronite Christian, and Druze interests as well as external players, such as France, Syria and Iran, who had their local allies, which complicated any attempt at a long-term settlement.

On June 26, 1998, while in Beirut, Eqbal went with Eric Rouleau (1926–2015), the veteran *Le Monde* Middle East correspondent and later French ambassador to Tunisia and Turkey, to interview the secretary-general of the Lebanese Hezbollah, Sayyad Hasan Nasrallah (b. 1960). The first thing he noticed were women within the Hezbollah compound who dressed modestly and did not wear *hijab*. Also, most people surrounding the leader of this highly militarized organization were civilians, not soldiers. In their conversation, Nasrallah pointed out that Shia Islam gave religious leaders the possibility of using *ijtihad*, independent reasoning applied to religious texts, which would make the *mujtahid* (the one who applies reason to texts) an important and influential figure. This ability at the core of Shia Islam, he claimed, allows for update and change as well as for the incorporation of modern notions in daily life and practice.[18]

From the same trip to Lebanon, Eqbal wrote about the Lebanese economy, which functioned mainly as a result of foreign remittances sent into Beirut banks by some eight million expatriates living abroad, helping to keep afloat the four million Lebanese left in the country. War had taken its toll on the country, but reconstruction had brought about a semblance of normality in Beirut, he reported, although investments in agriculture were low, providing small amounts of foreign exchange. Tourists helped the economy, especially Arabs coming from the Persian Gulf, but despite all the problems he discovered that the Lebanese were optimistic about their future and discounted the slowdown of business and high rates of unemployment. Their industriousness was evident everywhere that Eqbal went, and he was impressed with the upbeat conversations he had with Beirutis, many of whom thought that with time they would recover their prosperity.[19]

Eqbal had seen the late King Hussein Ibn Talal of Jordan (1935–1999) walking a tight rope to maintain his throne. He thought that the father of the present king, Abdullah II (b. 1962), was one of the brightest rulers in the Middle East, surviving on his throne despite multiple assassination attempts against his life and being caught between a majority population of Palestinians in his country, tribal shaykhs (*shuyukh*) favoring the status quo, Israel as a neighbor, Iraq and Syria disdaining his independence, and the United States demanding obedience. Eqbal considered the very fact that Hussein had survived in such a hostile environment as a credit to his far-sightedness and diplomacy. King Hussein had remained neutral through the 1991 American-led Operation Desert Storm, despite enormous pressures from the United States to join the war on the U.S. side. Eqbal, unlike many other Americans, recognized that if the king did otherwise, he could have lost his throne in an internal coup. Although he rarely complimented monarchs or any Middle Eastern and Asian rulers, he called Hussein "the wily old king" in an obituary he wrote of him.[20]

7

India, Pakistan, and Bangladesh

The Problem of Nuclear Proliferation and Views on Partitioning States

EQBAL VEERED FROM MAINSTREAM THINKING MOST OF ALL in his position on partitioning states. He came to believe that partition, though often desired by external powers to separate belligerents and momentarily tame conflicts, did not solve problems. Regarding Bosnian and Kosovar Muslims, he reluctantly advocated separation from the Serbs, mainly because he felt that these well-armed enemies would exterminate the Muslim minorities. Most partitions, he asserted, have reflected the failure of negotiating processes and the victory of supranationalism over rationalism and compromise. He argued that negotiated unity, even if imperfect, was most often better than creating sectarian states.

Despite his parents' cosmopolitanism and disdain for nationalism, Eqbal was consumed by the turbulence provoked by partition. He initially embraced Pakistan's creation with gusto. But he lived through the heady pre- and postindependence days, when many promises were made and then quickly postponed and forgotten. In the postcolonial period, optimism gave way to pessimism as liberal civilian governments fell to dictators. Pakistan was no exception. Nationalists had created myriad undeliverable expectations, and strong states were needed to contain mass aspirations and face the challenges ahead.

Pakistan's nationalist leader Muhammad Ali Jinnah was a British-educated barrister who spoke English in public, his native Gujarati in private, but his country's official language, Urdu, not at all. He believed that Pakistan had to forge a multicultural nation, an idea not at all liked by the country's religious elite, the ulema, who wanted to create an Islamic state. Eqbal argued that the population of the new Pakistan backed Jinnah in attempting to forge a modern nation. He pointed out that because later military dictators did not have Jinnah's charisma and nationalist credentials, they, unlike Jinnah, began to use Islam for their own political ends and to legitimize their rule by backing conservative ulema and their dogmas. In the process of historicization, Eqbal commented, Jinnah was converted into "a man of orthodox religious views who sought the creation of a theocratic state[,] and the Ulema, who with rare exceptions, had opposed Jinnah and the Pakistan movement, emerged as heroes and founding fathers of Pakistan."[1]

Dictators everywhere speeded the burial of expectations. Nationalism waned as manipulation and disillusionment grew. The new danger lay in authoritarianism. Military regimes often spent tax revenues on weapons and established kleptocracies that milked their nations of wealth. Small elites prospered at the expense of the increasingly impoverished masses. In Pakistan, dictatorship accompanied martial law, declared in October 1958, a little more than a year after Eqbal arrived in the United States.

In a lecture he delivered in 1998, Eqbal explained how he came to oppose that partition and to believe that "the break has to be mended." "[P]olitical boundaries were drawn on the basis of nationalism, and identities were asserted based on proclaimed and imagined differences" both in 1947 and again in 1972, when Bangladesh achieved its independence.[2] The work of Pakistani writer Saadat Hassan Manto (1912–1955), who wrote at the moment of partition in 1947, demonstrated the problem, according to Eqbal: his characters' indecision over what they should take of the old and which of the new places they should relate to lead to a confusion so profound that they end up in no man's land. For Eqbal, "no man's land" was the perfect metaphor for partition, which had to be rectified.

Eqbal always focused on people's basic humanity rather than on the ethnic or religious differences that divided them. This made him unpopular with the powers that be, for he opposed the trend of his times to separate warring parties while forgetting to settle the long-festering issues that brought them to war in the first place. Likewise, Eqbal's message was always antihegemonic. The people to whom he gravitated at the end of his life and his closest friends, such as Radha Kumar and Edward Said, examined partitions critically. After Radha wrote *The History of Doing: An Illustrated Account of Movements for Women's Rights and Feminism in India, 1800–1900*, she completed another book, *Divide and Fall? Bosnia in the Annals of Partition*, which criticized the partition of Bosnia.[3] At a memorial service for Eqbal in 1999, Radha stressed that "Eqbal was absolutely passionately committed to undoing the partition of India. He was committed to opposing partition wherever he found it. He believed very deeply that the problems of our individual countries would never be resolved as long as this partition lasted. He was much more optimistic than I. He believed this partition would in fact end and that the subcontinent would find another way of creating itself."[4]

Radha herself grappled with the problem of India's partition in her book *Making Peace with Partition*.[5] She concluded that the Indian partition may have been less painful than partitions in other countries. Although the split was accompanied by horrific violence and the experience was intense, she argued, on the Indian subcontinent the violence was short-lived, unlike in other partitioned regions such as Ireland, Korea, Palestine, Yugoslavia, and Cyprus. The Indian and Pakistani armies did not get involved in the mutual slaughter, she noted, and most of the people who unleashed the violence demobilized quickly in the aftermath of partition. Eqbal had already pointed out that the numbers of people killed in the partition were initially exaggerated: "Originally it was said that four or five million died. No. The number of deaths was minimal in view of the size of the catastrophe. Less than half a million died. But remember, twenty-two million people were displaced, moved from one place to another. To date it remains the largest migration in recorded history."[6]

Eqbal, Radha, and Edward argued in favor of a world devoid of artificial borders, a world where protagonists would work hard to sort out their problems through negotiations and would not accept having to live in small or large Bantustans because such partitioned areas only served the needs of narrow nationalists or those who governed the world. Their visionary message may seem utopian to many who think that separating warring parties is the best option to allow time to heal wounds and find relief in the fact that immediate killing has stopped. Eqbal, Radha, and Edward did not disagree with the need to put an end to violence, but they pushed for prolonged negotiations to sort out conflicting claims and establish a just peace. Their points of view certainly grated on policy makers, who wanted to end conflicts quickly at the lowest possible costs to themselves.

Just as Eqbal never became an American citizen,[7] long absences from Pakistan reinforced his outsider position there as well. Until the last years of his life, when he moved back to Pakistan but still spent some time in the United States, he had played little part in framing events in the newly created country, whose history unfolded while he lived abroad. He never established a solid base in Pakistan or involved himself in the rough and tumble politics there or spent years in jail to prove his mettle or confronted military dictatorship on a daily basis.

When young Pakistanis flocked around Eqbal and urged him to help establish a political party, he could not and did not do so; he instead attempted to create a new private university but failed. Outsiders, however, can do important things. First, the contradictions of Pakistan's politics had created a relatively free press. The print media there flourished, and Eqbal's columns, often condemning corruption, police brutality, and jingoism in Pakistan, were not censored. He thought they were published uncensored because less than 10 percent of the population were literate.[8] The state controlled local television stations more carefully because millions watched them. Satellite TV disrupted such control, however, as Pakistanis could watch a wide range of programs overseas. Eqbal's detachment and novel insights allowed him to contribute new ideas for many groups that he joined, helped form, or encouraged. He always felt that the subcontinent was his real home, and he never wanted to close the door to returning there one day.

Indian-Pakistani Citizen Exchanges

As Eqbal matured, he became more and more vocal in his opposition to the jingoistic nationalism emanating from both India and Pakistan, which prevented peaceful relations between the two neighbors. Starting in the 1970s, on his own initiative, he began traveling to India and established contacts with outstanding intellectuals there, such as Rajni Kothari (1928–2015), the founder of the Indian Center for the Study of Developing Societies. His trips were facilitated by the agreement of July 2, 1972, that Pakistan and India signed at Simla on bilateral relations, momentarily putting an end to the conflict and confrontation that marred their relations. The two countries had resolved to "work for the promotion of friendly and harmonious relationships and the establishment of a durable peace in the subcontinent."[9] Simla became the benchmark for future people-to-people exchanges.

Eqbal had scores of Indian friends and took on the task of personal diplomacy without conceiving of any institutional frameworks within which he could expand contacts between Indians and Pakistanis. The Indian peace activist and *Mainstream* editor Nikhil Chakravarty (1913–1998) led the way in organizing delegations of prominent Indians to visit Pakistan, and he spent twenty-five days in that country at the end of 1981. Dr. Mubashir Hassan (b. 1922), former Pakistani finance and planning minister and one of the principal organizers behind Zulfiqar Ali Bhutto's rise to power, recounted what happened next in an article on the history of the Indian-Pakistani peace movement published in 2003:

A significant event occurred when in April 1984, the English language newspaper *The Muslim* invited a number of eminent Indian journalists and intellectuals to Islamabad for a conference with Pakistani journalists, politicians, and retired civil and military officials. N[ikhil] C[hakravarty] was among the Indian delegation as was a retired Vice-Chief of the Army Staff of India, the first ever to visit Pakistan for such a conference. The rights and wrongs in the India-Pakistan relationship were aired by both sides with great frankness and candour. . . . Pakistanis and Indians during this conference were to go a long way in making joint efforts for peace in the following years.[10]

After Eqbal started returning to the subcontinent on a regular basis in the late 1980s and using the Indian friendships he had nurtured in the 1970s, he teamed up with Mubashir Hassan to expand those contacts and regularize cross-border visits by intellectuals and other prominent personalities. Both men saw an opportunity to broaden contacts between the civil societies of India and Pakistan and to end the cold war and arms race between them. Mubashir argued that it was "nothing short of tragic" that both countries missed opportunities to usher in progress and prosperity for the two people.[11] Each of the governments had long claimed that they could not enter into negotiations across their frontiers because of massive opposition from their civil societies against establishing such contacts. Eqbal and Mubashir wanted to demonstrate that little fierce opposition to a thaw existed within both societies, so they set out to establish and then broaden people-to-people contacts across the barriers that separated the two countries. They intended to build a social movement that would undercut the arguments for inaction of both governments and in that way help to create a groundswell to move both countries toward reconciliation and peace.

During the last decade of the twentieth century, as the cold war between the Soviet Union and the United States ended, it became possible to launch a campaign for peace and against war on the subcontinent. On April 9, 1990, a number of prominent Indians "appealed to all men and women of goodwill in both the countries, to make a united front to avoid a disastrous conflict, which will not solve any of the existing problems but will only aggravate and multiply them. We believe there are no outstanding problems, including Kashmir, which cannot be solved peacefully in a manner that could be acceptable to both the peoples and governments in India and Pakistan in the spirit of the Simla Agreement."[12] In another statement published in the *Hindustan Times* (New Delhi) about a week later, another group of prominent Indians, including the historian Romila Thapar (b. 1931) and Eqbal's friend Rajni Kothari, "appealed to India and Pakistan to refrain from taking any steps that might lead to a destructive war."[13] On April 25, 1990, seventy-eight South Asian academics and intellectuals, including Eqbal, "signed an appeal addressing all scholars and professionals, political leaders, academic associations and concerned citizens . . . for conciliation rather than confrontation and highlighted the futility of armed conflicts. Rather they advocated the resolution of disputes through discussions and negotiations."[14] On May 13, 1990, Eqbal and forty-nine other eminent Pakistanis, including jurists, parliamentarians, retired military officers, and even a retired cricket captain, issued another statement that received wide publicity in the Indian press. It said: "South Asia is haunted by the spectre of a fourth India-Pakistan war. The dispute is again over the unresolved question of Kashmir. As concerned Pakistanis, we urge the governments of India and Pakistan to refrain from seeking military solutions to an eminently political problem. Wars did not resolve this issue in the past. . . . We believe that Kashmir, which has so far been the primary cause of hostility between Pakistan and India, can well become the bridge to peace between the two countries."[15]

At the very end of May 1990, Eqbal and Mubashir, working with other Pakistani activists, formed a five-person delegation that included themselves, Asma Jahangir (b. 1952), secretary-general of the Human Rights Commission of Pakistan; Nisar Osmani (1931–1994), journalist and Human Rights Commission vice president; and Nasim Zehra (b. 1953), celebrated columnist and television talk-show hostess, to take part in a discussion with their counterparts in New Delhi on the Indo-Pakistan relationship. They met Shri I. K. Gujral (1919–2012), the minister for external affairs of the Indian government. Another informal meeting took place with an eminent member of Parliament and a leader of the Indian People's Party, Shri Jaswant Singh (b. 1938), at his residence. Rajiv Gandhi (1944–1991) had an informal discussion with them in his parliamentary office months before his assassination. The delegates

spent the rest of their time on tour in discussions with Indian intellectuals, especially political analysts, and retired diplomats at the Indo-Pakistan Friendship Society, the Council for South Asian Relations, Kothari's Center for the Study of Developing Societies, and, in a combined
meeting, the Indian Institute of Technology and Jawaharal Nehru
University.

While in Pakistan in 2004, I spoke with all but one member of this
delegation, Nisar Osmani, who wrote a column about the trip for the Karachi newspaper *Dawn*.[16] Members of the delegation praised Eqbal's role
in helping to organize the peace initiative. Clearly, Mubashir Hassan, as
a former Pakistani government minister, was the key figure among them,
but Eqbal, because of his previous frequent trips to India and his own notoriety, knew many intellectuals and drew Indian audiences to the talks
and discussions. He wore traditional Pakistani clothes, and in the debates
they participated in he came down hard on both Pakistan and India. He
already had an international reputation as being pro-Palestinian and had
been arrested and tried at the highest level by the U.S. government, so
he could not be accused of being a Zionist or a CIA agent, as other peacemakers invariably became labeled and dismissed in the press of both
countries. He had to be taken seriously. (Regarding an encounter he had
with Pakistan, a couple of his former friends and editorial collaborators
had ridiculously called him a U.S. spy, but I thought then that their
foolishness had more to do with his unwillingness to share their ideological choices than with anything based on fact.)

Asma Jahangir, human rights advocate and lawyer who sees clients
in her private practice while being guarded by two soldiers bearing machine guns, has a no-nonsense approach to life. She had lived through
years of repression in Pakistan, which steeled her resolve and courage to
carry on. In that way, she is representative of a growing number of
Pakistani women and men who have lived through a series of military dictatorships, suffered prison or state-sponsored terror, and finally have
emerged stronger and less afraid. It was gratifying on my most recent
visit to several cities in Pakistan that I met scores of people like her.

On the delegation's trip to India, she and her colleague Nisar Osmani
were impressed by India's democracy, its press freedom, and the sophis-

tication of in-depth analysis in the media. Jahangir at first had her doubts about the outsider Pakistani who did not live in Pakistan. Many intellectuals she knew, however, looked up to Eqbal as a demigod. She told me that "people around him made him into something that he was not." On the trip to India, she got to know him well. In some ways, she found him typical of a class of Indians who were truly great storytellers. In the process of spinning their yarns, they added some spice and elaborated to accommodate their audiences. She also later came to know the depths of his compassion and sensitivity. When they went out shopping together, she understood how down to earth he could be. She was impressed that he did not talk down to anyone. In the discussions among the five, she felt no gender pressures. She especially appreciated his ability to focus the group on elaborating structures for further exchanges.[17]

The exchange participants from both the Indian and the Pakistani sides thought that wars of the past had served no purpose and that an armed conflict in the future would be a disaster. They advocated government negotiations. They could not agree, however, on an agenda or priorities in those discussions. By the end of June, however, these Indian and Pakistani peacemakers had organized fifty-two politicians, former army officers, social workers, judges, teachers, and writers from across the divide to call on both governments to jointly reaffirm their commitment to peaceful resolution of all outstanding differences between the two countries.

In one of the South Asian dialogues in 1993, another delegation of Pakistani intellectuals, journalists, and human rights activists that Eqbal joined met with their counterparts in India and reached consensus on three points:

1. There cannot be any South Asian community without peace between Pakistan and India.
2. It is impossible to envisage normal relations between India and Pakistan until there is a settlement of the Kashmir question.
3. It is a duty and political obligation of South Asian intellectuals to protest violations of human rights wherever they occur. Kashmir was mentioned as a victim in extremis of such violations.

Kashmir was and still is a wedge dividing India and Pakistan. Periodically, as it did in August 2013, it explodes into violence and brings both states back to belligerency, jeopardizing all the gains made through people's exchanges and increases in trade relations between the two countries.

In 1996, Eqbal wrote perceptively of patterns that he saw then and that would still persist in 2015:

> In Kashmir, India is engaged as an incumbent; Pakistan supports the insurgency. . . . In the process an estimated 40,000 people are dead, and many more wounded. Kashmir's economy has been wrecked, and an entire generation of Kashmiri's has already been deprived of normal upbringing and education. Yet, armed struggle and Indian repression have not brought Kashmiri's closer to either self-determination, which is Pakistan's demand, or to the pacification which India seeks. In fact, both countries are further from attaining their goals in 1996 than they were in 1989.[18]

Eqbal did all this work on border crossings and writing about normalization between India and Pakistan as well as the Kashmiri issue as one of many projects that he participated in while living in Pakistan, but he did not see this work as the principal focus of his life there. In the end, however, these exchanges and visits to India as well as his and Mubashir Hassan's hosting of Indians when the latter in turn traveled to Pakistan may turn out to be the most significant contribution he made to the subcontinent's healthy future. As peacemakers, he and Mubashir deserve great credit for spearheading a movement that has mushroomed in recent years to include the exchange of parliamentarians, students, professionals, business leaders, and others as well as the establishment of bus service between the countries and with the contested region of Kashmir. When I was in Lahore in May 2004, I found it difficult to find a room in a hotel because of the influx of thousands of Indians there to attend a Pakistani-Indian cricket match, something inconceivable a decade earlier. Eqbal and Mubashir's contributions include preparing both India's and Pakistan's civil societies for such exchanges and ultimately forcing the governments to stop using their own people as an excuse for their belligerence.[19]

By the mid-1990s, Eqbal intensified his cross-border contacts. He traveled to Calcutta as a guest of the Bose Institute, headed by Sugata Bose (b. 1956), the grandson of the famous and controversial Subhas Chandra Bose (1897–1945) and now professor of Indian Ocean history at Harvard University.[20] Sugata, while still in India, invited Eqbal to give a series of talks there. In the early 1990s, few Indians came to Pakistan. Eqbal spoke before large audiences in traditional clothes and became the embodiment of civil society contacts between the two countries, organizing petition drives and the reciprocal exchanges of intellectuals that later blossomed. He also simultaneously engaged in a South Asian dialogue starting in 1990. He went to Nepal, Dakka, and Sri Lanka.[21]

Antinuclear Activities

When first the Indians and then the Pakistanis exploded their atomic bombs in full euphoria, Eqbal joined Pakistani physicists Abdul Hamid Nayyar (b. 1945)[22] and Pervez Hoodbhoy (b. 1950) in speaking out against the folly of a nuclear arms race in a part of the world where poverty degraded so many millions of people. He did so despite his gut feeling that if Pakistan would test an atomic bomb, it would give the Israelis a jolt. His fears of nuclear proliferation and atomic disaster on the subcontinent, however, outweighed his geopolitical concern that counterforces to Israel's power in the Middle East and the larger Muslim world needed to be established. He refused to follow the nationalists in Pakistan who celebrated Pakistan's explosion of its atomic bomb. In 1998, he told David Barsamian, "I don't believe in nuclear weapons. Therefore, I believe that just because India has nuclear weapons, Pakistan does not have to have them. I believe in unilaterally not having to compete with India in the nuclear arms race."[23] This was a lonely position, but that did not stop Eqbal from writing and lecturing in Pakistan and India against atomic diplomacy and exposing the political manipulations behind the detonations.

The lack of stability in Pakistan added to Eqbal's concern about the country possessing nuclear weapons. He told David Barsamian in 1998, "Out of the last fifty years since partition twenty-five have been spent under military rule and twenty-five under unstable, corrupt, and ineffi-cient civilian rule. People who have been living in that unstable fashion, facing a very large hostile neighbor, created out of historic India, therefore not certain whether their status is permanent or not, will feel insecure. That's another reason I feel we should have avoided the possession of nuclear weapons."[24]

Pervez Hoodbhoy began decrying nuclear arms on the subcontinent in 1978, four years after India exploded its first plutonium bomb. Eqbal vicariously followed Pervez as Pervez began writing more frequently on the question and had his uncle edit his articles before publishing them. When Pervez wrote something for the monthly magazine the *Karachi Herald* in 1980 and asked Eqbal to go over the article, he noticed that Eqbal was not as alarmed about the issue as he was.[25]

Pervez also shared his manuscripts for six pieces he wrote in 1993 for the *News* (Islamabad), which Eqbal said that he liked. In that year, Pervez had an interview with the chairman of the military Joint Chiefs of Staff Committee, General Shamin Alam Khan (b. 1937), and was troubled by the general's cavalier attitude toward nuclear arms. The general told him that Pakistan would use the bomb if the Indian army attempted to take over Pakistani cities, estimating that in a nu-clear war about 12 percent of the population would die. Most of the pop-ulation would survive, he concluded. Thumping the table, the general raised his voice and shouted that the Pakistani army would never be defeated. Eqbal was appalled when he heard Pervez's report on the conversation.[26]

Also in 1994, Zia Mian, the Islamabad-based Qaʿid al-Azam Univer-sity physicist and later, beginning in 1996, Princeton University research scientist, edited a collected work on nuclear proliferation issues, which Gautam Publications put out. When the book was published, the head of the press, Riaz, and his staff were arrested and tortured for seven months despite the fact that all the chapters in the book except Zia's had already been published elsewhere. Security forces put pressure on all Pakistani publishers to reject manuscripts by this group of antinuclear activists. Such realities began to change Eqbal's mind about the issue, and he became more and more involved.

Eqbal was shocked during an interview he had with General Pervez Musharraf (b. 1943) in March 1998, more than a year before the latter overthrew Prime Minister Nawaz Sharif in a coup. Musharraf told Eqbal that nuclear weapons would protect Pakistan from India and would change the strategic contours of South Asia. Eqbal immediately called Pervez and told him that the army thinks that it has a nuclear shield. "They are playing with fire," he said, "and when they are through with it, there will be tragedy."[27] On May 28, 1998, a few weeks after India set off its own round of nuclear explosions, Pakistan exploded five nuclear devices in underground steel-girded tunnels.

Four antinuclear activists—Pervez Hoodbhoy, Eqbal Ahmad, Zia Mian, and A. H. Nayyar—represented lonely voices in Pakistan. On June 2, a few days after Pakistan's nuclear tests, the Pakistan-India People's Forum for Peace and Democracy, which Eqbal helped animate, held a meeting in a hotel and a press conference on nuclear issues, in which Eqbal and Pervez participated. Some 120 journalists came, but so did a large number of belligerent spectators, and they disrupted the press briefing, making catcalls and derogatory comments. Others raised silly questions. Eqbal tried to pacify them and read a sura from the Qur'an praising differences of opinion. All this happened with much noise in the background. Suddenly fifteen people marched into the hall carrying signs and placards in favor of the nuclear detonations. They belonged to the youth movement of the Jammat al-Islam. They then circled around the stage, started chanting pro-bomb slogans, and shouted out that conference convenors were Indian agents and that there was no place in Pakistan for them. Nayyar, sharing the stage with Eqbal, reacted to the shouting, and the demonstrators pounced on him and started beating him up. Eqbal fruitlessly tried to protect him, and the security guards in the hall were useless. They were more afraid of the crowd than Eqbal and Nayyar were. About ten of the one hundred journalists present tried to protect

Nayyar, and they too were beaten up. The crowd roughed up but did not beat some women on the stage.[28]

Eqbal would, however, not be silenced. Two days later he published one of the most poignant columns he ever wrote on the subject:

> I saw on television a picture more awesome than the familiar mushroom cloud of nuclear explosion. The mountain had turned white. I wondered how much pain had been felt by nature, God's most wondrous creation. The great mountain in Chagai will turn in time to solid ash! . . .
>
> The leaders of India and Pakistan have now appropriated to themselves, as others had done before, the power that was God's alone— to kill mountains, make the earth quake, bring the sea to boil, and destroy humanity. I hope that when the muscle-flexing and cheering is over they will go on a retreat, and reflect on how they should bear this awesome responsibility.[29]

Beena Sarwar of Pakistan television, who produced a program on Eqbal as peacemaker, outlined for me later the story line of Eqbal's antinuclear activities:

> In May 1998, India exploded nuclear weapons, followed by Pakistan. Eqbal vociferously opposed both. . . . [H]e argued against Pakistan testing, and expressed his belief that the "celebrations" were not spontaneous but officially sponsored and engineered—"government agents ran around up and down Abpara market in Islamabad saying 'close your shops, come out to show your support for the bomb.' Then they said to the camera people, you can now take pictures. I did not see any expression of spontaneous joy either in Islamabad or in Rawalpindi." [Eqbal] argued that the Indian public and the Pakistani public, "even those who felt joy about it, know that this was too serious a matter to go about celebrating. . . . In both countries, on Hiroshima Day in 1998, large demonstrations took place. In India the demonstrations were much larger than in Pakistan. In Calcutta 250,000 people came out against nuclear weapons. In Delhi, 30,000."[30]

Eqbal joined Pervez about a half-dozen times in giving talks on the nuclear issue in different parts of Pakistan. When he agreed to speak, journalists turned out in large numbers to cover the event. Most audiences were initially not hostile, and each amounted to between two hundred and four hundred people, mainly from the liberal sectors of the society. However, when retired army officers appeared, they tended to be hostile. In 1996, some bearded people—Islamic radicals—showed up and objected to the talks. Nayyar told me that Eqbal was a great source of strength for this and many other movements, and when he died, they were so very much poorer. Before he joined them, they were working on impulse, Nayyar commented.[31]

Eqbal finally decided that he would live in Pakistan full time and get deeply involved in the day-to-day frays of civil society. His friend Raza Kazim thought that Eqbal would have had to do a long apprenticeship and learn how to operate in the treacherous political environment of Pakistan if he ever hoped to become deeply engaged. Raza told me that he himself had lived in Pakistan since 1947, had gone to jail five times, and managed to survive.[32] Others expected similar sacrifices from their populist leaders.

I had never seen Eqbal as happy as he was in India and Pakistan when we traveled there together during 1980. He beamed as he took me to the home of Raza Kazim, a lawyer who never gave up on political struggles and whom Eqbal got released from prison in November 1985, after mounting an international campaign over a period of nearly two years. A Pakistani military court acquitted the barrister.

Raza explained to me in 2004 that both he and Eqbal came from old feudal families who had fought their way into the Indian subcontinent, Raza's a millennium ago and Eqbal's beginning in the mid-fourteenth century. That history and shared background created a strong bond between them, which was cemented by their status as refugees from India. Political differences could not break their friendship. Raza also recalled that Eqbal had told him that he was his closest friend.[33]

Younger friends and associates urged Eqbal to get deeply involved and set up a mass-based party, especially beginning in 1987, when he returned to Pakistan with Julie and Dohra. Many people wanted him to lead a movement then, but Eqbal resisted the temptation to do so. Imran Hamid, a friend of Eqbal's from Islamabad, thought that Eqbal would have served as a father figure because they needed someone to strategize with them and direct a movement, but Eqbal's daughter, Dohra, did not believe that he would have been able to make the necessary compromises needed to run for office and legislate or govern. Imran mulled that "you can't spend most of your life subverting hierarchies and then construct a political organization. It just wouldn't have worked."[34] Zia Mian, a close friend of Eqbal, thought differently. He told me in 2004 that Eqbal had come to realize that the Pakistani state, sapped of its strength by years of official corruption, had become so weak and fragile that a successful oppositional movement would have only created anarchy and disorder. Eqbal wanted instead to work within state institutions to strengthen them.[35] In reiteration of what he told his friends, Eqbal wrote a few short months before his death, "Pakistan has been a parliamentary democracy for a decade, . . . [but] the democratic system is still in its infancy, feeble and malfunctioning. Its limbs, the institutions of governance and public service, have to be rebuilt and reinforced internally."[36]

Eqbal nevertheless encouraged nongovernment organization militants within Pakistan's civil society. For example, when in 1981–1982 a group of Pakistanis formed the Women's Action Forum, Eqbal understood what they were trying to do to widen women's rights and participation and endorsed their activities. When he first returned to his country on a regular basis in the late 1980s, he felt that the Left was out of touch with global realities. He had no faith in Zulfikar Ali Bhutto's Pakistan People's Party, which he viewed as the leader's feudal fiefdom. He encouraged young socialists who gathered around him to talk to and organize workers within the party and industrial laborers in general. Rani Mumtaz in Lahore told me that when she first met Eqbal, she was overawed by his persona, but as she got to know him, she saw his human side and appreciated him as a friend. What she liked best about him was his nonsexist approach; he became good friends of both men and women.[37]

In many discussions with groups of between fifty and one hundred people, Eqbal helped deepen these individuals' analysis of the current political situation and continuously argued that political parties were too corrupt to rely on in Pakistan, as were municipal governments. In a hard-hitting article that *Dawn* published in November 1998, he responded fearlessly to the growing violence engulfing the country's major city and economic capital, Karachi:

Terror in Karachi shall end only when the enforcement of law is lawfully carried out, and the purveyors of violence are isolated from the people by the assurance of the government's genuine commitment to restoring the city to health. On the other hand such practices as killings in custody, generalized torture, search-and-destroy operations, blanket arrests and extortions by the police shall reduce the government to the level of a criminal mafia and further undermine the legitimacy of the state. But even if the government is successful beyond expectations in restoring order, peace in Karachi cannot be sustained unless the city is invested with a viable new structure of governance that includes a meaningfully empowered city government and a metropolitan police force.[38]

As Eqbal matured, he criticized with unrelenting honesty the wrongs that he saw all around. His readers and audiences came to expect that of him. As he formulated his criticisms, he discarded any traces of his earlier nationalism and began applying universalist yardsticks to Pakistan's problems, as he had done earlier in the United States. Because most Pakistanis were nationalists to the core, his criticism shocked and sometimes bewildered his audiences and readers, but his logic was so clear and his persuasive force so great that they had to listen and pay attention to what he said and wrote. Educated people in Pakistan read him avidly, for few others took on the establishment and challenged consensus the way he did, consistently and devastatingly.

As he did with his students, he tried to empower the people he dealt with in Pakistan. Raza Kazim's half-sister, Nasim Zehra (or Chotti, as her friends call her), whom Eqbal befriended and encouraged, remembered the impact of their first encounter in 1985. She found him "extremely humane and a powerful intellectual. He made it sound as if anything was possible. It was . . . very inspiring," she told me in Islamabad. "In a world of hate and intolerance marked by an unethical use of power, Eqbal forced many people who became opinion makers and policy makers to value dialogue and peace without surrendering. He touched people intellectually and emotionally. He spoke of values and morality in the context of power. He was one of the few to do so," she remembered.[39] In the early years that she knew him, he addressed the most important challenges they faced and advocated not being reactive. He argued that one factor that pulled the Muslim world down and led to its intellectual depletion was its reactive and derivative tendencies.

One of the groups Eqbal worked with—led by I. A. Rehman (b. 1930), since 1990 the director of the Human Rights Commission, and Mubashir Hassan—organized encounters between South Asian citizens. Eqbal's outsider position facilitated interaction with the group's Indian interlocutors and lessened tensions in their meetings. These interchanges have grown more frequent since Eqbal's death in 1999 and constitute one of his significant accomplishments.

8

Critique of U.S. Foreign Policy, the Cold War, and Terrorism

IN THIS CHAPTER, I COVER ROUGHLY TWO SUBJECT AREAS, U.S. foreign policy during the Cold War and terrorism, reflecting the foreign-policy issues that preoccupied Eqbal. His writings on these subjects broke with the paradigms of the day, yet they stand the test of time and remain pertinent.

U.S. Foreign Policy

As the United States went down to defeat in Vietnam, Henry Kissinger, the architect of U.S. foreign policy under President Richard M. Nixon, changed the direction of American involvement overseas. The war had cost hundreds of billions of dollars and had overextended U.S. abilities to intervene abroad with flexibility. Political support for future direct U.S.

troop interventions had momentarily evaporated. Kissinger applied the program of Vietnamization (arming the Vietnamese allies of the United States to fight American enemies locally) throughout the world. He convinced President Nixon to supply weapons and money to national armies to fight Communist and radical nationalist insurgents everywhere. Eqbal was among the first to point out the scope of this transformation in U.S. foreign policy and its new implications.

Eqbal did not mince his words regarding either Nixon or Kissinger. He disliked them. "Richard Milhaus," he wrote in 1994, "was a devious, venal, and violent man. He began his political career as a witch hunter. . . . His career was built on red baiting and image making. . . . To Stephen Ambrose, historian of the cold war, Nixon 'was a McCarthyite before McCarthy.' He appealed to the dark side of the American psyche [and] . . . fed . . . on . . . the paranoid style in American politics. . . . He lied, manipulated, cheated, played dirty tricks, broke laws, obstructed justice."[1]

Kissinger played a prominent role in U.S. foreign policy between 1969 and 1977 and continued, reinforced, and established U.S. alliances with the world's worst dictators, including Franco in Spain, Salazar in Portugal, and the shah of Iran, as well as with right-wing military regimes in Greece and Turkey and with Israel increasingly after its decisive victory over the Arabs in 1967. The large Palestinian population in the Occupied Territories were denied their basic rights. The United States also established relationships with a series of dictators in Latin America, Indonesia, the Philippines, Thailand, and elsewhere. Eqbal saw a new pattern emerging whereby through military aid the United States was shoring up dictators and right-wing regimes everywhere. When all of the dictators and militaristic governments that the United States supported fell like a house of cards by the 1980s, Eqbal wondered in amazement how Kissinger with such a flawed global policy still remained a prized consultant of U.S. Republican presidents and corporate executives.

At the moment that his trial in the United States was about to take place in 1971, Eqbal published an important article on revolutionary warfare and counterinsurgency, which warned about the ways that organized attempts to eradicate revolutions overseas eroded democratic institutions at home:

The pursuit of counterrevolutionary foreign policy . . . enhances the power of the secret services of government over which parliamentary institutions can exercise little or no control and whose activities public organs (press, political parties, etc.) are normally not able to report and censure. The expanded role of the CIA and of the armed forces' special branches are examples. As their activities and influence increase, such agencies not only circumvent representative institutions but even begin to infiltrate and corrupt civilian life. . . . In order to overcome the checks of parliamentary institutions and public opinion, a government involved in counterinsurgency seeks ways to reduce its accountability to representative bodies and to bypass pressures of public opinion. A . . . favorite ploy is to employ puppet armies and experts to subvert foreign governments and fight wars by proxy. . . . Failure to defeat revolutionaries in protracted war alienates participants in counterinsurgency against the democratic values and institutions of their own country. The war is eventually seen as being lost at home rather than in the field . . . and democratic institutions increasingly appear as unworkable in revolutionary settings. . . . The divisions and disillusionments that follow involvements in counterrevolution ultimately reduce the legitimacy of existing institutions, inspire opposition to or contempt for them, and weaken the will to resist their corruption or destruction.

Above all, involvement in counterinsurgency politicizes the military and encourages its intrusion into civilian life.[2]

Early Confusion over the Issue of Terrorism

In a poignant analysis of the phenomenon of global terrorism, Eqbal had original, multipronged views. Regarding the Irangate affair in the mid-1980s, when President Ronald Reagan allowed Israel to arm Iran with U.S.-made weapons and the United States tried to placate and reach out to Ayatollah Ruhollah Khomeini despite Iran's status as a terrorist state, Eqbal already sensed a fundamental shift taking place in U.S. policy. With the onset of the decline of the Soviet Union as a world power, he saw U.S. leaders scurrying for a new overarching issue—this time antiterrorism—that would provide a new integrating principle of foreign policy in the same way that fear of the Soviet Union and the Cold War had effectively done since 1945. He recognized the beginning of the shift before other commentators did and pointed out the new principle's weakness at that specific point in time.

The brief U.S. embrace of Khomeini brought to the surface major contradictions in U.S. foreign policy. Since 1979, the United States had denounced Iran as a terrorist state, but by 1985 it began opening contacts with that same state. The American public could only be confused. For an integrative ideology on which the United States could base its foreign policy to be successful, there had to be continuous fear within the U.S. public, Eqbal argued. Also, policy makers had to be consistent and not contradict themselves. Terrorists and terrorist states had to incarnate evil and could not become parties to negotiations and arms transfers, lest the American public become confused and question the very rationale of their country's foreign policy.[3]

Therefore, long before September 11, 2001, Eqbal had begun analyzing the emerging U.S. foreign policy built around antiterrorism, as discussed in the introduction.[4] His ideas reflect the views of a critical outsider because they broke with the liberal consensus on the subject. Most liberal and conservative commentators viewed terrorism as irrational and terrorists as mad people intent on doing what they perceived to be God's will. Another problem arises, said Eqbal, when terrorist experts and Western officials do not bother to probe the issue of causation; for most of them, he thought, the phenomenon seems to have grown without identifiable causes. Some viewed terrorism as a manifestation of what Bernard Lewis and Samuel Huntington called the "clash of civilizations."[5]

Varieties of Terrorism

Eqbal's analysis revolved around four major points: (1) problems with the concept of terrorism; (2) the varieties of terrorism; (3) reasons terrorists act; and (4) what to do about terrorism. He identified five types of terrorism: state, religious, criminal, political, and oppositional—all deserving careful definitions and differentiation. He derided U.S. policy makers for bolstering the international radical Muslim movements by funding, arming, and training their members. As pointed out in the introduction, he predicted that these policies would have a spill-over effect, boomerang to haunt the larger Muslim world, and contribute to the escalating levels of violence there. Russia, the United States, and western Europe would pay the price as well, he argued starting in the late 1980s. He condemned Pakistan's military secret services for acting as surrogates for the United States by funding, arming, and training first the mujahideen and later the Taliban, who ultimately conquered Afghanistan from Pakistani bases using sophisticated U.S. weapons.[6]

Because the world economy and other areas of existence were increasingly global in scope, Eqbal was not surprised that terrorism too had become a global enterprise. At the same time, he pointed out that most nonstate terrorists had no revolutionary ideology but rather tended to look back to an often embellished, sometimes fictitious, glorious past, which they transformed into an idealistic vision for the future.

To the embarrassment of established states, Eqbal stressed that state-sponsored terrorism had flourished under the world order promoted in the 1970s and 1980s by the United States and western European states. These states had backed fascistic regimes in Asia, Africa, and Latin America, making their leaders heavily armed allies and in the process "committ[ing] a huge amount of terrorist violence."[7]

Eqbal did what most other commentators failed to do: he identified some of the causes of nonstate terrorism. First, terrorists needed to be heard, a characteristic of powerless people. Second, their acts were expressions of anger and helplessness. Third, they often felt betrayed (as Osama bin Laden did when America abandoned the U.S.-trained jihadists after the Soviet Union left Afghanistan, as explained in the introduction), a phenomenon tied to a tribal ethic of revenge.[8]

Eqbal raised finally the question, What can be done about terrorism? First, he advised, avoid double standards and condemn all terrorism, including that of allies and states. Second, concentrate on causes of terrorism and help ameliorate conditions, thereby removing those causes. Third, avoid military solutions because terrorism is a political problem. He argued that "military solutions cause more problems than they solve."[9] Fourth, the great powers should strengthen the framework of international law. In other words, they should treat terrorist acts as rational behavior subject to rational solutions.

U.S. Policy and Antiterrorism

Understanding that antiterrorism had become the paradigm of U.S. foreign policy, Eqbal was worried that "a single power [the United States] dominates the world militarily and dominates international institutions of peacekeeping and law without countervailing forces." Because of that domination, the weak and the poor are more vulnerable now, he thought, than during the Cold War. For that reason, he considered the present period, at the end of the twentieth century and beyond, to be much worse than the Cold War period.[10] Because there are no longer checks and balances in place within the international system, the present time is more dangerous for those who are poor and weak.[11]

Eqbal did not view U.S. power as a permanent phenomenon, though. First, he said, its economic capabilities do not match its military might. Second, the American public does not share the U.S. ruling class's will to dominate. To dominate in the world, a ruling power has to have an excess of morality, and its rulers have to set examples of uprightness. Without that, rulers cannot commit excesses throughout the rest of the world. Clinton and his shenanigans in the White House would not have been tolerated at the height of the British Empire, Eqbal argued. Americans continuing to like the president, allowing him to stay in power, and even resurrecting his reputation after the sex scandal passed demonstrate that they are not a people with a will to rule over the world.[12] Also, the U.S. population does not want to pay the price in American lives lost to maintain its dominance in the world. It enters wars reluctantly, and since the Vietnam War opponents of intervention have been able to mobilize millions against such policies. As noted earlier, President Ronald Reagan committed U.S. soldiers and organized an international jihadist crusade to help Afghanistan defeat Soviet troops there in the 1980s. Once that was done, the United States lost interest in Afghanistan, creating a power vacuum that the radical Taliban, allied with Osama bin Laden's al-Qaeda, filled. They took over the country, only to provoke a new intervention of U.S. troops to neutralize or eliminate radical Muslims there. The new Afghan government, approved by the Americans and led by President Hamid Karzai (b. 1957), had little real power beyond the capital Kabul and proved to be extremely corrupt, giving the Taliban a chance to regroup and challenge the state for control of large areas of the country.[13] President George W. Bush, erroneously claiming that Saddam Hussein's Baath regime possessed weapons of mass destruction, orchestrated an invasion of Iraq, with some North Atlantic Treaty Organization support, starting on March 20, 2003. Western troops overturned the state and three years later executed the dictator. Shiites, with close ties to Iran and the majority of the population emerged as the dominant political force in the country and lorded over the once dominant Sunni population. Once again, the U.S. public pressured the president to withdraw U.S. troops, which President Barack Obama did in 2013, leaving a precarious situation wherein sectarian violence has spread.

Eqbal described the early stages of this same process as it had occurred under President Bill Clinton—the imperial presidency thriving amid a great deal of "muck"—and revealed how "deeply flawed" American democracy is. The United States, he argued,

exercises power abroad, often in an arbitrary fashion, frequently in criminal ways that have devastating effects on people's lives and future. It does so without accountability, at home or abroad. Even officially acknowledged crimes of the American government and officials routinely go unremarked and unpunished. Thus in the last five decades not one president nor one of his high officials has been censured by the congress, convicted by the courts, or investigated by an independent counsel for the myriad crimes they have committed against individuals and peoples abroad. Some of these are officially acknowledged crimes, among which are the multiple attempts to kill Fidel Castro, the targeted killing of some 10,000 Vietnamese under the

Phoenix Program, the participation in the overthrow of elected governments such as those of Arbenz [in Guatemala], Mossadegh [in Iran], and Allende [in Chile], and the waging of secret wars that caused the destruction of Laos and Cambodia. All of these were illegal acts, none was carried out with congressional consent, and none was a subject of inquiry and censure. It is this fact which renders the American a narrow and sectarian democracy unworthy, still, of universal respect.[14]

Eqbal's anti-imperialism did not abate with age but rather became more focused and fierce. He did not mince his words, spoke what he felt and saw, and in return gained the respect of a wide readership outside of the United States who appreciated his forthrightness.

CONCLUSION

EQBAL'S FRIENDS, COLLEAGUES, AND STUDENTS GATHERED AT Hampshire College in October 1997 to commemorate his retirement from teaching. The five colleges in Amherst transformed the event into a memorable weekend-long celebration of his life and organized a series of talks by his friends, including Edward Said, Noam Chomsky, and Daniel Ellsberg.[1] Edward opened the event with a lecture, "Clash or Definition of Civilizations," at the University of Massachusetts. In his critique of the notion of a clash of civilizations, which Harvard professor Samuel Huntington had popularized,[2] he observed that civilizations do not fall along discreet geographical boundaries, that the exchange and intermixing of ideas and forms are more discernable, deeper, and more endearing realities than separation and clash, and that the ideas of civilizational clash have their roots in a history of domination and discrimination.

On identifying imperialism and superpower intervention in the Third World as among the issues that engaged Eqbal, Noam Chomsky delivered a devastating critique of the rhetoric of human rights and globalization that emanated from Washington, D.C., and the American media. Globalization, he argued, was a project to perpetuate imperial domination and advance the interests of international capital and vested interests linked to money. Globalization affected people unevenly, he continued, and always to the detriment of the Third World's vulnerable economies. Citing U.S. patronage and support of such gross human rights violators as South Korea, Israel, and Indonesia, Chomsky exposed official U.S. advocacy of democracy and human rights as a cruel joke. He argued that the hope for humanity lay in people organizing to resist in multiple ways the symbiotic partnership of imperialism, international capital, and local elites. After Chomsky's talk before thousands of people coming from the five colleges in the Pioneer Valley and the town of Amherst itself, Eqbal thanked his friend for taking the time to attend this event. Noam in turn thanked Eqbal for his many contributions over the years in helping him clarify his own ideas.[3]

Daniel Ellsberg spoke next. As a high-level national-security adviser to the Pentagon and the State Department in the 1960s, he had earned a place in history when he divulged the Pentagon Papers, a large body of secret documents revealing that the highest U.S. officials had been deliberately deceiving the American people and Congress by knowingly pursuing a policy in Vietnam that broke American as well international laws.[4] Ellsberg began by quoting from Eqbal's writings to show how uncannily Eqbal had understood and analyzed Washington's policies without the benefit of inside information. He cited documents to show that the Vietnam War may have endured longer and could have ended in the use of nuclear weapons had it not been for the fact that the antiwar movement made continuing the war untenable at home.

Many more of Eqbal's activist friends contributed memories of their interaction with their Pakistani friend. Howard Zinn, whose book *People's History of the United States* is regarded as a classic of revisionist historiography,[5] had everyone laughing with his witty narration of how he and Eqbal beat the FBI at its own game when Father Daniel Berrigan became a fugitive from the law (see chapter 1). For health reasons, Father Berrigan was not present, but his poem to commemorate the occasion was read out to an applauding audience.

Cora Weiss spoke next, reading a humor-filled paper entitled "What If Eqbal Ran the United Nations." It was in effect a well-thought-out program for reforming the world organization. Iqbal Riza, then Secretary-General Kofi Anan's chief of cabinet at the United Nations and Eqbal's longtime friend, remarked ruefully that Cora had suggested "all the good things we would like to do and cannot."[6] In his turn, Peter Weiss (b. 1925), one of the founders of the New York–based Center for Constitutional Rights, argued that Western liberal governments' concern for human rights goes only so far as it suits their interests. Furthermore, they engage the softer issue of violations of procedural rights (e.g., imprisonment without trial) while ignoring distributive injustices and people's substantive rights, such as freedom from want. He also narrated in some detail the austere and imaginative ways in which Eqbal founded and led the Transnational Institute. "And now," he said, turning toward him, "you are planning to establish a university in Pakistan. I am sure that your country will have one great institution to be proud of."

Eqbal's persistent ambition to establish Khaldunia University in Pakistan was on many minds. Masao Miyoshi (1928–2009), a Japanese literary critic who taught at the University of California at San Diego, also analyzed the problems of globalization and spoke of the ill effects on teaching and scholarship of the increasing "corporatization" of the university. Corporations and governments now set the agenda of teaching and research, he argued, gently warning Eqbal that he ought to watch out for this trend as he built Khaldunia in Pakistan.

Adele Simmons, former president of Hampshire College and then later of the John D. and Catherine T. MacArthur Foundation, narrated stories of Eqbal's unusual gifts as a teacher and educationist. She concluded with thoughts on the need to plug the brain drain and create a favorable environment for scientific research and higher learning in the Third World, a mission that she said Eqbal was undertaking in Pakistan with his characteristic quiet dedication.

In her talk, eccentrically entitled "Whither Hypochondria?" Sara Suleri (b. 1953), a Lahori professor of English at Yale University, used hypochondria as a metaphor for a country, Pakistan, that despite its enormous strengths refuses to be healthy. Eqbal, she said, was typically headed for Pakistan against the traffic, and she warned of the chances of "his magnificent failure."

Several others, especially Eqbal's Middle Eastern and North African friends and former students, spoke of the ways in which he influenced their lives and work and then read passages from their recent work. Mohammed Guessous (1938–2014), sociologist at Mohammad V University in Rabat (Morocco), impressed the audience with his reflections on the challenges of the intellectual in the Third World. He argued that intellectual engagement as viewed by Western intellectuals is not possible to sustain in Third World conditions unless it is undertaken as a mission of militancy. I read a paper that I had written with Eqbal on the courageous Tunisian Tahar Haddad, the early advocate of Muslim women's emancipation.

Edward Said and Eqbal concluded the formal proceedings. Speaking from a prepared text, the Palestinian critic analyzed in detail what he described as "Eqbal's special blend of intellectual brilliance and courage, supernally accurate analysis, and consistently humane and warm presence [that] make of him—to paraphrase from Kipling's *Kim*—a friend of the whole world." Palestinian leaders and cadres trusted him even though he was not an Arab and criticized their policies. "Anyone who knows Eqbal in conditions of struggle," Edward continued, "knows subliminally that his loyalty and solidarity need never be questioned. He is a genius at sympathy . . . but never at the expense of his honesty or of his critical faculties, which reign supreme. That is why Eqbal comes as close to being a really free man as anyone can be."

Edward began his detailed appraisal of Eqbal's literary contributions, noting that Eqbal wrote as a dissenter against empire and its sorry products—postcolonial elites and dependant societies—with acuity and without bitterness because he appeared always

more interested in creativity than in vindictiveness, in originality of spirit and method rather than mere radical, in generosity and complexity of analysis over the tight neatness of his fellow political scientists. In fact, it is only now as I write these lines that I recall with surprise that although Eqbal is a trained political scientist, I have never thought of him as one. When I dedicated my book *Culture and Imperialism* to him[,] it was, I realized, because in his activity, life, and thinking, Eqbal embodied not just the politics of empire but the whole fabric of experience expressed in human life itself, rather than economic rules and reductive formulae. What Eqbal understands about the experience of empire is the domination of empire in all its forms, but also the creativity, originality, and vision created in resistance.[7]

Eqbal followed his friend. The audience had waited eagerly to hear him, but he said he would like first to give the floor to friends who had come from far away and had not been heard. He would invite at least some to speak. He called on Kashmiri educationist Agha Ashraf Ali (b. 1923); Pakistani physicist and peace activist Dr. Pervez Hoodbhoy; and his own cardiologist, Dr. Bernard Lown (b. 1921). When they had had their turn, Eqbal then spoke of the lessons he had learned through a life that spanned from childhood in an Indian village to migration to Pakistan, engagements with the peace movement in America, the Algerian war of independence, and the Palestinian struggle for self-determination.

The event concluded with a dinner attended by three hundred guests. It was an emotion-filled evening. The Kashmiri poet and Eqbal's friend Agha Shahid Ali (1949–2001) read his own poems and his English translations of four poems from Faiz, with Eqbal reading the original Urdu versions. Students, colleagues, and friends took turns at the rostrum to describe an affectionate and authoritative teacher who changed their lives, a friend who was always there in times good and sad, a scholar who with great generosity of spirit nurtured and guided younger colleagues. Edward Said's words echoed through the evening: "Eqbal is a genius at sympathy." It was past midnight, and many were still awaiting their turn to speak when Hampshire College deans Margaret Cerullo and Michael Ford reluctantly closed the proceedings.

Eqbal's cardiologist, Bernard Lown, whose organization International Physicians for the Prevention of Nuclear War won the 1985 Nobel Peace

Prize, sent a note of thanks to Eqbal following the celebration at Hampshire. It best reflects who Eqbal was and what he represented for his friends: "You have demonstrated that one identity need not overwhelm another," Dr. Lown wrote. "A single person can integrate several identities and be the richer for it. Indeed, your life demonstrates that encompassing several particularities does not preclude harboring universal values. You did not deliver a speech but etched before our eyes an instructive and uplifting novella."[8]

Eqbal, Julie, and Dohra

Soon after marrying, Eqbal and Julie faced an ordeal together and had to cope with the difficulties of mounting a defense against his indictment and trial in Harrisburg. Their daughter, Dohra, was born a little before the trial began in 1971, and the trio moved to Pennsylvania to face the court.[9] After many years of marriage, Eqbal and Julie separated amicably, in part due to his long absences when he traveled to the subcontinent. They afterward remained good friends while living their separate lives.

Dohra gave Eqbal's life great meaning. He adored her, and as she grew up, he was proud to have an accomplished, intelligent, and caring daughter. Both of her parents had instilled in her a profound moral sense, given her necessary work habits to succeed, and prepared her for both having fun in life and contributing to society's needy. I remember vividly how excited Eqbal became on one of our frequent walks when I visited him in Amherst. He described what Dohra had accomplished in San Francisco, where she had moved after graduating from Yale University. She had gotten a job as a community organizer with a social agency, the Telegraph Hill Neighborhood Center. She spent the first few months in San Francisco listening to the complaints of the people she met, cataloging their demands, and prioritizing their needs. She then convinced her agency to embark on a series of projects that fulfilled the community's desires. When she went to graduate school at Columbia University, she left behind self-sustainable programs that continued to function after her departure. Eqbal beamed as he described her work there and reveled in her success.

Eqbal involved himself in Dohra's education and enjoyed doing so. As she defined her dissertation topic on the imperial background of early-modern English literature, Eqbal read some early-modern authors for the first time and discovered that the theme of imperialism registered even in a mythic text such as Milton's *Paradise Lost*. He offered her some bibliographic suggestions and proffered some theoretical approaches that crossed over from fatherhood to professorship.

In their voluminous correspondence, Eqbal confided in her and at times remembered his parental duties. In that vein, he would offer her recipes so that she could develop her "aesthetic appreciation" of fine cooking. In one letter he wrote to her, I discovered one such recipe for a famous marinade.

Eqbal's Chicken Tikka/Masala Marinade

Eqbal was a gourmet chef, and many friends and strangers who were lucky to taste his curries left his table with fond memories of wonderful meals and excellent conversation. This is the recipe for a marinade that Eqbal invented.*

> Grate 1 or 2 large-size onions
> Crush or finely chop 6–12 cloves garlic (more if you are garlic lovers)
> Chop 2–4 tablespoons fresh ginger
> Add 2 tablespoons coriander
> Add ½ tablespoon turmeric
> Add 1 tablespoon garam masala
> Add 1½ tablespoons cumin
> Add ¼ to ½ tablespoon cayenne pepper
> Salt to taste
> Add 2–4 tablespoons olive oil or vegetable oil

Mix all ingredients together. In skillet or pot, cook until brownish or until the sharp smell/taste of turmeric is gone.
Add 2, 3, or 4 tablespoons of plain yogurt. Cook for a minute or two.
*Included in Eqbal Ahmad to Dohra Ahmad, Amherst, August 17, 1993, zipped files on disks, filed under "DOHR," Box 12, Eqbal Ahmad Papers, Johnson Library, Hampshire College, Amherst, Mass.

While pursuing her doctorate at Columbia University, Dohra married and soon had two daughters. She lives with her husband, Orin, and the girls in a house in downtown Brooklyn. Wanting to stay in New York City, she found a job teaching English literature at St. John's University, where she is now an associate professor.

Radha Kumar and Eqbal

Near the end of his life, after Eqbal and Julie separated, he often saw Radha Kumar, who loved him selflessly. I first met Radha at Eqbal's home in Hampshire College and again on a few occasions in New York and Amherst. In the last years of his life, she visited him frequently in Islamabad, and when in India, he stayed with her family. Pakistani human rights activist and lawyer Asma Jahanghir remembers how relaxed and fun he was in India when Asma visited Radha's place and stayed up until three in the morning with them, celebrating a major victory their allies had won in the Indian Supreme Court.

Otherwise, Eqbal spent most of his time in Islamabad during the last two years of his life, but he told me that he no longer liked living in Pakistan. Already in 1992, in a letter he wrote to Dohra from Islamabad, he complained that he was "working to avoid boredom. This is a very boring place, not just Islamabad. I think it is true of all of Pakistan. There is an intellectual indolence here which combines with an excess of interest in political intrigues and the bane of my life—gossip."[10]

Eqbal intended to marry Radha. He was due to join her in New York, where she had taken a fellowship, but ill health complicated the matter. Dr. Lown, his cardiologist, had recommended that he have heart surgery, but Julie told me that Eqbal came away from that medical visit with only a vague idea about a timetable. After his last visit to Lown, he told Radha that Lown was pleased by his progress and thought that he could avoid heart surgery. Eqbal thought that he could return to Pakistan and then at a later date return to the United States for treatment. Also he had developed colon cancer, which had to have taken a heavy toll on his spirit. His cancer was discovered just a few weeks before he died, and then he was rushed into surgery. Lown was concerned about whether his heart could withstand the operation and liaised with the doctors in Islamabad on methods to inflate his heart while he underwent the surgery. He told me when I last saw him in 1998 that he lived mainly by himself in Islamabad and saw few friends. His project to establish Khaldunia University faced insurmountable hurdles, he said, and it seemed to him that it would never happen. Some friends had advised him to start the school as a small venture just to get it off the ground. He refused to do so because he wanted to establish a full-fledged university, which would help set standards for Pakistan's higher education.

I discounted his words about being alone often because I knew that Eqbal could never really be alone, for friends and family who loved him always surrounded him. But loneliness is, after all, often an existential condition and a perception of reality, not necessarily a real condition. Someone can be alone but not lonely, just as a busy person surrounded by a multitude of close friends and loved ones might feel deep depression and isolation. Nevertheless, I did not at all like what I saw and heard. His fire was gone. My friend, who always had projects, who continually mobilized others, seemed quiescent and resigned. Some other friends in Pakistan and the United States who saw him daily at the end of his life later confirmed what I had felt.[11] I remember feeling very sad when I left him for what I didn't realize would be the last time in 1998, and I afterward suffered for weeks from a terrible depression. I had premonitions of disaster and wondered to myself how much longer he would live. His premature death ended his and Radha's plans to live together as husband and wife.

Surrounding Eqbal's hospital bed in Islamabad in May 1999 were some of the people closest to him: Dohra, Rashida and Raza Kazim, and his nephew and collaborator Pervez Hoodbhoy. Pervez, a nuclear physicist, had first met Eqbal in the United States in 1971 as a member of an audience at an anti–Vietnam War teach-in at MIT at which Eqbal spoke.[12] He later worked with Eqbal on the Khalduniya University project as well as on Eqbal's antinuclear work near the end of his life. Pervez was a staunch secularist. When Rashida took out her Qur'an and started reciting suras, Pervez begged Eqbal to have her stop. Eqbal looked at his dear friend and nephew, whom he loved, and whispered, "Pervez, I *am* a Muslim."[13]

On his hospital bed, the recital of the Qur'an celebrated who he was. His attachment to Islamic culture gave him the strength to be an outsider, to criticize fearlessly, to speak truth to power. Despite his outsider status, he was rooted in the culture and traditions of Islam, which gave him the wherewithal to stand up to injustice and hypocrisy and to feel right about doing so because, for him, striving for social justice represented the very essence of Islamic culture and polity and therefore the core of the religion itself.

NOTES

Introduction

1. No one except Eqbal's older sister, Sharfa Jahani Khanum (b. 1920), claimed to know his exact birth date. She told me that he was ten years her junior, putting his birth on December 30, 1930. His mother delivered him on his family's estate in Bihar near West Bengal in India, and there, as was the case with most infants on the subcontinent in the colonial period, births were not normally recorded. Eqbal claimed that he did not know his exact date of birth, but he thought that he was fifteen years old at the moment of partition of the Indian subcontinent, which would place his birthday in 1932. His widow, Julie Diamond, thought 1932 was correct, but his grade transcript from Occidental College in California, his driver's license, and hospital records (Ali Medical Center from March 1991) list his date of birth as December 30, 1930. A biography, with information provided by Eqbal and issued in a press packet by the Harrisburg Defense Committee on January 24, l972, lists his birth date as December 31, 1930. Other documents in the Eqbal Ahmad Papers at Hampshire

College's Johnson Library in Amherst, Massachusetts, give the year of his birth as 1932. When I first met him at Princeton University in 1958, he thought that he was seven years my senior. I was born in 1937. His widow, however, does not believe that he was seven years old when his father died in 1937. She thought he was closer to five. Copies of the hospital bill and his driver's license are located in Box 12, Eqbal Ahmad Papers (EAP), 1956–1999, Johnson Library, Hampshire College, Amherst, Mass.

2. Eqbal Ahmad, "After the Winter Bombs," *Dawn* (Karachi), December 20, 1998, reprinted in Eqbal Ahmad, *The Selected Writings of Eqbal Ahmad*, ed. Carollee Bengelsdorf, Margaret Cerullo, and Yogesh Chandrani (New York: Columbia University Press, 2006), 287–290, quote on 289.

3. This lecture was published as Eqbal Ahmad, *Terrorism: Theirs and Ours*, foreword and interview by David Barsamian, Open Media Pamphlet Series (New York: Seven Stories Press, 2001), quote on 12–15, reprinted as "Terrorism: Theirs and Ours," in Ahmad, *Selected Writings of Eqbal Ahmad*, 257–266.

4. Eqbal Ahmad, "Osama bin Laden Is a Sign of Things to Come" [interview by David Barsamian], *Progressive*, November 1998, http://mar1209.tripod.com /2001okt/2001-3367i.htm (accessed January 22, 2015).

5. Ahmad, *Terrorism*, 24.

6. Ahmad, "Osama bin Laden Is a Sign of Things to Come."

7. Richard Falk, who was part of the delegation, told me that its members changed their opinion about Eqbal, whom they at first resented for monopolizing the conversations as he deconstructed the plans of the Iranian revolutionaries for their new state. His analysis proved to be correct (conversation with the author, Santa Barbara, Calif., November 2012).

8. I had hoped to get Eqbal a job in New York City at Brooklyn College in 1975, and Eqbal went there for an interview with the dean of the School of Social Science, who very much wanted him on the faculty. The dean later told me that the appointment could not go through because of opposition by pro-Zionist faculty and administrators. The same happened at Rutgers University, where the associate provost told me a similar story.

9. Edward W. Said, "Eqbal Ahmad; He Brought Wisdom and Integrity to the Cause of Oppressed Peoples" [obituary], *Guardian* (London), May 14, 1999.

10. Eqbal Ahmad, "History Is a Weapon: Cold War from the Stand Points of Its Victims" (1991), http://www.historyisaweapon.com/defcon1/eqbalahmad coldwar.html (accessed January 22, 2015). Eqbal delivered his talk "The Cold War from the Standpoint of Its Victims" at the conference "Rethinking the Cold War" in honor of William Appelman Williams at the University of

Wisconsin–Madison, October 18–20, 1991. Its original title was "Victims of the Long Peace," and it is reprinted in Ahmad, *Selected Writings of Eqbal Ahmad*, 219–227.

11. Ahmad, "Osama bin Laden Is a Sign of Things to Come."

12. Amitava Kumar, novelist, professor of English at Vassar College, and fellow Bihari, understood Eqbal's outsider status. He could not imagine Eqbal running a university such as the one he wanted to build in Pakistan because Eqbal "was too much the congenital outsider" ("On Eqbal Ahmad," *Nation*, November 27, 2006, http://www.amitavakumar.com/?page_id-29 [accessed January 22, 2015]).

13. George Simmel, "The Stranger," in *Social Theory: The Multicultural and Classic Readings*, ed. Charles C. Lemert (Boulder, Colo.: Westview Press, 1993), 139–141; Richard Wright, *The Outsider* (New York: Harper, 1953); Colin Wilson, *The Outsider* (Boston: Houghton Mifflin, 1956); James Baldwin, "Stranger in the Village," *Harper's Magazine*, October 1953; Albert Camus, *The Outsider*, trans. Stuart Gilbert (New York: Knopf, 1970); Edward W. Said, *Out of Place: A Memoir* (New York: Knopf, 1999).

14. Judith M. Brown, "The Making of a Critical Outsider," in Judith M. Brown and Martin Prozesky, *Gandhi and South Africa: Principles and Politics* (New York: St. Martin's Press, 1996), 21–33.

15. Tom Hayden, ed., *Radical Nomad: C. Wright Mills and His Times* (Boulder, Colo.: Paradigm, 2006).

16. On witnessing, see Sheila Kennedy, "Witness," *Sheila Kennedy Thinking About Liberty*, May 11, 2005, http://sheilakennedy.net/content/view/654/50/.

17. Marty Jezer, *The Power of the People: Active Nonviolence in the U.S.*, ed. Robert Cooney and Helen Michalawski (Philadelphia: New Society, 1987), specifically the chapters "World War II and the Pacifist Movement," 96–97, and "Direct Action for Disarmament," 138–139. Don Will, who knew Eqbal well and whose father, Herman Will, had organized with Mustie, clarified for me some of these points (interview with the author, Orange, Calif., November 2011). See Herman Will, *A Will for Peace: Peace Action in the United Methodist Church: A History* (Washington, D.C.: General Board of Church & Society of the United Methodist Church, 1984).

18. Charles De Benedetti, *An American Ordeal: The Antiwar Movement of the Vietnam War* (Syracuse, N.Y.: Syracuse University Press, 1990), 20–26.

19. Don Will to Stuart Schaar, e-mail, November 24, 2010; Will, interview.

20. David Barsamian, *Eqbal Ahmad, Confronting Empire: Interviews with David Barsamian* (Cambridge, Mass.: South End Press, 2000), 33.

21. Cora Weiss to Stuart Schaar, March 2, 2013, author's correspondence files.
22. Barsamian, *Eqbal Ahmad, Confronting Empire*, 153.
23. Falk was the first well-known antiwar activist to fly to Chicago to meet Eqbal after his indictment, despite the fact that they did not yet know each other well. He was invaluable in helping Eqbal work out an initial defense strategy. See Barsamian, *Eqbal Ahmad, Confronting Empire*, 27. Noam Chomsky was the second to arrive.
24. Ted Glick (b. 1939), the layman whose name was added in a second indictment, decided to defend himself. His case was thereupon separated from that of the others, so the group thenceforth was known as the Harrisburg 7. Glick went on to become a leader of the Green Party in New Jersey and unsuccessfully ran for the U.S. Senate on that party's ticket. He remains an activist, staging many fasts, and has led many demonstrations on environmental issues.
25. Harrisburg [Pennsylvania] Defense Committee Collected Records, 1970–1973, Collection CDG-A, Peace Collection, Swathmore College, Swathmore, Pa., http.//www.swarthmore.edu/Library/peace/ (accessed July 13, 2013). I also collected a personal archive of materials from the pretrial and trial proceedings, which I have used to write this book and will eventually deposit in the Swathmore College Peace Collection.
26. For more on Boudin, see Leonard Boudin, "Reminiscences of Leonard Boudin," 1983 interview, Individual Interview List Oral History Project, RLIN NXCP86-A42, Document OHI0016726-12169, Oral History Research Office, Columbia University, New York. Boudin's daughter, Kathy Boudin (b. 1943), joined the Weather Underground and was convicted in a felony murder case for participating in an armed robbery that led to the murder of two police officers and a security guard. She served twenty-two years in prison. When she got out of jail, she earned her Ph.D. and later taught as an adjunct lecturer in the School of Social Work at Columbia University.
27. Jay Schulman to Stuart Schaar, personal communication, New York City, June 25, 1972. The survey was carried out by Eqbal's friend, Professor Jay Schulman (1927–1987), sociologist at City College of New York, who pioneered the techniques of jury selection at this trial.
28. The charges against Berrigan and McAlister were later dropped on appeal. The prosecutor in the case, William S. Lynch, claimed that fourteen letters came into Lewiston Prison for Phil and ten went out to Liz.
29. Besides short stories, Julie Diamond wrote the book *Kindergarten: A Teacher, Her Students, and a Year of Learning*, foreword by Jules Feiffer (New York: New Press, 2011).

30. The quote from Perrin comes from a handout composed by the Defense Committee and distributed to reporters; copy in author's Harrisburg files.

31. Eqbal Ahmad, statement, Chicago Federal Court Building, January 14, 1971, copy in author's Harrisburg files.

32. Garry Wills, "A Revolution in the Church," *Playboy*, November 1971.

33. For instance, Thomas Jeannot reports that the American historian Howard Zinn, from Boston University, drove the fugitive Dan Berrigan from New Jersey to Boston, beginning Dan's four-month evasion of the FBI ("Berrigan Underground," in *Faith, Resistance, and the Future: Daniel Berrigan's Challenge to Catholic Social Thought*, ed. James L. Marsh and Anna J. Brown [New York: Fordham University Press, 2012], 174).

34. Lee Lockwood, "How the 'Kidnap Conspiracy' Was Hatched," *Life*, May 21, 1971. Lockwood (1932–2010) here acknowledged for the first time publicly that "Ahmad . . . is widely reported to have been a main organizer of Dan Berrigan's underground movements."

35. Douglas received more than $9,000 in 1970 for his services as an informant plus the use of a government credit card for three months. Beginning in December 1971, he also received a per diem of $36 as a government witness (Homer Bigart, "Berrigan Trial Witness Says He Weighed Informer Career," *New York Times*, March 9, 1972, and "Prosecutor Lauds Berrigan Informer," *New York Times*, March 17, 1972).

36. More information on the Davidons can be found in the Ann Morrissett Davidon and William C. Davidon Papers, 1949–, Collection DG144, Swarthmore College Peace Collection, http.//www.swathmore.edu/Library/peace/ (accessed July 13, 2013). Journalist Betty Medsger, who covered the Harrisburg trial, later published *The Burglary: The Discovery of J. Edgar Hoover's Secret FBI* (New York: Knopf, 2014), which indicated that Bill Davidon was the mastermind behind the break-in of FBI offices in Media, Pennsylvania, near Philadelphia, forty-three years ago, in which peace activists stole FBI records. These records revealed the existence of "Cointelpro" set up by the FBI in 1956 to investigate and disrupt dissident political groups in the United States. Davidon and the other Media raiders were never caught.

37. For details of Dan's arrest, see Jim Forest, "Harrisburg Conspiracy: The Berrigans and the Catholic Left," *Win* (Ripon, N.Y.), March 15, 1973, 13.

38. Quoted from my hand-written notes of a meeting with the defendants in New York City before the Harrisburg trial began, n.d., to be deposited in the Harrisburg Defense Committee Collected Records, 1970–1973, Swarthmore College.

39. Eqbal's arguments against draft board raids and in favor of large mass actions are given in Justin Jackson, "Kissinger's Kidnapper: Eqbal Ahmad, the US New Left, and the Transnational Romance of Revolutionary War," *Journal for the Study of Radicalism* 4, no. 1 (2010): 101.

40. Cited in "Eqbal Ahmad: Odd Man Out," *Washington Post*, February 13, 1972, which is quoted in Jackson, "Kissinger's Kidnapper," 103.

41. Quoted in Lockwood, "How the 'Kidnap Conspiracy' Was Hatched."

42. A copy of the letter is included in Forest, "Harrisburg Conspiracy," 16.

43. Homer Bigart, "Informer Says Berrigan Told of Entering Tunnels," *New York Times*, February 29, 1972, and "Two Quote Priest on Tunnel System," *New York Times*, March 21, 1972.

44. Homer Bigart, "Tunnels' Destruction Is Topic of Purported Berrigan Letter," *New York Times*, March 2, 1972; Forest, "Harrisburg Conspiracy," 10.

45. Jack Anderson, "The Berrigan Fiasco," *New York Post*, June 21, 1972.

46. The May 21, 1971, issue of *Life* had a nine-page photo essay on the defendants: Lockwood, "How the 'Kidnap Conspiracy' Was Hatched." Lee Lockwood, a photo journalist who had made a film about Dan Berrigan while Dan was underground, *The Holy Outlaw*, wrote an informative article. Several of the defendants and some of their close friends spoke to Lockwood confidentially.

47. David E. Rosenbaum, "Senate Panel Concludes Inquiry into Amnesty for Draft Evaders," *New York Times*, March 3, 1972.

48. The best books on these two movements are Joshua Bloom and Waldo F. Martin Jr., *Black Against Empire: The History and Politics of the Black Panther Party* (Berkeley: University of California Press, 2013); and Daniel Erick-Wanzer, *The Young Lords: A Reader* (New York: New York University Press, 2010).

49. Dan Berger, *Outlaws of America: The Weather Underground and the Politics of Solidarity* (Oakland, Calif.: AK Press, 2005).

50. A copy of the letter can be found in Forest, "Harrisburg Conspiracy," 18.

51. Garry Wills, "Love on Trial: The Berrigan Case Reconsidered," *Harper's*, July 1972.

52. Forest, "Harrisburg Conspiracy," 19. Jim Forest had converted to Catholicism and in 1964, after being dismissed from the U.S. Navy as a conscientious objector, was one of the founders of the Catholic Peace Fellowship. He worked for a time as the managing editor of Dorothy Day's *Catholic Worker*, later writing her biography. In 1969, he served as the Vietnam Program Coordinator of the Fellowship of Reconciliation and received a prison sentence for raiding a Milwaukee draft board and removing and burning files. In 1971, he worked on the Harrisburg Defense Committee. In 1989, he converted to Orthodox Chris-

tianity and from his base in the Netherlands soon became secretary of the Orthodox Peace Fellowship. Besides working in journalism, he has written several adult and children's books.

53. Homer Bigart, "Berrigan Defense Calls No Witnesses and Rests Its Case," *New York Times*, March 25, 1972.

54. Quoted from notes I took at the strategy session with the defendants, n.d., New York City.

55. The Harrisburg Defense Committee published both Phil's intended opening statement as well as a copy of the statement he would have presented in his defense if he had been allowed to speak publicly at the trial.

56. The Chicago Seven, originally the Chicago Eight, included antiwar activists Abbie Hoffman (1936–1989), Jerry Rubin (1938–1994), David Dellinger, and Tom Hayden (b. 1939), all of whom were charged with conspiracy, inciting riots, and other crimes relating to the protests that took place in 1968 at the Democratic National Convention. Black Panther activist Bobby Seale (b. 1936) was originally one of those charged, but his case was severed from the others.

57. I have in my possession the account records, while in New York City, of all the Harrisburg Defense Committee's disbursements to the lawyer working on the case.

58. For a compendium of Dan's work, see Daniel Berrigan, *Writings*, Modern Spiritual Masters (Maryknoll, N.Y.: Orbis Books, 2009).

59. For Elizabeth McAlister's life after the trial, including several stints in prison amounting to some four years for antimilitaristic activities, see "Peace Train: Nearly Forty Years After Its Founding a Radical Catholic Commune Finds New Allies," *Baltimore Magazine*, March 2012, http://www.baltimoremagazine.net /peole/2012/03/peacetrain (accessed July 13, 2013). Phil and Liz Berrigan founded a commune in Baltimore at Jonah House in 1973. After twenty years, they moved into St. Peter's Cemetery in West Baltimore as caretakers of the grounds for the archdiochese. Phil Berrigan was buried in that cemetery. When the Occupy movement came to Baltimore in 2011/2012, the young organizers of the new movement sought out the members of Jonah House and linked up with these older pacifists.

60. For an update on Frida Berrigan's life, see "Marriages/Celebrations: Frida Berrigan and Patrick Sheehan-Gaucher," *New York Times*, July 15, 2011.

61. A copy of Eqbal's evaluation of Frida Berrigan's student work is included in EAP, Box 4, evaluations.

1. Eqbal's Life

1. This was the way Eqbal's friend Raza Kazim explained Bihar's cultural legacy to me in Pakistan in the spring of 2004.

2. Eqbal Ahmad, comments prepared for his retirement celebration, Hampshire College, 1997, zip files on disks made as backup of Eqbal's computer hard drive, March 25, 1998, under "my files" and "veiled," Box 12, Eqbal Ahmad Papers (EAP), Johnson Library, Hampshire College, Amherst, Mass.

3. Arlie Russell Hochschild to Stuart Schaar, January 2011, author's correspondence files.

4. Ahmad, comments prepared for his retirement celebration, 3.

5. Amrik Singh Nimbran, *Poverty, Land, and Violence: An Analytical Study of Naxalism in Bihar* (Patna, India: Layman's Publication, 1992), 3, 11.

6. Ahmad, comments prepared for retirement celebration. According to Eqbal's nephew Kamran Ali in Pakistan in 2004, other Maliks before Eqbal had married outside the clan but were stigmatized for doing so.

7. Eqbal Ahmad, conversation with the author, 1964.

8. Ahmad, comments prepared for his retirement celebration.

9. David Barsamian, *Eqbal Ahmad, Confronting Empire: Interviews with David Barsamian* (Cambridge, Mass.: South End Press, 2000), 3.

10. Ahmad, comments prepared for his retirement celebration.

11. Ibid.

12. Regarding his mother's pilgrimage, see "To Whom It May Concern," Correspondence 1970, Box 1, EAP.

13. For the Punjab land-resettlement program, see Tarlochan Singh, *Land Resettlement Manual*, part I, http://www.Punjabrevenue.nc.in/manuel.htm (accessed February 24, 2014), and for the program in all of India and Pakistan, see Joseph B. Schechtman, "Evacuee Property in India and Pakistan," in *50 Years of Indo-Pakistani Relations*, vol. 1, ed. Verinder Groever and Ranjara Arora (New Delhi: Deep and Deep, 1955), 55.

14. John Berger memorializes the story in "Two Recumbent Male Figures Wrestling on a Sidewalk," in *Photocopies: Encounters* (New York: Vintage, 1998), 94–101.

15. Khwaja Habiballah, conversation with the author, Lahore, April 8, 2004.

16. The interview was never published. Copy in author's files and used with Dohra Ahmad's permission.

17. This story is based on "Correspondence. Sailor, Randolph," Box 1, EAP. The Yale Divinity School Library contains Randolph Sailor's papers.

18. Khwaja Habiballah, conversation.

19. Arshad Durrani, conversation with the author, Lahore, April 8, 2004.

20. Syad Abid Hussein to Eqbal Ahmad, December 9, 1983, Correspondence 1980–1983, Box 1, EAP.

21. Barsamian, *Eqbal Ahmad, Confronting Empire*, 120–121.

22. Eqbal's comments on Lenin's disdain of democracy are in ibid., 123–124.

23. Ibid., 63.

24. Ibid., 152.

25. Iqbal Riza, conversation with the author, New York City, September 15, 2005. Iqbal Riza was Eqbal's close friend and a Pakistani diplomat who quit the foreign service. He worked from 1997 to 2005 at the United Nations as Secretary-General Kofi Anan's cabinet chief.

26. Eqbal Ahmad to David Hochschild, August 25, 1993, 5¼-inch diskette, Box 2, EAP.

27. Donald R. Hamilton, dean, Graduate School, Princeton University, to Eqbal Ahmad, April 1, 1960, file "certificates, fellowships," Box 2, EAP. I bought a new Volkswagen convertible in Gibraltar in 1962 for $1,000, which would cost about $17,000 today. Therefore, $2,450 in 1960/1961 represented a very generous fellowship equivalent to around $40,000 today.

28. James I. Armstrong, assistant dean, Graduate School, Princeton University, to Eqbal Ahmad, November 9, 1960; and "Advanced Fellows Feted by University," *Princeton Herald*, November 11, 1960, file "certificates, fellowships," Box 2, EAP. Princeton gave out about ten Proctor Fellowships each year to the Graduate School's best students.

29. JL [Jean Lacouture], "La Mort de Roger Le Tourneau: L'homme tranquille de l'islamologie française," *Le Monde* (Paris), April 10, 1971.

30. Eqbal Ahmad to Stuart Schaar, December 19, 1961, author's correspondence files.

31. The chronology for this period was provided by letters that Eqbal and I exchanged and that we happily dated. I kept these letters and will eventually deposit them with the rest of the papers I have relating to Eqbal in the Stuart Schaar Special Collection at the Brooklyn College Library.

32. I have in my files copies of letters that Tlili wrote to Eqbal in January and February 1967, when the trade union leader, fearful of being assassinated by the Tunisian secret police, lived in Geneva. The January 17, 1967, letter begins with the salutation "Very dear brother Eqbal." The letters, including that one, are scanned in an electronic folder of 152 pages in pdf format, file mg5 (mg5_02_ctliliahmed.pdf), copy in Box 2, EAP, and can also be downloaded from http://hdl.handle.net/10009/642 (accessed July 25, 2013).

33. Tâhir al-Hadâd [Tahar Haddad], *Al-ʾummâl al-tûnisiyûn wa dhuhûr al-harakah al-niqâbiya* (The Tunisian workers and the birth of the trade union movement) (Tunis: Arab Printers, 1927), translated as *Les travailleurs tunisiens et l'émergence du mouvement syndical*, trans. Abderrazak Halioui (Tunis: Maison Arabe du Livre, 1985).

34. Tâhir al-Hadâd [Tahar Haddad], *Imraʾ atunâ fi al-shariʿah wa a mujtamaʾ* (Our women in Islamic law and society) (Tunis: Artistic Printers, 1930; reprint, Tunis: Maison Tunisienne de l'Edition, 1978), partially translated into French by M. Mutafarrij in *Revue des Etudes Islamiques* 3 (1935): 201–230; completely but less adequately translated as *Notre femme, la législation islamique et la société* (Tunis: Maison Tunisienne d'Edition, 1978).

35. Eqbal Ahmad and Stuart Schaar, "M'hamed Ali et les fondements du Mouvement syndical tunisien," in *Les Africains*, vol. 11, ed. Charles-André Julien (Paris: Editions Jeune Afrique, 1978), 13–46, translated as "M'hamed Ali and the Tunisian Labor Movement," *Race & Class* 19, no. 3 (1978): 253–276, and "M'Hammad Ali: Tunisian Labor Organizer," in *Struggle and Survival in the Middle East*, 2nd ed., ed. Edmund Burke III and David Yaghoubian (Berkeley: University of California Press, 2005), 264–277. See also Eqbal Ahmad and Stuart Schaar, "Tahar Haddad: A Tunisian Intellectual [1920s]," *Maghreb Review* 21, nos. 3–4 (1996): 240–255.

36. Abdelhai Choikha to Eqbal Ahmad, n.d. (early 1970s), Correspondence 1957–1999, Box 2, EAP. See also Ahmed Mestiri, *Temoignage pour l'histoire* (Tunis: Sud Editions, 2011), 260–261.

37. See, for example, Eqbal Ahmad and Stuart Schaar, "Human Rights in Morocco and Tunisia: A Critique of State Department Findings," *MERIP Reports*, no. 67 (1978): 15–17, reprinted in *Congressional Record* H2514–15, H2518–19 (April 5, 1978).

38. Clement Henry Moore (after 1995 Clement Moore Henry), *Tunisia Since Independence: The Dynamics of a One-Party Government* (Berkeley: University of California Press, 1965; reprint, Westport, Conn.: Greenwood Press, 1982).

39. Eqbal Ahmad to Stuart Schaar, August 29, 1963, author's correspondence files.

40. Charles B. Hagen, chairman, Department of Political Science, University of Illinois, to Eqbal Ahmad, April 29, 1964, Correspondence 1951–1999, file "certificates and fellowships," Box 2, EAP.

41. Eqbal Ahmad to Stuart Schaar, September 22, 1965, author's correspondence files.

42. Feldstein was president of the New Hampshire Charitable Association from 1986 to 2010.

43. Margaret Burnham, conversation with the author about Eqbal in Mississippi, New York City, November 2012.

44. Eqbal Ahmad to Professor T. Cuyler Young, April 29, 1969, Correspondence, Box 1, EAP.

45. Eqbal Ahmad to Dorothy Nelkin, May 22, 1969, Correspondence, Box 1, EAP.

46. Eqbal Ahmad to Dohra Ahmad, Islamabad, October 25, 1992, disk, files "my files," "letters," "Dohra," Box 12, EAP.

47. Eqbal Ahmad, "Radical but Wrong," in *Régis Debray and the Latin American Revolution*, ed. Leo Huberman and Paul M. Sweezy (New York: Monthly Review Press, 1968), 70–83. Eqbal reconciled with Debray by the early 1970s after Debray published *Revolution in the Revolution*, trans. Bobbye Ortiz, new ed. (1967; New York: Grove Press, 2000), which Eqbal liked, and he invited the Frenchman to participate in programs organized by the Harrisburg Defense Committee around his trial in 1972. See Eqbal Ahmad to Régis Debray, March 12, 1972, author's correspondence files.

48. Six years after Eqbal passed away, there was a controversy between Noam Chomsky and the British newspaper the *Guardian* over an interview regarding Bosnia that he had given to a hostile reporter, Emma Brockes, on October 31, 2005. The *Guardian* pulled the story from its website on November 17, 2005.

49. Quoted in Michael McAuliffe, "U.S. Policy Blamed for 'Genocide,'" *Sunday Republican* (Amherst, Mass.), December 4, 1994.

50. Ahmad to Hochschild.

51. Eqbal Ahmad, "At Cold War's End," *Boston Review*, June–August 1993, and "Welcome War in Bosnia," *Dawn* (Karachi), 1994 (specific date unknown), both reprinted in Eqbal Ahmad, *The Selected Writings of Eqbal Ahmad*, ed. Carollee Bengelsdorf, Margaret Cerillo, and Yogesh Chandrani (New York: Columbia University Press, 2006), 249–252, 271–273.

52. "Eqbal Ahmad, India, Pakistan, Bosnia, etc.: Interviewed by David Barsamian," August 4, 1993, http://www.geocities.com/CollegePark/Library/9803/eqbal_ahmad/Barsamwint.hmtl (accessed October 4, 2004, but no longer available).

53. Eqbal Ahmad, "NATO Has Failed," *Al-Ahram Weekly* (Cairo), April 8–14, 1999, and "NATO: The Controversy over Kosovo," *Dawn* (Karachi), April 11, 1999. See also *Al-Ahram Weekly*, April 15–21, 1999, and, on Kosovo and Russia, *Dawn*, April 25, 1999.

54. Raza Kazim, conversation with the author, Lahore, March 2004.

55. See, for example, Eqbal Ahmad, "On Arab Bankruptcy," *New York Times*, August 10, 1982, reprinted in Ahmad, *Selected Writings of Eqbal Ahmad*, 357–359.

56. Eqbal Ahmad and Richard J. Barnet, "A Reporter at Large: Bloody Games," *New Yorker*, April 11, 1988, 44–86, reprinted as "Bloody Games," in Eqbal Ahmad, *Between Past & Future: Selected Essays on South Asia*, ed. Dohra Ahmad, Iftikhar Ahmad, and Zia Mian (Karachi: Oxford University Press, 2004), 153–194, and *Selected Writings of Eqbal Ahmad*, 453–492.

57. See the introduction, example 2.

58. Barsamian, *Eqbal Ahmad, Confronting Empire*, 48.

59. Eqbal Ahmad to Dohra Ahmad.

60. Professor Carollee Bengelsdorf, ten-year evaluation of Eqbal Ahmad, November 14, 1989, Correspondence 1957–1999, "Hampshire College reappointment," Box 2, EAP.

61. Disk, 1972, Box 12, EAP.

62. Adele Simmons, former president of Hampshire College, to Stuart Schaar, January 12, 2011, author's correspondence files.

2. Reflections on Eqbal's Life

1. Eqbal Ahmad to Tim May and Frank Hanly, December 7, 1992, p. 1, file "Said, Edward," Correspondence, Box 1, Eqbal Ahmad Papers (EAP), Johnson Library, Hampshire College, Amherst, Mass. Quotations in the next four paragraphs are from this letter.

2. Stuart Schaar, "Orientalism at the Service of Imperialism," in *Orientalism: A Reader*, ed. A. L. Macfie (New York: New York University Press, 2001), 181–193.

3. Eqbal Ahmad to Edward Said, September 25, 1997, Box 12, EAP.

4. Said's reading of this letter Edward Said and Radha Kumar, "Remembering Eqbal Ahmad," reminiscences given at the celebration of his life, Hampshire College, Amherst, Mass., September 18, 1999, recorded by David Barsamian for Alternative Radio, Program SAIE-KUMR001. The talk can be purchased from the site http://www.alternativeradio.orgkproducts/saie-kumr001 (accessed January 22, 2015).

5. Edward W. Said to the Search Committee, Middle East Studies, Hampshire College, April 6, 1983, Correspondence 1957–1999, Box 2, EAP.

6. Eqbal Ahmad, "Commencement Address," Hampshire College, May 17, 1997, 3, in zip files on disks made as backup of Eqbal's computer hard drive, March 25, 1998, files "Eudora," "Attack," "hamp.wp," Box 12, EAP.

7. Zia Mian, conversation with the author, New York City, March 17, 2004.

8. The chronology and details of the land grant for the university as well as Prime Minister Bhutto's opposition to the project are detailed in Eqbal Ahmad to Dr. Saidar Mahmoud, Secretary of the Ministry of Education, Pakistan, January 6, 1998, file "Khal" (for "Khaldunia"), Box 12, EAP.

9. Najeeb Omar, conversation with the author, Karachi, April 12, 2004.

10. A week and a half before Eqbal died, he wrote a devastating article, "Bonnie and Clyde in Karachi," *Al-Ahram Weekly* (Cairo), April 29–May 5, 1999, in response to the conviction of Benazir Bhutto and her husband, Asif Zardari, for having taken $4.3 million in kickbacks from a Swiss Company. Zardari, around whom corruption scandals continually surfaced, spent time in prison and then went into self-exile to Dubai. He returned to Pakistan in December 2007, taking over the Pakistan People's Party after his wife's assassination. He then was elected president of Pakistan and served from 2009 to 2013.

11. Pamela Collett, "A New University for Pakistan: Institution's Organizers Seek to Break from a Long Tradition of Colonial Education," *Chronicle of Higher Education*, April 27, 1994.

12. Eqbal Ahmad to Dohra Ahmad, Amherst, Mass., August 17, 1993, disk, file "DOHR," Box 12, EAP.

13. Eqbal Ahmad, letter to the editor, *Times Literary Supplement*, April 2, 1993.

14. Rumors abound that Eqbal was part of the Algerian delegation to the Evian Peace Conference in 1962, which ended the eight-year Algerian War. The historian Mohamed Harbi, to whom I introduced Eqbal in the 1990s in New York City and who was at Evian, told me in Paris in 2005 that Eqbal was not there.

3. Polemics

1. Abderrahmane Moussaoui, *De la violence en Algérie: Les lois du chaos* (Arles, France: Actes Sud and MMSH, 2006). Harbi told me in Paris a few years ago that he had turned some seventeen hundred documents detailing past violence in Algerian society over to the Algerian national archives for the use of future historians.

2. There are rumors afloat that Eqbal worked with Fanon in Tunis. There is no definitive evidence one way or the other as to whether they met. Dated letters that we exchanged show that Eqbal arrived in Tunis in early 1962, but Fanon, who lived there, died of leukemia on December 6, 1961, in a Bethesda, Maryland, hospital. Eqbal did befriend Fanon's widow, Josie, and gave a reception for her in his New York apartment after Fanon died. He was going to organize

a tour for her around the United States to spread Fanon's message, but she tragically committed suicide in 1989 in Algiers before any plans could materialize.

3. Faiz Ahmad Faiz, "Dawn of Freedom," trans. Agha Shahid Ali, in David Barsamian, *Eqbal Ahmad, Confronting Empire: Interviews with David Barsamian* (Cambridge, Mass.: South End Press, 2000), viii–ix.

4. Barsamian, *Eqbal Ahmad, Confronting Empire*, 127.

5. See the excellent study of Gellner by John A. Hall, *Ernest Gellner: An Intellectual Biography* (London: Verso, 2012).

6. Letters flew back and forth between Gellner and Said starting with Gellner's review of Edward Said's book *Culture and Imperialism* (London: Chatto and Windus, 1993; New York: Vintage, 1994): Ernest Gellner, "The Mightier Pen? Edward Said and the Double Standards of Inside-Out Colonialism," in "The Bogy of Orientalism," special issue, *Times Literary Supplement*, February 19, 1993. The issue had an Orientalist painting by Ludwig Deutsh on the front cover. The letters can be seen in the February 26; March 5, 19; April 2, 9, 16; and June 4 and 11, 1993, issues. John M. Mackenzie, emeritus professor of imperial history at Lancaster University in Great Britain, called this memorable debate "a near defamatory correspondence" ("Edward Said and the Historians," *Nineteenth Century Contexts* 18, no. 1 [1994]: 9–28).

7. Ernest Gellner, *Words and Things: A Critical Account of Linguistic Philosophy and a Study in Ideology* (London: Gallancz, 1959).

8. Sarah Gellner, "Letter: Memories of Ernest Gellner," *London Review of Books*, August 25, 2011, http://www.lrb.co.uk/v33/n16//letters (accessed January 22, 2015).

9. Ibid.

10. Hall, *Ernest Gellner*, 272.

11. Two of Robert Montagne's most important publications were *Les Berbères et le Makhzen dans le sud du Maroc* (Paris: Félix Alcan, 1930), and *Naissance du prolétariat marocain* (Paris: Peyonnet, 1952).

12. In 2002, Michael Cook received a $1.5 million Distinguished Achievement Award from the Mellon Foundation.

13. Patricia Crone and Michael A. Cook, *Hagarism, the Making of the Islamic World* (Cambridge: Cambridge University Press, 1971). In this book, Crone and Cook argued that Islam had deep roots in Judaism. They saw early Islam as a tribal rebellion of Arabs and Jews against Byzantine and Persian domination, a controversial viewpoint informed by Armenian, Syriac, Greek, Hebrew, and Aramaic texts. Ironically, the book's central theses were rejected later, even by the authors themselves. Another early book by Crone, *Meccan*

Trade and the Rise of Islam (Princeton, N.J.: Princeton University Press, 1987), caused further stir because she took on the dean of early Islamic studies, Montgomery Watt (1909–2006), a Marxist Scottish Episcopal minister who taught at Edinburgh University from 1964 to 1979. Watt examined the material roots of early Islam in his classic works *Muhammad at Mecca* (Oxford: Oxford University Press, 1953) and *Muhammad at Medina* (1953; reprint, Oxford: Oxford University Press, 1956). He argued that Mecca was an important commercial hub in the trade between Arabia and the heartland of the Middle East and that a rudimentary form of capitalism was developing there at the time of the prophet Muhammad that challenged the value system of the town's tribal peoples. Muhammad's prophecy was the answer to the population's problems in their attempts to adjust to the new situation created by these material shifts. Crone challenged Watt's thesis, pointing out in a long section of her book that frankincense, the basis of Meccan prosperity, was no longer traded with the Fertile Crescent during the prophet's lifetime, as Watt had asserted, but rather that Arabian traders enriched themselves with the trade in camel skins. So, Crone argued, it turns out that Muhammad probably engaged in the camel-skin trade, and he would have been very successful at it—leaving the reader to wonder why a local capitalism could not develop around that commerce. The significance of Crone's work was her anti-Marxist bias hidden behind a curtain of erudition.

14. Chris Hann, "Obituary: Professor Ernest Gellner," *Independent* (London), November 8, 1995.

15. For Lewis's and Said's contrasting views, see Bernard Lewis, "The Clash of Civilizations," 363–366, and Edward W. Said, "The Clash of Ignorance," 367–372, in *The Middle East and Islamic World Reader*, 3rd ed., ed. Marvin E. Gettleman and Stuart Schaar (New York: Grove Press, 2012).

16. Eqbal Ahmad to Ernest Gellner, March 9, 1993, and a copy of his *Times Literary Supplement* letter, zip files on disks made as backup of Eqbal's computer hard drive on March 25, 1998, Box 12, Eqbal Ahmad Papers (EAP), Johnson Library, Hampshire College, Amherst, Mass.

17. The original French title of Franz Fanon's book is *Sociologie d'une révolution: L'an V de la Révolution algérienne* (Paris: Maspero, 1959). It was translated into English as *A Dying Colonialism* (New York: Grove Press, 1959).

18. Eqbal Ahmad, letter to the editor, *Times Literary Supplement*, March 9, 1993.

19. Eqbal Ahmad, "Trade Unionism in the Maghreb," in *State and Society in Independent North Africa*, ed. Leon Carl Brown (Washington, D.C.: Middle East Institute, 1964), 146–191.

20. Ahmad, letter to the editor.
21. Samir al-Khalil [Kanan Makiya], *The Republic of Fear: The Inside Story of Saddam's Iraq* (New York: Pantheon, 1990). For details of U.S. aid to Iraq during that war, see Stuart Schaar, "Irangate: The Middle East Connections," in *The United States and the Middle East: A Search for New Perspectives*, ed. Hooshang Amirahmadi (Albany: State University of New York Press, 1993), 177–210.
22. Kanan Makiya, *Cruelty and Silence: War, Tyranny, Uprising, and the Arab World* (New York: Norton, 1993).
23. Geraldine Brooks, "Bookshelf: Stories of Suffering in Saddam's Iraq," *Wall Street Journal*, April 7, 1993; Michael Massing, "Book Review: *Cruelty and Silence*," *New Yorker*, April 26, 1993.
24. Edward Said, interview by Nabeel Abraham, *Lies of Our Times* (*LOOT*), May 1993, 13.
25. Eqbal Ahmad, "Cruelties Compounded" [review of *Cruelty and Silence*, by Kanan Makiya], *Nation*, August 9, 1993.
26. Eqbal Ahmad to Elsa Dixler and Victor Navasky, August 5, 1993, disk, Box 1, EAP.
27. Eqbal speaks of his problems with the *Nation* over "Cruelties Compounded" in Eqbal Ahmad to Dohra Ahmad, August 17, 1993, disk, file "DOHRA," Box 12, EAP.
28. Christopher Lydon, "He Got It Wrong, Alas: Kanan Makiya," *Open Source Radio* 69 (November 7, 2007), http://he-got-itg-Wrong-alas;Kanan Makiya //radioopenaource.org/vol.69 (accessed January 22, 2015).
29. Aijaz Ahmad, "The Politics of Literary Postcoloniality," *Race & Class* 36, no. 3 (1995): 1–20. According to Eqbal's nephew Kamran Asdar Ali, Aijaz had called Eqbal a CIA agent without having proof. As a committed Communist, Aijaz must have resented Eqbal's independence on the left. The two broke over Aijaz's attack on Edward W. Said in the pages of *Race & Class*.
30. The letters between Eqbal Ahmad, Ambalavaner Sivanandan, and Hazel Waters about this affair are in Correspondence 1995–1996, Box 1, EAP.

4. Islam and Islamic History

1. Bernard Lewis, *The Emergence of Modern Turkey* (Oxford: Oxford University Press, 1961).
2. His opponents' arguments are summarized in Eqbal Ahmad to Stuart Schaar, June 3, 1992, author's correspondence files.

3. For example, Eqbal Ahmad and Stuart Schaar, "Tahar Haddad: A Tunisian Activist Intellectual," *Maghreb Review* 21, nos. 3–4 (1996): 240–255.

4. Eqbal Ahmad, "Islam and Politics," in *The Islamic Impact*, ed. Yvonne Haddad, Byron Haines, and Ellison Findly (Syracuse, N.Y.: Syracuse University Press, 1984), 7–26, reprinted in Eqbal Ahmad, *The Selected Writings of Eqbal Ahmad*, ed. Carollee Bengelsdorf, Margaret Cerillo, and Yogesh Chandrani (New York: Columbia University Press, 2006), 160–178, and excerpted in Eqbal Ahmad, *Between Past & Future: Selected Essays on South Asia*, ed. Dohra Ahmad, Iftikhar Ahmad, and Zia Mian (Karachi: Oxford University Press, 2004), 260–280.

5. These ideas began to be discussed in academic circles in the early 1960s and were incorporated in Lloyd Rudolph and Susanne H. Rudolph, *The Modernity of Tradition: Political Development of India* (Chicago: University of Chicago Press, 1967). In fieldwork in Java and Bali and in books published in the early 1960s, the anthropologist Clifford Geertz at the University of Chicago dealt with similar themes.

6. Jinnah's views are summarized in Eqbal Ahmad, "The Betrayed Promise," *Dawn* (Karachi), June 18, 1993, reprinted in Ahmad, *Between Past & Future*, 27–30, quotes on 27–28. For more of Eqbal's views on Jinnah, see "Pakistan's Endangered History" and "Jinnah, in a Class of His Own," in Ahmad, *Between Past & Future*, 19–22, 23–26.

7. David Barsamian, *Eqbal Ahmad, Confronting Empire: Interviews with David Barsamian* (Cambridge, Mass.: South End Press, 2000), 140. In the same vein, see Eqbal Ahmad, "Islam as Refuge from Failure," *Dawn* (Karachi), September 6, 1998, and *Al-Ahram Weekly* (Cairo), September 10–16, 1998.

8. Eqbal Ahmad, "An Islamic Predicament," *Dawn* (Karachi), February 22, 1998, reprinted in Ahmad, *Between Past & Future*, 256–259, quote and estimation on 257, 258.

9. Ahmad, "Islam and Politics," 270–271.

10. Eqbal Ahmad, "A *Jihad* Against Time," *Al-Ahram Weekly* (Cairo), February 4–10, 1999.

11. Eqbal Ahmad, "Roots of the Religious Right," *Dawn* (Karachi), January 24, 1999, reprinted in Ahmad, *Between Past & Future*, 281–285, and *Selected Writings of Eqbal Ahmad*, 179–190, quote on 190. See also Eqbal Ahmad, "The Grim Reaper Is Everywhere," *Al-Ahram Weekly* (Cairo), March 11–17, 1999, and "Profile of the Religious Right," *Dawn*, March 17, 1999.

12. Eqbal Ahmad to Israel Shahak , n.d., under recipient's name, Box 1, EAP.

13. Eqbal Ahmad, "In a Land Without Music," *Dawn* (Karachi), July 13, 1995, reprinted in Ahmad, *Selected Writings of Eqbal Ahmad*, 500–503.

14. Edward W. Said, Aga Shahid Ali, Ibrahim Abu Lughod, Akeel Bilgrami, and Eqbal Ahmad, "'The Satanic Verses'" [letter to the editor], *New York Review of Books*, March 16, 1989, http://www.nybooks.com/articles/archives/1989/mar/16/the-satanic-verses/ (accessed January 22, 2015).

15. Ibid.

16. Ahmad, "Roots of the Religious Right," 186–187.

5. Imperialism, Nationalism, Revolutionary Warfare, Insurgency, and the Need for Democracy

1. Eqbal Ahmad, "The Iranian Revolution: A Landmark for the Future," in "On the Iranian Revolution," ed. Eqbal Ahmad, special issue, *Race & Class* 21, no. 1 (1979): 3–11, reprinted as *The Iranian Revolution* (Lahore: Vanguard, 1980).

2. Raza Kazim, conversation with the author, Pakistan, April 7, 2004.

3. Eqbal Ahmad, "Iran and the West: A Century of Subjugation," *Christianity & Crisis*, March 3, 1980, 37–44, reprinted in *Tell the American People: Perspectives on the Iranian Revolution*, ed. David H. Albert (Philadelphia: Movement for a New Society, 1980), 28–43.

4. Frank Wisner Jr. was studying for a bachelor's of arts degree at the time Eqbal was at Princeton. He was the son of Frank G. Wisner (1909–1965), the CIA director of operations for Eastern Europe, including the Soviet Union, during the Cold War. The older Wisner committed suicide in 1965. Frank Jr. went on to become U.S. ambassador to India, the Philippines, and Egypt before ending his government service as undersecretary of defense for policy (1993–1994). Since retiring from the government, he has engaged in business and has served on several boards of large corporations such as Enron and AIG. In June 2013, he joined the board of Ergo, a global intelligence and advisory corporation.

5. Eqbal Ahmad, "Revolutionary Warfare: How to Tell When the Rebels Have Won," *Nation*, August 30, 1965, 95–100, reprinted in Eqbal Ahmad, *The Selected Writings of Eqbal Ahmad*, ed. Carollee Bengelsdorf, Margaret Cerullo, and Yogesh Chandrani (New York: Columbia University Press, 2006), 13–23.

6. H. O. Nazareth, prod., *Stories My Country Told Me: The Meaning of Nationhood* (Bremerton, Wash.: Penumbra Productions for the BBC Arena, 1996).

7. Mahatma Gandhi, *The Mahatma and the Poet: Letters and Debates Between Gandhi and Tagore, 1915–1941*, comp. and ed. with an introduction by Sabyasachī Bhattacharya (New Delhi: National Book Trust, 1997).

8. David Barsamian, *Eqbal Ahmad, Confronting Empire: Interviews with David Barsamian* (Cambridge, Mass.: South End Press, 2000), 4.

9. Zulfikar Ahmad, conversation with the author, Islamabad, March 2004.

10. Barsamian, *Eqbal Ahmad, Confronting Empire*, 139.

11. Eqbal Ahmad to Stuart Schaar, December 4, 1978, author's correspondence files.

12. Eqbal Ahmad, "From Potato Sack to Potato Mash: The Contemporary Crisis of the Third World," *Arab Studies Quarterly* 2, no. 3 (1980): 223–234, quote on 223, 236, reprinted in *Monthly Review* 32, no. 10 (1981): 8–21; Eqbal Ahmad, *Between Past & Future: Selected Essays on South Asia*, ed. Dohra Ahmad, Iftikhar Ahmad, and Zia Mian (Karachi: Oxford University Press, 2004), 3–15, quote on 3, 15; and *Selected Writings of Eqbal Ahmad*, 116–127. The second article in this series is "Postcolonial Systems of Power," *Arab Studies Quarterly* 2, no. 4 (1980): 350–363, reprinted in Ahmad, *Selected Writings of Eqbal Ahmad*, 128–141. The third article is "The Neo-fascist State: The Pathology of Power in the Third World," *Arab Studies Quarterly* 3, no. 2 (981): 170–180, reprinted in *First Harvest: The Institute for Policy Studies, 1963–1983*, ed. John S. Friedman (New York: Grove Press, 1983), 68–78, and Ahmad, *Selected Writings of Eqbal Ahmad*, 142–153.

13. Eqbal Ahmad, "Beyond Blown Bridges," *Al-Ahram Weekly* (Cairo), January 14–20, 1999.

14. Eqbal Ahmad, "Intellectuals' Role in Society," *Dawn* (Karachi), December 10, 1995, reprinted in Ahmad, *Between Past & Future*, 316–319, quote on 318–319.

15. Barsamian, *Eqbal Ahmad, Confronting Empire*, 65.

16. Eqbal Ahmad, "The Betrayed Promise," *Dawn* (Karachi), June 18, 1993, reprinted in Ahmad, *Between Past & Future*, 27–30, and *Selected Writings of Eqbal Ahmad*, 419–422, quote on 420.

17. Eqbal Ahmad, "Notes on South Asia in Crisis," *Bulletin of Concerned Asian Scholars* 4, no. 1 (1972): 23–29, reprinted in Ahmad, *Between Past & Future*, 38–48, quote on 46–47.

18. Eqbal Ahmad, "Pakistan in Crisis: An Interview with Eqbal Ahmad by Nubar Hovsepian," *Race & Class* 22, no. 2 (1980): 135, reprinted in Ahmad, *Between Past & Future*, 68–88, quote on 75.

19. Eqbal Ahmad, "Islam and Politics," in *The Islamic Impact*, ed. Yvonne Haddad, Byron Haines, and Ellison Findly (Syracuse, N.Y.: Syracuse University Press, 1984), 7–76, reprinted in Ahmad, *Selected Writings of Eqbal Ahmad*, 160–178, and excerpted in Ahmad, *Between Past & Future*, 260–280, quote on 263.

20. For more on this concept of a social democracy, see Omid Safi, ed., *Progressive Muslims: On Justice, Gender, and Pluralism* (Oxford: One World, 2003).

6. The Middle East and the Palestinian-Israeli Conflict

1. "Eqbal Ahmad, India, Pakistan, Bosnia, etc.: Interviewed by David Barsamian," August 4, 1993, http://www.geocities.com/CollegePark/Library/9803/eqbal_ahmad/Barsamwint.hmtl, (accessed October 4, 2004, but no longer available).
2. David Barsamian, *Eqbal Ahmad, Confronting Empire: Interviews with David Barsamian* (Cambridge, Mass.: South End Press, 2000), 32.
3. Eqbal Ahmad, "Pioneering in the Nuclear Age: An Essay on Israel and Palestinians," *Race & Class* 25, no. 4 (1984): 1–7, reprinted in Eqbal Ahmad, *The Selected Writings of Eqbal Ahmad*, ed. Carollee Bengelsdorf, Margaret Cerillo, and Yogesh Chandrani (New York: Columbia University Press, 2006), 298–317, quote on 302.
4. The society website's listing of conferences for 1994 does not include the one that Eqbal participated in on September 13, 1994: "Jerusalem: Between the Past and the Future" (see http://www.passia.org/ [accessed August 6, 2013]). Although Eqbal was the main speaker on the panel, he so shocked his audience with his proposals that the organization removed all traces of what he said from its website.
5. Eqbal Ahmad, remarks at the conference "Jerusalem," 2, 3, 4.
6. Eqbal Ahmad, "An Essay in Reconciliation" [review of *The Question of Palestine*, by Edward W. Said], *Nation*, March 22, 1980. Eqbal repeated this statement in Eqbal Ahmad, introduction to David Barsamian, *The Pen and the Sword: Conversations with Edward Said* (Monroe, Me.: Common Courage Press, 1994), 1–16.
7. Eqbal Ahmad and Ibrahim Abu-Lughod, eds., "The Invasion of Lebanon," special double issue, *Race & Class* 24, no. 4 (1983). See also Ahmad, "Pioneering in the Nuclear Age."
8. Edward W. Said, "Foreword: Cherish the Man's Courage," in Barsamian, *Eqbal Ahmad, Confronting Empire*, xxix.
9. Ibid., xxix–xxx.
10. Ibid.
11. Eqbal Ahmad to Tim May and Frank Hanly, December 7, 1992, p. 1, file "Said, Edward," Box 1, Eqbal Ahmad Papers (EAP), Johnson Library, Hampshire College, Amherst, Mass.

12. Eqbal Ahmad to Israel Shahak, October 22, 1969, file "Shahak, Israel," Box 1, EAP.

13. Barsamian, *Eqbal Ahmad, Confronting Empire*, 98.

14. Ahmad, "Pioneering in the Nuclear Age," 305.

15. See the article Eqbal wrote, published in different journals with different titles but otherwise is the same article, that deals with this subject: "Born Again Apartheid," *Dawn* (Karachi), October 25, 1998, and "After the Peace of the Weak," *Al-Ahram Weekly* (Cairo), November 5–11, 1998.

16. Eqbal Ahmad, "The Hundred Hour War," *Dawn* (Karachi), March 17, 1991, reprinted in Ahmad, *Selected Writings of Eqbal Ahmad*, 278–281, quote on 278.

17. Ahmad and Abu-Lughod, eds., "Invasion of Lebanon."

18. Eqbal Ahmad, "Encounter with an Islamist," *Dawn* (Karachi), July 26, 1998, reprinted as "Encounter with a Fighter," *Al-Ahram Weekly* (Cairo), July 30–August 5, 1998.

19. Eqbal Ahmad, "Lebanon's Economic Mystery," *Dawn* (Karachi), July 19, 1998, and *Al-Ahram Weekly* (Cairo), July 23–29, 1998.

20. Eqbal Ahmad, "King Hussein's Dual Legacy," *Dawn* (Karachi), February 14, 1999, reprinted in Ahmad, *Selected Writings of Eqbal Ahmad*, 381–385, quote on 385.

7. India, Pakistan, and Bangladesh

1. Eqbal Ahmad, "Pakistan's Endangered History," *Dawn* (Karachi), June 4, 1995, first delivered as a speech at the introduction of the Jinnah Papers (curated by Dr. Z. H. Zaidi) and reprinted in Eqbal Ahmad, *Between Past & Future: Selected Essays on South Asia*, ed. Dohra Ahmad, Iftikhar Ahmad, and Zia Mian (Karachi: Oxford University Press, 2004), 19–22, quote on 22.

2. Eqbal Ahmad, "India's Partition—History, Memory, & Loss," *Hindu* (Chennai, India), December 27, 1998.

3. Radha Kumar, *The History of Doing: An Illustrated Account of Movements for Women's Rights and Feminism in India, 1800–1900*, 2nd ed. (New Delhi: Kali for Women, 2002), and *Divide and Fall? Bosnia in the Annals of Partition* (London: Verso, 1997).

4. Edward Said and Radha Kumar, "Remembering Eqbal Ahmad," reminiscences given at the celebration of his life, Hampshire College, Amherst, Mass., September 18, 1999, recorded by David Barsamian for Alternative Radio, Program SAIE-KUMR001. The talk can be purchased from the site http://www.alternativeradio.orgkproducts/saie-kumr001 (accessed January 22, 2015).

5. Radha Kumar, *Making Peace with Partition* (New Delhi: Penguin, 2005).

6. David Barsamian, *Eqbal Ahmad, Confronting Empire: Interviews with David Barsamian* (Cambridge, Mass.: South End Press, 2000), 13.

7. According to Eqbal's widow, "Eqbal was going through the process of applying for U.S. citizenship at the time of his death" (Julie Diamond to Stuart Schaar, e-mail, March 3, 2014).

8. Eqbal Ahmad, "'Democrats' Against Democracy," *Dawn* (Karachi), March 14, 1999.

9. Ministry of External Affairs, Government of India, "Documents: Simla Agreement," July 2, 1972, quote from point 1, http://mea.gov.in/in-focus -article.htm?19005/Simla+Agreement+July+2+1972 (accessed November 20, 2004).

10. Dr. Mubashir Hassan, "India-Pakistan: 'Walls Must Come Down': Nikhil Chakravartty and the Growing Momentum of Peace," *Mainstream* (New Delhi), November 22, 2003, 8.

11. Ibid., 7.

12. Quoted in ibid., 8.

13. Reported in ibid., 8–9, citing *Hindustan Times* (New Delhi), April 16, 1990.

14. Ibid., 9.

15. Quoted in ibid.

16. Nisar Osmani, "Pakistan Group Discusses Kashmir with Indian Intellectuals," *Dawn* (Karachi), June 5, 1990.

17. Asma Jahangir, conversation with the author, Lahore, April 8, 2004.

18. Quoted in Agha Imran Hamid, "The Amazing Eqbal Ahmad," *Friday Times* (Lahore), May 20, 2000. See also Pervez Hoodbhoy, "Eqbal Ahmad: Post-Pokhran Days," *Chowk*, May 11, 2000, http://www.chowk.com/show_article .cgi?aid=00000768&channel=covic%20center&start=0&end=9&chapte . . . (accessed October 4, 2004, no longer available because the online magazine *Chowk* crashed).

19. Eqbal wrote a number of columns about the need for peace between India and Pakistan. See, for example, "The Bus Can Bring a Nobel Prize," *Dawn* (Karachi), February 21, 1999, and "No Alternative to Dialogue," *Dawn*, June 28, 1998.

20. Subhas Chandra Bose was a controversial Indian nationalist who, in order to end British rule in India, wanted to ally his country with Nazi Germany and fascist Japan during World War II, according to Leonard A. Gordon, *Brothers Against the Raj: A Biography of Indian Nationalists Surat and Subhas Chandra Bose* (New York: Columbia University Press, 1990).

21. For an overview of such exchanges, see Smithu Kothari, Zia Mian, Kamla Bhasla, and A. H. Nayyar, *Bridging Partition: People's Initiatives for Peace Between India and Pakistan* (Hyderabad: Orient Black Swan, 2010).

22. Abdul Hamid Nayyar specializes in solid-state and quantum physics and quantum mechanics. He has been a visiting research scholar at Princeton University since 1998 and a faculty member at Lahore University of Management Sciences. In addition to his antinuclear work and publications, he has been actively engaged in public-school curriculum and textbook reform in Pakistan.

23. Barsamian, *Eqbal Ahmad, Confronting Empire*, 86.

24. Ibid., 8.

25. Pervez Hoodbhoy, conversation with the author, Islamabad, April 8, 2004.

26. Ibid.

27. Ibid.

28. Abdul Hamid Nayyar, conversation with the author, Islamabad, April 9, 2004. See Eqbal's recounting of the press conference in "Reason as Spectator," *Dawn* (Karachi), June 11, 1998, and "Reason on the Side Lines," *Al-Ahram Weekly* (Cairo), June 6, 1998, both reprinted in Ahmad, *Between Past & Future*, 107–111.

29. Eqbal Ahmad, "When Mountains Die," *Dawn* (Karachi), June 4, 1998, reprinted in Ahmad, *Selected Writings of Eqbal Ahmad*, 543–547, quote on 543, 547. See four other articles that Eqbal wrote on the nuclear issue in South Asia: "India's Obsession, Our Choice," *Dawn*, May 17, 1998, reprinted in Ahmad, *Between Past & Future*, 93–96; "Atomic Gains, Nuclear Losses," *Dawn*, June 18, 1998, and *Al-Ahram Weekly* (Cairo), June 18–24, 1998, reprinted as "Nuclear Gains and Losses," in Ahmad, *Between Past & Future*, 102–106; *Testing the Limits: Pakistan, Following India into the Pit* [brochure] (Amsterdam: Transnational Institute; Washington, D.C.: Institute of Policy Studies, August 1998); and review of *India 2020: A Vision for the New Millennium*, by A. P. J. Abdul Kalam and Y. S. Rajan, *Foreign Policy*, no. 115 (1999): 122–125, http://www.foreignpolicy.com/sumbookpage.htm (accessed January 22, 2015), written just before he died in May 1999.

30. Beena Sarwar to Stuart Schaar, e-mail, September 13, 2004.

31. Abdul Hamid Nayyar, conversation.

32. Raza Kazim, conversation with the author, Lahore, April 7, 2004. Eqbal remembered Raza as a well-known Communist leader and activist at their alma mater, Foreman Christian College in Lahore. Raza had heard about Eqbal from other Pakistanis and from the notoriety of the Harrisburg trial. They met again in 1972, the year that Eqbal's mother and younger brother Saghir died, and

Eqbal traveled to Pakistan from the United States. Raza removed Eqbal's bags from the hotel room and took him to his home to live with his family. In this way, every time Eqbal went to Lahore, he moved into Raza's house and stayed there for as long as he pleased.

33. Raza Kazim, conversation.

34. Dohra Ahmad, conversation with the author, New York City, March 2004; Imran Hamid, conversation with the author, Islamabad, April 3, 2004.

35. Zia Mian, conversation with author, New York City, March 13, 2004.

36. Eqbal Ahmad, "Shotgun Governance," *Dawn* (Karachi), March 21, 1999, reprinted in Ahmad, *Selected Writings of Eqbal Ahmad*, 563–566, quote on 565–566.

37. Rani Mumtaz, conversation with the author, Lahore, April 8, 2004.

38. Eqbal Ahmad, "The Governor's Challenge," *Dawn* (Karachi), November 10, 1998.

39. I first met Chotti in Eqbal's apartment in Amherst when she was studying at Tufts University. I reconnected with her in Islamabad on April 9, 2004.

8. Critique of U.S. Foreign Policy, the Cold War, and Terrorism

1. Eqbal Ahmad, "Yet Again, a New Nixon," *Dawn* (Karachi), May 7, 1994, reprinted in Eqbal Ahmad, *The Selected Writings of Eqbal Ahmad*, ed. Carollee Bengelsdorf, Margaret Cerullo, and Yogesh Chandrani (New York: Columbia University Press, 2006), 228–231, quote on 229.

2. Eqbal Ahmad, "Revolutionary Warfare and Counterinsurgency," *Journal of International Affairs* 25, no. 1 (1971): 1–47, excerpts reprinted as "Counterinsurgency" in Ahmad, *Selected Writings of Eqbal Ahmad*, 36–64, quote on 62–63.

3. This discussion is based on a conversation I had with Eqbal in 1987 about Irangate. See also Stuart Schaar, "Irangate: The Middle East Connections," in *The United States and the Middle East: A Search for New Perspectives*, ed. Hooshang Amirahmadi (Albany: State University of New York Press, 1993), 177–210.

4. For Eqbal's ideas on terrorism, see Eqbal Ahmad, *Terrorism: Theirs and Ours*, foreword and interview by David Barsamian, Open Media Pamphlet Series (New York: Seven Stories Press, 2001).

5. Eqbal mentioned this in his closing remarks at a conference he attended on November 10, 1998, transcript, 6, Eqbal Ahmad Papers, Johnson Library, Hampshire College, Amherst, Mass. (no specific information is available on the conference).

6. Eqbal Ahmad and Richard J. Barnet, "A Reporter at Large: Bloody Games,"
New Yorker, April 11, 1988, 44–86, reprinted as "Bloody Games," in Eqbal Ahmad, *Between Past & Future: Selected Essays on South Asia*, ed. Dohra Ahmad,
Iftikhar Ahmad, and Zia Mian (Karachi: Oxford University Press, 2004),
153–198, and *Selected Writings of Eqbal Ahmad*, 453–492.

7. David Barsamian, *Eqbal Ahmad, Confronting Empire: Interviews with David
Barsamian* (Cambridge, Mass.: South End Press, 2000), 95.

8. Ibid., 96.

9. Ibid., 93.

10. Ibid., 94.

11. Ibid., 99–100.

12. Eqbal Ahmad, "Bill Clinton Turns to God," *Al-Ahram Weekly* (Cairo), September 17–23, 1998.

13. Pressures to withdraw U.S. troops from Afghanistan grew in the United States,
and President Hamid Karzai, in an attempt to appease the Taliban, refused to
sign a security agreement defining the terms of U.S. military presence in the
country after 2014. As a result, President Barack Obama threatened to pull all
U.S. military personnel out of the country by the end of 2014. As soon as the
new Afghan president, Ashraf Ghani, assumed his office, he signed an agreement with the United States allowing almost 10,000 U.S. troops to remain in
the country as advisers.

14. Eqbal Ahmad, "Imperial Presidency Under Siege," *Al-Ahram Weekly* (Cairo),
August 13–19, 1998.

Conclusion

1. Unless otherwise noted, my descriptions of and quotations from the talks given
at the commemoration of Eqbal's retirement from Hampshire College come
from a transcript of his retirement celebration, October 4, 1997, Box 12, filed
under "my files," and "veiled," Eqbal Ahmad Papers (EAP), Johnson Library,
Hampshire College, Amherst, Mass.

2. Samuel P. Huntington, *The Clash of Civilizations and the Remaking of World
Order* (New York: Touchstone, 1996).

3. The Eqbal Ahmad Papers at Hampshire College contain letters from Eqbal
Ahmad to Noam Chomsky from the 1970s and one from Chomsky to Eqbal
in 1992 (file "Chomsky," Box 1). They deal with organizing antiwar and
anti-imperialist events, writings, and solidarity movements with Palestinians
and Vietnamese. In a review of David Barsamian's book *Eqbal Ahmad*,

Confronting Empire: Interviews with David Barsamian (Cambridge, Mass.: South End Press, 2000) in 2000, Chomsky called Eqbal a "secular Sufi" who opposed "the twin curse of nationalism and religious fanaticism" ("Thoughts of a Secular Sufi," n.d., http://www.chomsky.info/articles/2000----.htm [accessed November 7, 2014]). Chomsky delivered the third Eqbal Ahmad Distinguished Lecture in Lahore in 2001, sponsored by the Eqbal Ahmad Foundation and the newspapers *Dawn* (Islamabad) and *Friday Times* (Islamabad). See Najam Sethi, "Chomsky's Relevance" [editorial], *Friday Times*, November 30, 2001. In a lecture that Chomsky delivered by Skype from his MIT office to an audience at Café Bol in the Maine Market in Gulberg, Lahore, in May 2011, he referred to his late friend's views on Pakistan. See Maria Amir, "In US-Pakistan Relations Stability Means Obedience: Chomsky," *Express Tribune* (Karachi), May 26, 2011.

4. Daniel Ellsberg, *Papers on the War* (New York: Simon and Schuster, 1972).

5. Howard Zinn, *A People's History of the United States, 1492–Present*, rev. and updated ed. (New York: Harper Perennial, 1995).

6. Eqbal met Iqbal Riza in 1972 in Washington, D.C., during the Bangladesh crisis. On December 15, when Dacca fell, Iqbal became despondent and told his wife, Parveen, that he could not remain a diplomat for Pakistan if the army fired on its own people. He would resign his diplomatic post if that happened. Early in 1972, Iqbal read one of Eqbal's columns, which so impressed him that he made it his business to find him. Tracking him down, Iqbal went to Eqbal's house in Washington, D.C., beginning a long friendship. In 1977, Iqbal was posted to Paris as deputy chief of the Pakistani embassy. During elections in Pakistan in 1977, however, the military fired on civilians, triggering Iqbal's dramatic response. He consulted with his wife, called Eqbal, and announced his decision to resign from the Pakistan foreign service. Eqbal approved of the move and in doing so cemented their friendship. Iqbal set up a meeting between Eqbal and Mubashir Hassan, who later worked closely with Eqbal to facilitate exchanges between Indian and Pakistani intellectuals and politicians in order to break the deadlock in the peace process between the two countries. Iqbal also introduced Eqbal in the 1990s to the chief of staff and commander in chief of the Pakistani army from 1998 to 2007 and Pakistan's tenth president from 2001 to 2008, Pervez Musharraf (b.1943), who told Iqbal that he had read with great interest Eqbal's columns in the Pakistani press. Iqbal's position as Secretary-General Kofi Anan's chief of cabinet at the United Nations opened up many new contacts for Eqbal within the United Nations and larger diplomatic circles.

7. This talk was expanded in Edward Said, "Foreword: Cherish the Man's Courage," in Barsamian, *Eqbal Ahmad, Confronting Empire*, quote on xxi–xxii.

8. Bernard Lown, M.D., to Eqbal Ahmad, October 20, 1997, Correspondence 1996–1998, Box 1, EAP.

9. The trial took place in 1972, but pretrial motions were heard in 1971.

10. Eqbal Ahmad to Dohra Ahmad, Islamabad, October 25, 1992, zip files on disks made as backup to Eqbal's computer hard drive on March 25, 1996, files "my files," "letters," "Dohra," Box 12, EAP.

11. David Barsamian, who interviewed Eqbal extensively at the end of his life, wrote that during a walk he took with Eqbal between interviews in Mount Holyoke, Massachusetts, in August 1998, Eqbal "was in a pensive and reflective mood. It was then that he told me that his health was not so good. Ten months later, he was dead" (*Eqbal Ahmad, Confronting Empire*, xvi).

12. Pervez Hoodbhoy, foreword to Eqbal Ahmad, *Between Past & Present: Selected Essays on South Asia*, ed. Dohra Ahmad, Iftikhar Ahmad, and Zia Mian (Karachi: Oxford University Press, 2004), vii.

13. Pervez Hoodbhoy, conversation with the author, Pakistan, 2004. Pervez interpreted Eqbal's response differently than I did. He thought that Eqbal did not want to hurt Rashida's feelings and therefore let her continue reciting the Qur'an. But I do not think that he realized the depth of Eqbal's attachment to Islamic culture, which was a profound aspect of his being. On Pervez's view, see Hoodbhoy, foreword to Ahmad, *Between Past & Future*, xxiv.

BIBLIOGRAPHY

Archives

Ahmad, Eqbal. Papers. Johnson Library, Hampshire College, Amherst, Mass.

Boudin, Leonard. "Reminiscences of Leonard Boudin." Interview, 1983. Individual Interview List Oral History Project, RLIN NXCP86-A42, Document OHI0016726-12169. Oral History Research Office, Columbia University, New York.

Davidon, Ann Morrissett and William C. Papers, 1949–. Collection DG144. Peace Collection, Swathmore College, Swathmore, Pa. http.//www.swathmore.edu /Library/peace/.

Harrisburg [Pennsylvania] Defense Committee Collected Records, 1970–1973. Collection CDG-A. Peace Collection, Swathmore College, Swathmore, Pa. http.//www.swarthmore.edu/Library/peace/.

Schaar, Stuart. Personal archives. Includes Eqbal Ahmad–Stuart Schaar correspondence, 1960–1998 (letters to and from Eqbal Ahmad), to be deposited in the author's archive at Brooklyn College's Special Collections in the Library; Harrisburg trial archive, to be deposited in the Swathmore Peace Archive,

Swathmore College, Swathmore, Pa. Materials relating to Eqbal Ahmad, to be deposited in the author's archive in Special Collections, Brooklyn College Library.

Books and Articles

Ahmad, Aijaz. "The Politics of Literary Postcoloniality." *Race & Class* 36, no. 3 (1995): 1–20.

Ahmad, Aijaz, Walter Abish, Aijaz Ahmad, Eqbal Ahmad, Edward Albee, John Ashbery, John Barth, Donald Barthelme, Heinrich Böll, Kamal Boullata, et al. "Death in Iran" [letter to the editor]. *New York Review of Books*, August 13, 1981. http://www.nybooks.com/articles/archives/1981/aug/13/death-in-iran /?insrc=toc. Accessed January 22, 2015.

Ahmad, Dohra. *Landscapes of Hope: Anti-colonial Utopianism in America.* New York: Oxford University Press, 2009.

——. *Rotten English: A Literary Anthology.* New York: Norton, 2007.

Ahmad, Eqbal. "After the Peace of the Weak." *Al-Ahram Weekly* (Cairo), November 5–11, 1998.

——. "After the Winter Bombs." *Dawn* (Karachi), December 20, 1998. Reprinted in Eqbal Ahmad, *The Selected Writings of Eqbal Ahmad*, 287–290.

——. "At Cold War's End." *Boston Review*, June–August 1993. Reprinted in Eqbal Ahmad, *The Selected Writings of Eqbal Ahmad*, 249–252.

——. "Atomic Gains, Nuclear Losses." *Dawn* (Karachi), June 18, 1998, and *Al-Ahram Weekly* (Cairo), June 18–24, 1998. Reprinted as "Nuclear Gains and Losses" in Eqbal Ahmad, *Between Past & Future*, 102–106.

——. "Autoportrait de H. Kissenger: Une nouvelle doctrine de l'impérialisme." *Le Monde Diplomatique* (Paris), May 1975.

——. "The Betrayed Promise." *Dawn* (Karachi), June 18, 1993. Reprinted in Eqbal Ahmad, *Between Past & Future*, 27–30, and *The Selected Writings of Eqbal Ahmad*, 419–422.

——. *Between Past & Future: Selected Essays on South Asia.* Edited by Dohra Ahmad, Iftikhar Ahmad, and Zia Mian. Karachi: Oxford University Press, 2004.

——. "Beyond Blown Bridges." *Al-Ahram Weekly* (Cairo), January 14–20, 1999.

——. "Bill Clinton Turns to God." *Al-Ahram Weekly* (Cairo), September 17–23, 1998.

——. "Bonnie and Clyde in Karachi." *Al-Ahram Weekly* (Cairo), April 29–May 5, 1999.

——. "Born Again Apartheid." *Dawn* (Karachi), October 25, 1998.

——. "The Bus Can Bring a Nobel Prize." *Dawn* (Karachi), February 21, 1999.

——. "Campagne pour la démocratie au Pakistan." *Le Monde Diplomatique* (Paris), December 1983.

——. "The Cold War from the Standpoint of Its Victims." Talk delivered at the "Rethinking the Cold War" conference in honor of William Appelman Williams, University of Wisconsin, Madison, October 18–20, 1991. Reprinted in Eqbal Ahmad, *The Selected Writings of Eqbal Ahmad*, 219–227, and published online as "History Is a Weapon: Cold War from the Stand Points of Its Victims (1991), http://www.historyisaweapon.com/defcon1/eqbalahmadcoldwar.html. Accessed January 23, 2015.

——. "Comments on Skocpol: The Rentier State and Shi'a Islam in the Iranian Revolution." *Theory and Society* 11, no. 3 (1982): 293–300.

——. "Comprehending Terror." *Middle East Report* 16, no. 140 (1986). http://www.merip.org/mer/mer140/comprehending-terror. Accessed January 23, 2015.

——. "Cruelties Compounded." Review of *Cruelty and Silence*, but Kanan Makiya. *Nation*, August 9–16, 1993.

——. "Democracy in Pakistan." Parts 1, 2, 3, 4, and 5. *The Nation* (Lahore), March 23 and 31, April 7, 13, and 28, 1989.

——. "'Democrats' Against Democracy." *Dawn* (Karachi), March 14, 1999.

——. "Encounter with an Islamist." *Dawn* (Karachi), July 26, 1998. Reprinted as "Encounter with a Fighter," *Al-Ahram Weekly* (Cairo), July 30–August 5, 1998.

——. "Espoirs et uncertitude en Inde: M. Rajiv Gandhi sur la ligne de départ." *Le Monde Diplomatique* (Paris), March 1985.

——. "An Essay in Reconciliation" [review of *The Question of Palestine*, by Edward Said]. *Nation*, March 22, 1980.

——. "Fall and Rise of the Bhuttos of Pakistan." *Book World* (*Washington Post*), March 26, 1989.

——. "From Potato Sack to Potato Mash: The Contemporary Crisis of the Third World." *Arab Studies Quarterly* 2, no. 3 (1980): 223–234. Reprinted in *Monthly Review* 32, no. 10 (1981): 8–21; and Eqbal Ahmad, *Between Past & Future*, 3–15, and *The Selected Writings of Eqbal Ahmad*, 116–127.

——. "The Governor's Challenge." *Dawn* (Karachi), November 10, 1998.

——. "The Grim Reaper Is Everywhere." *Al-Ahram Weekly* (Cairo), March 11–17, 1999.

——. "How We Look to the Third World." *Nation*, March 3, 1969.

——. "The Hundred Hour War." *Dawn* (Karachi), March 17, 1991. Reprinted in Eqbal Ahmad, *The Selected Writings of Eqbal Ahmad*, 278–281.

——. " 'I Am the Destiny.' " *London Review of Books*, June 18, 1998.

——. "Imperial Presidency Under Siege." *Al-Ahram Weekly* (Cairo), August 13–19, 1998.

——. "In a Land Without Music." *Dawn* (Karachi), July 13, 1995. Reprinted in Eqbal Ahmad, *The Selected Writings of Eqbal Ahmad*, 500–503.

——. "India's Obsession, Our Choice." *Dawn* (Karachi), May 17, 1998. Reprinted in Eqbal Ahmad, *Between Past & Future*, 93–96.

——. "India's Partition—History, Memory, & Loss." *Hindu* (Chennai, India), December 27, 1998.

——. "Intellectuals' Role in Society." *Dawn* (Karachi), December 10, 1995. Reprinted in Eqbal Ahmad, *Between Past & Future*, 316–319.

——. Introduction to David Barsamian, *The Pen and the Sword: Conversations with Edward Said*, 1–16. Monroe, Me.: Common Courage Press, 1994.

——. "Introduction: Portent of a New Century." In *Beyond the Storm*, edited by Phyllis Bennis and Michel Moushabeck, 7–30. Northampton, Mass: Interlink, 1998.

——. "Iran and the West: A Century of Subjugation." *Christianity and Crisis*, March 3, 1980, 37–44. Reprinted in *Tell the American People: Perspectives on the Iranian Revolution*, edited by David H. Albert, 28–43. Philadelphia: Movement for a New Society, 1980.

——. "The Iranian Revolution: A Landmark for the Future." In "On the Iranian Revolution," edited by Eqbal Ahmad, special issue, *Race & Class* 21, no. 1 (1979): 3–11. Reprinted as *The Iranian Revolution*. Lahore: Vanguard, 1980.

——. "Islam and Politics." In *The Islamic Impact*, edited by Yvonne Haddad, Byron Haines, and Ellison Findly, 7–76. Syracuse, N.Y.: Syracuse University Press, 1984. Reprinted in Eqbal Ahmad, *The Selected Writings of Eqbal Ahmad*, 160–178; excerpted in Eqbal Ahmad, *Between Past & Future*, 260–280.

——. "Islam as Refuge from Failure." *Dawn* (Karachi), September 6, 1998, and *Al-Ahram Weekly* (Cairo), September 10–16, 1998.

——. "An Islamic Predicament." *Dawn* (Karachi), February 22, 1998. Reprinted in Eqbal Ahmad, *Between Past & Future*, 256–259.

——. "A *Jihad* Against Time." *Al-Ahram Weekly* (Cairo), February 4–10, 1999.

——. "Jinnah, in a Class of His Own." In Eqbal Ahmad, *Between Past & Future*, 23–26.

——. "King Hussein's Dual Legacy." *Dawn* (Karachi), February 14, 1999. Reprinted in Eqbal Ahmad, *The Selected Writings of Eqbal Ahmad*, 381–385.

——. "Lebanon's Economic Mystery." *Dawn* (Karachi), July 19, 1998, and *Al-Ahram Weekly* (Cairo), July 23–29, 1998.

———. "Letter to a Pakistani Diplomat." *New York Review of Books*, September 2, 1971. http://www.nybooks.com/issues/1971/sep/02/?insrc=wai. Accessed January 23, 2015. Reprinted in Eqbal Ahmad, *The Selected Writings of Eqbal Ahmad*, 425–430.

———. "NATO: The Controversy over Kosovo." *Dawn* (Karachi), April 11, 1999.

———. "NATO Has Failed." *Al-Ahram Weekly* (Cairo), April 8–14, 1999.

———. "The Neo-fascist State: The Pathology of Power in the Third World." *Arab Studies Quarterly* 3, no. 2 (1981): 170–180. Reprinted in *First Harvest: The Institute for Policy Studies, 1963–1983*, edited by John S. Friedman, 68–78. New York: Grove Press, 1983; and Eqbal Ahmad, *The Selected Writings of Eqbal Ahmad*, 142–153.

———. "No Alternative to Dialogue." *Dawn* (Karachi), June 28, 1998.

———. "Notes on South Asia in Crisis." *Bulletin of Concerned Asian Scholars* 4, no. 1 (1972): 23–29. Reprinted in Eqbal Ahmad, *Between Past & Future*, 38–48.

———. "On Arab Bankruptcy." *New York Times*, August 10, 1982. Reprinted in Eqbal Ahmad, *The Selected Writings of Eqbal Ahmad*, 357–359.

———. "Osama bin Laden Is a Sign of Things to Come" [nterview by David Barsamian]. *Progressive*, November 1998. http://mari209.tripod.com/200i0kt /2001-3367i.htm. Accessed January 22, 2015.

———. "Pakistan in Crisis: An Interview with Eqbal Ahmad by Nubar Hovsepian." *Race & Class* 22, no. 2 (1980): 129–149. Reprinted in Eqbal Ahmad, *Between Past & Future*, 68–88.

———. "Pakistan: L'intervention de l'armée a accru les risques d'explosion." *Le Monde Diplomatique* (Paris), October 1977.

———. "Pakistan's Endangered History." *Dawn* (Karachi), June 4, 1995. Reprinted in Eqbal Ahmad, *Between Past & Future*, 19–22.

———. "Pakistan: Signposts to a Police State." *Journal of Contemporary Asia* 4, no. 4 (1974): 423–438. Reprinted in Eqbal Ahmad, *Between Past & Future*, 49–67.

———. "Pioneering in the Nuclear Age: An Essay on Israel and Palestinians." *Race & Class* 25, no. 4 (1984): 1–7. Reprinted in Eqbal Ahmad, *The Selected Writings of Eqbal Ahmad*, 298–317.

———. "Political Culture and Foreign Policy: American Intervention in the Third World." In *For Better or Worse: America's Influence in the World*, edited by Allen F. Davis, 119–131. Westport, Conn.: Greenwood Press, 1980. Reprinted as *Political Culture and Foreign Policy: Notes on American Interventions in the Third World*. Washington, D.C.: Institute for Policy Studies, 1982.

———. "Postcolonial Systems of Power." *Arab Studies Quarterly* 2, no. 4 (1980): 350–363. Reprinted in Eqbal Ahmad, *The Selected Writings of Eqbal Ahmad*, 128–141.

——. "Profile of the Religious Right." *Dawn* (Karachi), March 17, 1999.

——. "Proposal to Establish the Khaldunia: A College of the Arts and Sciences in Pakistan. Unpublished paper, March 12, 1992.

——. "Radical, but Wrong." In *Régis Debray and the Latin American Revolution*, edited by Leo Huberman and Paul M. Sweeny, 70–83. New York: Monthly Review Press, 1968. Reprinted in Eqbal Ahmad, *The Selected Writings of Eqbal Ahmad*, 24–35; abridged as "Debray: ABC for Revolution," *Nation*, July–August 1968.

——. "Reason as Spectator." *Dawn* (Karachi), June 11, 1998. Published as "Reason on the Side Lines." *Al-Ahram Weekly* (Cairo), June 6, 1998. Reprinted in Eqbal Ahmad, *Between Past & Future*, 107–111.

——. Review of *India 2020: A New Vision for the New Millennium*, by A. P. J. Abdul Kalam and Y. S. Rajan, *Foreign Policy*, no. 115 (1999): 122–125. http://www.foreignpolicy.com/sumbookpage.htm. Accessed January 22, 2015.

——. "Revolutionary Warfare and Counterinsurgency." *Journal of International Affairs* 25, no. 1 (1970): 1–47. Excerpted as "Counterinsurgency," in Eqbal Ahmad, *The Selected Writings of Eqbal Ahmad*, 36–64.

——. "Revolutionary Warfare: How to Tell When the Rebels Have Won." *Nation*, August 30, 1965. Reprinted in Eqbal Ahmad, *The Selected Writings of Eqbal Ahmad*, 13–23.

——. "Roots of the Religious Right." *Dawn* (Karachi), January 24, 1999. Reprinted in Eqbal Ahmad, *Between Past & Future*, 281–285, and *The Selected Writings of Eqbal Ahmad*, 179–190.

——. "Security." In *Draft Report: Federal & Sovereign: A Policy Framework for the Economic Development of Pakistan*, 49–69. Lahore: Independent Planning Commission of Pakistan, 1985.

——. *The Selected Writings of Eqbal Ahmad*. Edited by Carollee Bengelsdorf, Margaret Cerillo, and Yogesh Chandrani. New York: Columbia University Press, 2006.

——. "Shotgun Governance." *Dawn* (Karachi), March 21, 1999. Reprinted in Eqbal Ahmad, *The Selected Writings of Eqbal Ahmad*, 563–566.

——. "The Taliban's Unlikely Story." *Al-Ahram Weekly* (Cairo), October 17, 1996.

——. "Terrorism: Theirs and Ours." In Eqbal Ahmad, *The Selected Writings of Eqbal Ahmad*, 257–266.

——. *Terrorism: Theirs and Ours.* Foreword and interview by David Barsamian. Open Media Pamphlet Series. New York: Seven Stories Press, 2001.

——. *Testing the Limits: Pakistan, Following India into the Pit* [brochure]. Amsterdam: Transnational Institute; Washington, D.C.: Institute of Policy Studies, August 1998.

———. "Trade Unionism in the Maghreb." In *State and Society in Independent North Africa*, edited by Leon Carl Brown, 146–191. Washington, D.C.: Middle East Institute, 1964.

———. "The Tunisian Trade Union Movement." Ph.D. diss., Princeton University, 1965.

———. "Welcome War in Bosnia." *Dawn* (Karachi), 1994 (specific date unknown). Reprinted in Eqbal Ahmad, *The Selected Writings of Eqbal Ahmad*, 271–273.

———. "When Mountains Die." *Dawn* (Karachi), June 4, 1998. Reprinted in Eqbal Ahmad, *The Selected Writings of Eqbal Ahmad*, 543–547.

———. "'A World Restored' Revisited: American Diplomacy in the Middle East." *Race & Class* 17, no. 3 (1976): 223–252. Reprinted in Eqbal Ahmad, *The Selected Writings of Eqbal Ahmad*, 318–349.

———. "Yet Again, a New Nixon." *Dawn* (Karachi), May 7, 1994. Reprinted in Eqbal Ahmad, *The Selected Writings of Eqbal Ahmad*, 228–231.

Ahmad, Eqbal, and Ibrahim Abu-Lughod, eds. "The Invasion of Lebanon." Special double issue, *Race & Class* 24, no. 4 (1983).

Ahmad, Eqbal, and Richard J. Barnet. "A Reporter at Large: Bloody Games." *New Yorker*, April 11, 1988. Reprinted as "Bloody Games," in Eqbal Ahmad, *Between Past & Future*, 153–194, and *The Selected Writings of Eqbal Ahmad*, 453–492.

Ahmad, Eqbal, and David Barsamian. "Distorted Histories." *HIMĀL South Asian* 12, no. 3 (1999): 12–29.

Ahmad, Eqbal, Richard Bulliet, Irene Gendzier, Don Peretz, George Saliba, and Stuart Schaar. "Bona Fide Archives of Palestinian History" [letter to the editor]. *New York Times*, March 16, 1983.

Ahmad, Eqbal, Edmund Burke III, Irene Gendzier, Clement Henry, Stuart Schaar, and John Waterbury. "Carter's Wrong Prescription for the Western Saharan War" [letter to the editor]. *New York Times*, November 3, 1979.

Ahmad, Eqbal, and David Caploe. "The Logic of Military Intervention." *Race & Class* 17, no. 3 (1976): 319–332.

Ahmad, Eqbal, and Stuart Schaar. "Human Rights in Morocco and Tunisia: A Critique of State Department Findings." *MERIP Reports*, no. 67 (1978): 15–17. Reprinted in *Congressional Record* H2514–15 and H2518–19 (April 5, 1978).

———. "M'hamed Ali et les fondements du Mouvement syndical tunisien." In *Les Africains*, vol. 11, edited by Charles-André Julien, 13–46. Paris: Editions Jeune Afrique, 1978. Also published as "M'hamed Ali and the Tunisian Labor Movement," *Race & Class* 19, no. 3 (1978): 253–276, and "M'hammad Ali: Tunisian Labor Organizer," in *Struggle and Survival in the Modern Middle East*, 2nd ed., edited by Edmund Burke III and David Yaghoubian, 264–277. Berkeley: University of California Press, 2005.

———. "Tahar Haddad: A Tunisian Activist Intellectual." *Maghreb Review* 21, nos. 3–4 (1996): 240–255.

———. "Tension in Tunisia" [op-ed]. *New York Times*, February 13, 1978.

Ahmad, Eqbal, and Nassim Zehra. "Pakistan After Zia." In "The Middle East After Reagan," special issue, *Middle East Report* 155 (1988): 31–32.

Ahmed, Khaled. "Obituary: An Intellectual Unintimidated by Power or Authority." *HIMĀL South Asian*, June 1999. http://old.himalmag.com/component/content/article/2258-Eqbal-Ahmad.html. Accessed January 23, 2015.

Alam, M. Shahid. "U.S. Imperialism and the Third World." Review of *The Selected Writings of Eqbal Ahmad*, by Eqbal Ahmad. *Monthly Review* 58, no. 8 (2007): 55–62.

Amir, Maria. "In US-Pakistan Relations Stability Means Obedience: Chomsky." *Express Tribune* (Karachi), May 26, 2011.

Anderson, Jack. "The Berrigan Fiasco." *New York Post*, June 21, 1972.

Aslam, Abid. "Politics: Memories of Eqbal Ahmad, Hopeful Prankster." IPS-Inter Press Service, May 18, 1999.

Baghdadi, Ali. "A Talk with Eqbal Ahmad." *Muhammad Speaks*, February 19, 1971.

Baldwin, James. "Stranger in the Village." *Harper's Magazine*, October 1953.

Barsamian, David. *Eqbal Ahmad, Confronting Empire: Interviews with David Barsamian.* Cambridge, Mass.: South End Press, 2000.

———. "Interview & Tribute." *Massachusetts Review* 41, no. 4 (2000–2001): 449–464.

Berger, Dan. *Outlaws of America: The Weather Underground and the Politics of Solidarity.* Oakland, Calif.: AK Press, 2005.

Berger, John. *Photocopies: Encounters.* New York: Vintage, 1998.

Berrigan, Daniel. *Writings.* Modern Spiritual Masters. Maryknoll, N.Y.: Orbis Books, 2009.

Berrigan, Daniel, David McReynolds, Eqbal Ahmad, Eric Bentley, George Novak, Jules Feiffer, and Kate Millett. "Release Dzhemilev" [letter to the editor]. *New York Review of Books*, May 17, 1979. http://www.nybooks.com/articles/7795. Accessed January 23, 2015.

Berrigan, Phil. "Phil Berrigan on Trial." *Win* (Rifton, N.Y.), March 15, 1973, 32–41.

Bidwai, Praful. "Afghanistan-Pakistan: Taliban Gives Neighbors the Jitters." IPS-Inter Press Service, November 17, 1995.

Bigart, Homer. "Berrigan Case a Mistrial on Main Plotting Charges." *New York Times*, April 6, 1972.

———. "Berrigan Case: A Strategy That Backfired." *New York Times*, April 9, 1972.

———. "Berrigan Defense Calls No Witnesses and Rests Its Case." *New York Times*, March 25, 1972.

———. "Berrigan Trial Witness Says He Weighed Informer Career." *New York Times*, March 9, 1972.

———. "F.B.I. Informer Says Pakistani Plotted Kidnapping of Kissinger." *New York Times*, March 16, 1972.

———. "Informer Says Berrigan Told of Entering Tunnels." *New York Times*, February 29, 1972.

———. "Prosecutor Lauds Berrigan Informer." *New York Times*, March 17, 1972.

———. "Tunnels' Destruction Is Topic of Purported Berrigan Letter." *New York Times*, March 2, 1972.

———. "Two Quote Priest on Tunnel System." *New York Times*, March 21, 1972.

Bloom, Joshua, and Waldo F. Martin Jr. *Black Against Empire: The History and Politics of the Black Panther Party*. Berkeley: University of California Press, 2013.

Brooks, Geraldine. "Bookshelf: Stories of Suffering in Saddam's Iraq." *Wall Street Journal*, April 7, 1993.

Brown, Judith M. "The Making of a Critical Outsider." In Judith M. Brown and Martin Prozesky, *Gandhi and South Africa: Principles and Politics*, 21–33. New York: St. Martin's Press, 1996.

Camus, Albert. *The Outsider*. Translated by Stuart Gilbert. New York: Knopf, 1970.

Cargas, Harry J. "Sister Elizabeth McAlister: An Interview." *Commonweal*, October 13, 1971.

Chaudhury, P. C. Roy. *Gandhi and His Contemporaries*. New Delhi: Sterling, 1972.

Chomsky, Noam. "Thoughts of a Secular Sufi." N.d. http://www.chomsky.info/articles/2000----.htm. Accessed November 7, 2014.

Choudhary, Radhakrishna. *History of Bihar*. Patna, India: Motilalall Bandarsidass, 1958.

Collett, Pamela. "A New University for Pakistan: Institution's Organizers Seek to Break from a Long Tradition of Colonial Education." *Chronicle of Higher Education*, April 27, 1994.

Crone, Patricia. *Meccan Trade and the Rise of Islam*. Princeton, N.J.: Princeton University Press, 1987.

Crone, Patricia, and Michael A. Cook. *Hagarism, the Making of the Islamic World*. Cambridge: Cambridge University Press, 1971.

Datta, K. K. *History of the Freedom Movement in Bihar*. 3 vols. Patna, India: Government of Bihar, 1958.

De Benedetti, Charles. *An American Ordeal: The Antiwar Movement of the Vietnam War*. Syracuse, N.Y.: Syracuse University Press, 1990.

Debray, Régis. *Revolution in the Revolution.* Translated by Bobbye Ortiz. New ed. 1967. New York: Grove Press, 2000.

Diamond, Julie. *Kindergarten: A Teacher, Her Students, and a Year of Learning.* Foreword by Jules Pfeiffer. New York: New Press, 2011.

Dryland, Estelle. *Faiz Ahmad Faiz: Urdu Poet of Social Realism.* Lahore: Vanguard Books, 1993.

Ellsberg, Daniel. *Papers on the War.* New York: Simon and Schuster, 1972.

"Eqbal Ahmad" [obituary]. *Times* (London), June 25, 1999.

"Eqbal Ahmad, Historian and Rebel, Died on May 11th, Aged 67." *Economist*, May 29, 1999.

"Eqbal Ahmad, India, Pakistan, Bosnia, etc.: Interviewed by David Barsamian." August 4, 1993. http://www.geocities.com/CollegePark/Library/9803/eqbal _ahmad/Barsamwint.hmtl. Accessed October 4, 2004, but no longer available.

Erick-Wanzer, Daniel, ed. *The Young Lords: A Reader.* New York: New York University Press, 2010.

Erikson, Erik H. *Gandhi's Truth: On the Origins of Militant Nonviolence.* New York: Norton, 1969.

Faiz, Ahmad Faiz. "Dawn of Freedom." Translated by Agha Shahid Ali. In David Barsamian, *Eqbal Ahmad, Confronting Empire: Interviews with David Barsamian*, viii–ix. Cambridge, Mass.: South End Press, 2000.

Faiz, Ahmed Faiz, and Naomi Lazard. *The True Subject: Selected Poems of Faiz Ahmed Faiz.* Princeton, N.J.: Princeton University Press, 1988.

Fanon, Frantz. *Sociologie d'une révolution: L'an V de la Révolution algérienne.* Paris: Maspero, 1959. Translated as *A Dying Colonialism.* New York: Grove Press, 1959.

"54 Eminent Men for VP-Benazir Meet." *Indian Express* (New Dehli), June 27, 1990.

Findley, Paul. *They Dare to Speak Out: People and Institutions Confront Israel's Lobby.* Westport, Conn.: Hill, 1985.

Fischer, Louis. *The Life of Mahatma Gandhi.* New York: Harper, 1950.

FitzGerald, Frances. *Fire in the Lake: The Vietnamese and the Americans in Vietnam.* New York: Random House, 1972.

Forest, Jim. "Harrisburg Conspiracy: The Berrigans and the Catholic Left." *Win* (Rifton, N.Y.), March 15, 1973, 5–31.

Gandhi, Mahatma. *The Mahatma and the Poet: Letters and Debates Between Gandhi and Tagore, 1915–1941.* Compiled and edited with an introduction by Sabyasachī Bhattacharya. New Delhi: National Book Trust, 1997.

Ganguly, Šumit. *The Crisis in Kashmir: Portents of War, Hopes of Peace.* Woodrow Wilson Center Series. New York: Cambridge University Press, 1997.

Gellner, Ernest. "The Mightier Pen? Edward Said and the Double Standards of Inside-Out Colonialism." In "The Bogy of Orientalism," special issue, *Times Literary Supplement*, February 19, 1993.

——. *Words and Things: A Critical Account of Linguistic Philosophy and a Study in Ideology*. London: Gallancz, 1959.

Gellner, Sarah. "Letter: Memories of Ernest Gellner." *London Review of Books*, August 25, 2011. http://www.lrb.co.uk/v33/n16//letters. Accessed January 22, 2015.

Gettleman, Marvin E., and Stuart Schaar, eds. *The Middle East and Islamic World Reader*. 3rd ed. New York: Grove Press, 2012.

Gordon, Leonard A. *Brothers Against the Raj: A Biography of Indian Nationalists Surat and Subhas Chandra Bose*. New York: Columbia University Press, 1990.

Gupta, Sisir. *Kashmir: A Study in India-Pakistan Relations*. Bombay: Asia Publishing House, 1966.

al-Hadâd, Tâhir [Tahar Haddad]. *Imra' atunâ fi al-sharî'ah wa a mujtama'* (Our women in Islamic law and society). Tunis: Artistic Printers, 1930. Reprint, Tunis: Maison Tunisienne de l'Edition, 1978. Partially translated into French by M. Mutafarrij in *Revue des Etudes Islamiques* 3 (1935): 201–230. Completely but less adequately translated as *Notre femme, la législation islamique et la société*. Tunis: Maison Tunisienne d'Edition, 1978.

——. *Al-'ummal al-tûnisîyûn wa dhuhûr al-harakah al niqâbîya* (The Tunisian workers and the birth of the trade union movement). Tunis: Arab Printers, 1927. Translated as *Les travailleurs tunisiens et l'émergence du mouvement syndical*, translated by Abderrazak Halioui. Tunis: Maison Arabe du Livre, 1985.

Hall, John A. *Ernest Gellner: An Intellectual Biography*. London: Verso, 2012.

Hamid, Agha Imran. "The Amazing Eqbal Ahmad." *Friday Times* (Lahore), May 20, 2000.

Hassan, Mubashir. "India-Pakistan: 'Walls Must Come Down': Nikhil Chakravartty and the Growing Momentum of Peace." *Mainstream* (New Delhi), November 22, 2003, 7–15.

——. "On a New Vision for South Asia." In *Perspectives on South Asia*, edited by V. A. Pai Ppanandiker and Navnita Chadha Behara, 3–11. New Delhi: Konark, 2000.

Hayden, Tom, ed. *Radical Nomad: C. Wright Mills and His Times*. Boulder, Colo.: Paradigm, 2006.

Hoodbhoy, Pervez. "Eqbal Ahmad: Post-Pokhran Days." *Chowk*, May 11, 2000. http://www.chowk.com/show_article.cgi?aid=00000768&channel=covic %20center&start=0&end=9&chapte . . . . Accessed October 4, 2004, but no longer available.

———. Foreword to Eqbal Ahmad, *Between Past & Present: Selected Essays on South Asia*, edited by Dohra Ahmad, Iftikhar Ahmad, and Zia Mian, vii–xxv. Karachi: Oxford University Press, 2004.

HTC. "70 Prominent Citizens Appeal to India, Pakistan Govts." *Hindustan Times* (New Delhi), December 20, 1998.

Huntington, Samuel P. *The Clash of Civilizations and the Remaking of World Order.* New York: Touchstone, 1996.

Husain, Imdad. *An Interpretation to the Poetry of Faiz Ahmed Faiz.* Lahore: Vanguard Books, 1989.

Hussain, Syed Talat. "Helping Education the Wrong Way." *News* (Islamabad), August 7, 1994.

Iqbal, Jonaid. "Islamabad: Tribute Paid to Eqbal Ahmad." *Dawn* (Karachi), September 19, 2004.

Jackson, Justin. "Kissinger's Kidnapper: Eqbal Ahmad, the U.S. New Left, and the Transnational Romance of Revolutionary War." *Journal for the Study of Radicalism* 4, no. 1 (2010): 75–120.

Jeannot, Thomas. "Berrigan Underground." In *Faith, Resistance, and the Future: Daniel Berrigan's Challenge to Catholic Social Thought*, edited by James L. Marsh and Anna J. Brown, 155–182. New York: Fordham University Press, 2012.

Jezer, Marty. *The Power of the People*: *Active Nonviolence in the U.S.* Edited by Robert Cooney and Helen Michalawski. Philadelphia: New Society, 1987.

JL [Jean Lacouture]. "La Mort de Roger Le Tourneau: L'homme tranquille de l'islamologie française." *Le Monde* (Paris), April 10, 1971.

Kahin, George McT. *Intervention: How America Became Involved in Vietnam.* New York: Knopf, 1986.

Kahin, George McT., and John W. Lewis. *The United States in Vietnam.* New York: Dial Press, 1967.

Kennedy, Sheila. "Witness." *Sheila Kennedy Thinking About Liberty*, May 11, 2005. http://sheilakennedy.net/content/view/654/50/.

Al-Khalil, Samir [Kanan Makiya]. *The Republic of Fear: The Inside Story of Saddam's Iraq.* New York: Pantheon, 1990.

KM. "External Affairs, Defense: A Policy That Fails Every Test." *Viewpoint*, November 21, 1985.

Kothari, Smithu, Zia Mian, Kamla Bhasla, and A. H. Nayyar. *Bridging Partition: People's Initiatives for Peace Between India and Pakistan.* Hyderabad: Orient Black Swan, 2010.

Kumar, Amitava. "On Eqbal Ahmad." *Nation*, November 27, 2006. http://www.amiutavakumar.com/?page_id=29. Accessed January 22, 2105.

Kumar, Radha, *Divide and Fall? Bosnia in the Annals of Partition*. London: Verso, 1997.

———. *The History of Doing: An Illustrated Account of Movements for Women's Rights and Feminism in India, 1800–1900*. 2nd ed. New Delhi: Kali for Women, 2002.

———. "In Memoriam: Eqbal Ahmad 1933–1999." *Seminar: Something Like a War: A Symposium on Low Intensity Conflicts*, no. 479 (1999). http://www.india-seminar .com/1999/479/479%20memoriam.htm. Accessed January 23, 2015.

———. *Making Peace with Pakistan*. New Delhi: Penguin, 2005.

Lamb, Alastair. *Crisis in Kashmir, 1947–1966*. London: Routledge & Kegan Paul, 1966.

Latif, Asad. "A Life That Made a Great History." *Straits Times* (Singapore), July 3, 1999.

Lewis, Bernard. *The Emergence of Modern Turkey*. Oxford: Oxford University Press, 1961.

Lockwood, Lee. "How the 'Kidnap Conspiracy' Was Hatched." *Life*, May 21, 1971.

"The Loss of a Friend" [editorial]. *Al-Ahram Weekly* (Cairo), May 13–19, 1999.

Lydon, Christopher. "He Got It Wrong, Alas: Kanan Makiya." *Open Source Radio* 69 (November 7, 2007). http://he-got-itg-Wrong-alas;Kanan Makiya//radioo penaource.org/vol.69. Accessed January 22, 2015.

Mackenzie, John. "Edward Said and the Historians." *Nineteenth Century Contexts* 18, no. 1 (1994): 9–28.

Makiya, Kanan. *Cruelty and Silence: War, Tyranny, Uprising, and the Arab World*. New York: Norton, 1993.

Massing, Michael. "Book Review: *Cruelty and Silence*." *New Yorker*, April 26, 1993.

McAuliffe, Michael. "US Policy Blamed for 'Genocide.'" *Sunday Republican Hampshire* (Amherst, Mass.), December 4, 1994.

Medsger, Betty. *The Burglary: The Discovery of J. Edgar Hoover's Secret FBI*. New York: Knopf, 2014.

Mestiri, Ahmed. *Temoignage pour l'histoire*. Tunis: Sud Editions, 2011.

Mian, Zia. "Recent Nonfiction. Striking Back at Empire: The Steady Resistance of Noam Chomsky and Eqbal Ahmad." *Peace Work* (American Friends Service Committee), July–August 2000. http://www.peaceworkmagazine.org/pwork /0700/072k05.htm.

Ministry of External Affairs, Government of India. "Documents: Simla Agreement." July 2, 1972. http://mea.gov.in/in-focus-article.htm?19005/Simla+Agreement +July+2+1972. Accessed November 20, 2004.

Montagne, Robert. *Les Berbères et le Makhzen dans le sud du Maroc.* Paris: Félix Alcan, 1930.

——. *Naissance du prolétariat marocain, enquête collective exécutée de 1948 à 1950.* Paris: Peyonnet, 1952.

Moore, Clement Henry. *Tunisia Since Independence: The Dynamics of a One-Party Government.* Berkeley: University of California Press, 1965. Reprint, Westport, Conn.: Greenwood Press, 1982.

Moussaoui, Abderrahmane. *De la violence en Algérie: Les lois du chaos.* Arles, France: Actes Sud and MMSH, 2006

Naeem, Raza. "Remembering Eqbal" [letter to the editor]. *Al-Ahram Weekly* (Cairo), May 16–22, 2002.

Nandy, Ashis. "The Itinerant Intellectual." *HIMĀL South Asian* 12, no. 6 (1999): 45.

Nazareth, H. O., prod. *Stories My Country Told Me: The Meaning of Nationhood.* Bremerton, Wash.: Penumbra Productions for the BBC Arena, 1996.

Nelson, Jack. *The FBI and the Berrigans: The Making of a Conspiracy.* New York: Coward, McCann & Geoghegan, 1972.

Nimbran, Amrik Singh. *Poverty, Land, and Violence: An Analytical Study of Nationalism in Bihar.* Patna, India: Layman's Publication, 1992.

Oppetit, Dennis. "Roger Le Tourneau (1907–1971): Un intellectuel français et le Maghreb." *Correspondances, Institut de Recherche sur le Maghreb Contemporain,* no. 51 (1998): 9–16.

O'Rourke, William. *The Harrisburg 7 and the New Catholic Left.* New York: Cromwell, 1972.

Osmani, Nisar. "Pakistan Group Discusses Kashmir with Indian Intellectuals." *Dawn* (Karachi), June 5, 1990.

"Peace Train: Nearly Forty Years After Its Founding a Radical Catholic Commune Finds New Allies." *Baltimore Magazine,* March 2012. http://www.baltimore magazine.net/peole/2012/03/peacetrain.

"People Asked to Forge India, Pak Ties." *Hindu* (Chennai, India), December 27, 1998.

Pfeffer, Richard M., ed. *No More Vietnams: The War and the Future of American Foreign Policy.* New York: Harper & Row, 1968.

"Public Opinion Leaders Call for Peace." *Dawn* (Karachi), June 27, 1990.

Qazi, Ashraf Jehangir. "Eqbal Ahmad—a Writer with Deep Insight." *Dawn* (Karachi), May 12, 1999.

Quiros de Quetzalcoatl, Juan Jose Chacon. "Professor Sees Little Peace Movement." *Massachusetts Daily Collegian* (Amherst), December 5, 1994.

Quraishi, Emran. "Ahmad, Eqbal." In *The Oxford Encyclopedia of the Islamic World*, edited by John L. Esposito. Oxford Islamic Studies. Oxford: Oxford University Press, 2009. http://www.oxfordislamicstudies.com/article/opr/t236 /e0990. Accessed January 23, 2015.

Rahman, Tariq. "Book Review: The Legacy of an Intellectual." *Daily Times* (Lahore), August 23, 2004.

Raines, John C., ed. *Conspiracy: The Implications of the Harrisburg Trial for the Democratic Tradition*. New York: Harper & Row, 1974.

Rashid, Abbas. "Eqbal Ahmad: A Voice of Conscience." *Daily Times* (Lahore), October 4, 2004. http://www.dailytimes.com/pk/default.asp?page-story_17-7 -2004_pg3_2.

Raza, S. Abbas. "Monday Musing: Eqbal Ahmad." *3 Quarks Daily*, August 21, 2008. http://3quarksdaily.blogs.com/3quarksdaily/2006/08/monday_musing. Accessed July 24, 2013.

Rosenbaum, David E. "Senate Panel Concludes Inquiry Into Amnesty for Draft Evaders." *New York Times*, March 3, 1972.

Rudolph, Lloyd, and Susanne H. Rudolph. *The Modernity of Tradition: Political Development of India*. Chicago: University of Chicago Press, 1967.

Russell, Ralph, ed. *The Oxford India Ghalib: Life, Letters, and Ghazals*. New Delhi: Oxford University Press, 2003.

Safi, Omid, ed. *Progressive Muslims: On Justice, Gender, and Pluralism*. Oxford: One World, 2003.

Said, Edward. *Culture and Imperialism*. London: Chatto and Windus, 1993. Reprint, New York: Vintage, 1994.

——. "Eqbal Ahmad; He Brought Wisdom and Integrity to the Cause of Oppressed Peoples." *Guardian* (London), May 14, 1999.

——. "Foreword: Cherish the Man's Courage." In David Barsamian, *Eqbal Ahmad, Confronting Empire: Interviews with David Barsamian*, xix–xxxv. Cambridge, Mass.: South End Press, 2000.

——. Interviewed by Nabeel Abraham. *Lies of Our Times* (*LOOT*), May 1993, 13.

——. *Out of Place: A Memoir*. New York: Knopf, 1999.

——. *The Question of Palestine*. New York: Vintage, 1979.

Said, Edward W., Eqbal Ahmad, George Wald, Marcus G. Raskin, Ramsey Clark, and Richard A. Falk. "The Case of Raza Kazim" [letter to the editor]. *New York Review of Books*, May 31, 1984. http://www.nybooks.com/articles/5824. Accessed January 23, 2015.

Said, Edward W., Aga Shahid Ali, Ibrahim Abu Lughod, Akeel Bilgrami, and Eqbal Ahmad. " 'The Satanic Verses' " [letter to the editor]. *New York Review of Books*,

March 16, 1989. http://www.nybooks.com/articles/archives/1989/mar/16/the-satanic-verses/. Accessed January 22, 2015.

Sarwar, Beena. "Afghanistan: Pakistan Caught in Afghan Vortex." IPS-Inter Press Service, September 19, 1995.

Schaar, Stuart. "Ahmad Eqbal et son époque: Le récit d'une vie." *Naqd*, nos. 14–15 (2001): 67–93.

——. "Irangate: The Middle East Connections." In *The United States and the Middle East: A Search for New Perspectives*, edited by Hooshang Amirahmadi, 177–210. Albany: State University of New York Press, 1993.

——. "Orientalism at the Service of Imperialism." In *Orientalism: A Reader*, edited by A. L. Macfie, 181–193. New York: New York University Press.

——. "Teaching Global Justice" [review of *The Selected Writings of Eqbal Ahmad*, edited by Carollee Bengelsdorf, Margaret Cerullo, and Yogaish Chandrani]. *Journal of Palestine Studies* 37, no. 1 (2007): 115–116.

Schechtman, Joseph B. "Evacuee Property in India and Pakistan." In *50 Years of Indo-Pakistani Relations*, vol. 1, edited by Verinder Groever and Ranjara Arora, 102–161. New Delhi: Deep and Deep, 1955.

Sethi, Najam. "Chomsky's Relevance" [editorial]. *Friday Times* (Islamabad), November 30, 2001.

Simmel, George. "The Stranger." In *Social Theory: The Multicultural and Classic Readings*, edited by Charles C. Lemert, 139–141. Boulder, Colo.: Westview Press, 1993.

Singh, Tarlochan. *Land Resettlement Manual*. http://www.Punjabrevenue.nc.in/manuel.htm. Accessed February 24, 2014.

Small, Helen. *The Public Intellectual*. Oxford: Blackwell, 2002.

Spivak, Lawrence E. "Transcript of Interview with the Reverend Daniel J. Berrigan." *Meet the Press* 16, no. 9 (1972): 1–10.

"UN Secretary-General Says Restoring Global Culture of Knowledge Must Be UN Priority in Next Century." First Eqbal Ahmad Lecture at Hampshire College, Amherst, Mass. M2 Presswire, September 17, 1998.

Varma, Paan K. *Ghalib: The Man, the Times*. New Delhi: Penguin, 1989.

"War in Kargil, Peace in Lahore" [editorial]. *Hindu* (Chennai, India), June 3, 1999.

Watt, Montgomery. *Muhammad at Mecca*. Oxford: Oxford University Press, 1953.

——. *Muhammad at Medina*. 1953. Reprint. Oxford: Oxford University Press, 1956.

"Weak Pak Leaders Using Islam." *Hindustan Times* (New Delhi), December 29, 1998.

Will, Herman. *A Will for Peace: Peace Action in the United Methodist Church: A History.* Washington, D.C.: General Board of Church & Society of the United Methodist Church, 1984.

Wills, Garry. "Love on Trial: The Berrigan Case Reconsidered." *Harper's,* July 1972.

——. "A Revolution in the Church." *Playboy,* November 1971.

Wilson, Colin. *The Outsider.* Boston: Houghton Mifflin, 1956.

Wright, Richard. *The Outsider.* New York: Harper, 1953.

Yacoobali, Vazira Fazila. "In Retrospect: Edward Said and Eqbal Ahmad: Anti-imperialist Struggles in a Post-colonial World." *ISIM Newsletter* 13 (2003): 36–37.

Yacoubi, Youssef. "Edward Said, Eqbal Ahmad, and Salman Rushdie: Resisting the Ambivalence of Postcolonial Theory." *Alif: Journal of Comparative Poetics,* January 1, 2005, 193–213.

Yasin, Muhammad. "A Democrat to Be Remembered." *Dawn* (Karachi), May 21, 1999.

Zeddour, Ibrahim. "Hommage Ahmad Eqbal . . . L'ami de l'humanité." *La Nouvelle République* (Algiers), August 6, 2006.

Zinn, Howard. *A People's History of the United States, 1492–Present.* Rev. and updated ed. New York: Harper Perennial, 1995.

INDEX

Ahmad, Eqbal (*continued*)
childhood and upbringing of,
10–12, 25–32, 105–106, figure 2;
citizenship of, 126, 180n.7;
commencement speech given by, 74;
conformity avoided by, 44;
dependents of, 60; deportation of,
threatened, 53; discouraged with
U.S., 54–55; driving ability of,
63–64; education of, 30–31, 35,
37–47, 167n.27, 28, figure 3 (*see also*
Tunisia); ideals and beliefs of, 11–12
(*see also* anti–Vietnam War
movement; nonviolent resistance);
illness and death of, 65, 156–158,
185n.11; influence of, on students,
62–64, 74–75; intellectual gifts of, 1,
11, 27, 37, 44–45, 67, 73–74, 102–103,
152 (*see also* Ahmad, Eqbal: teaching
positions and skills of); lecturing by,
61; loyalty of, 73, 152; and morality,
63, 74, 140; in New York City, 44,
60–62, 71; nonviolent resistance
espoused by, 6, 9–11, 16; in North
Africa (*see* Algeria; Tunisia); outsider
status of, 8–9, 11, 68, 70, 75, 101,
126–127, 161n.12; and Pakistan
(*see* Pakistan); and Palestinian cause
(*see* Palestinians); parents of
(*see* Khartoon; al-Rahman, Atta);
and partition of India, 34–35 (*see also*
partition); polemics of, 81–92
(*see also specific individuals*); politics
of, 110–111, 137–139 (*see also* Ahmad,
Eqbal: activism by; anti–Vietnam
War movement; partition);
reflections on own life, 56, 153–154;

remembrance of life of, 72; roots of,
in Muslim culture, 95, 100, 158,
185n.13; salons of, 45, 55, 62; siblings
of (*see* Ahmad, Ghaffar; Ahmad,
Zafar; Khanum, Sharfa Jahani);
social and speaking skills of, 10–11,
38–39, 62, 67, 131, 139–140; teaching
positions and skills of, 5, 52–53, 56,
60, 61–65, 74–75, 160n.8; university
project of, 65, 75–77, 94–95, 151, 157,
161n.12; unpredictability of, 67;
and war in Kashmir, 35–37;
wide-ranging contacts of, 7–8
(*see also specific individuals*); writing
of, 1, 8, 50, 61, 74, 152–153 (*see also*
specific works, periodicals, and topics).
See also *specific friends, colleagues,
and topics*

ACTIVISM BY: antinuclear activities, 65,
133–137; Daniel Berrigan hidden,
15–16, 99, 150–151, 163n.34;
Indian-Pakistani citizen exchanges,
127–133, 135, 140; at Princeton
University, 43. See also anti–Vietnam
War movement; Harrisburg 7

INFLUENCES ON: brother (Zafar), 12,
32, 37; former opium addict, 34–35;
Gandhi, 11; Greenwich Village and
counterculture, 44; Le Tourneau,
46–47; Marxism, 39–40; mother, 11,
12, 29, 32–33; Princeton graduate
studies, 12, 42, 44–45, 46; Tagore, 9,
11–12, 106–108; Tunisian trade union
movement, 47–49

PREDICTIONS BY: Arab Spring, 6–7, 97;
basis for, 102–103; chaos following
overthrow of Saddam Hussein, 1–2;

post-revolutionary Iran, 5; rise of
jihadist terrorism, 2–5; rise of radical
Muslim movements, 59–60
Ahmad, Ghaffar (brother of Eqbal),
30, 60
Ahmad, Husnara (wife of Ghaffar),
xi–xii, 31
Ahmad, Iftikhar (nephew of Eqbal),
xi, 99
Ahmad, Nasir, xi
Ahmad, Saghir (brother of Eqbal), 30,
figure 4
Ahmad, Zafar (brother of Eqbal), 5, 12,
30–35, 37
Ahmad, Zulfikar (nephew of Eqbal), xi,
107
Algeria: after independence, 77–79,
86–87; and Fanon, 82–83, 86; and Le
Tourneau, 46–47; occupation of, by
France, 46; radical Muslim
movement in, 59; revolution in,
46–47, 49, 82–83, 101–102, 104,
171n.14
Ali, Agha Ashraf, 153
Ali, Agha Shahid, 153
Ali, Kamran Asdar, xii
Alliston, Sue, 50
American Left, 56, 57–58. *See also*
anti–Vietnam War movement
anti–Vietnam War movement: Ahmad
and organization of, 50; Ahmad's
criticism of, 56; Daniel Berrigan
hidden, 15–16, 99, 150–151, 163n.34;
demise of, 61; and draft board office
raids, 13, 15–20; and FBI offices
broken into, 163n.36; and Harrisburg
7, 14–15, 17–20 (*see also* Harrisburg

7); and Tougaloo College teach-in,
53–54; war possibly shortened
by, 150
Arab-Israeli conflict, 53, 69, 113–120.
See also Israel; Palestinians
Arab Spring, 6–7, 97
Arab world, Western myths/anxieties
about, 69–70
Arafat, Yasser, 5–6, 116, 117, 119. *See
also* Palestine Liberation
Organization
Atatürk (Mustapha Kemal), 94
Ayub Khan, Mohammad, 51, 54

Bangladesh, 124, 184n.6
Barnet, Richard J., 55, 59
Barsamian, David, interviews with
Ahmad: on Ahmad's health, 184n.6;
on Ahmad's politics, 110–111; on
Bosnian crisis, 57; on Faiz, 83; on
Gramsci, 40; on large-scale Arab
uprising, 6–7; on Middle East as
point of convergence, 113–114; on
nuclear weapons, 133–134; on
pathology of power, 108–109; on
Tagore, 106
Ben Badis, Abdelhamid, 86
Ben Bella, Ahmed, 78, 87
Bengelsdorf, Carollee, 62–63
Ben Seddik, Mahjoub, 48
Bernstein, Leonard, 22
Berrigan, Daniel, 15–16, 22, 99,
150–151, 163nn.33, 34, 164n.46.
See also Harrisburg 7
Berrigan, Frida, 22–23
Berrigan, Phillip, 13–21, 162n.28,
165n.59. *See also* Harrisburg 7

Henry, Clement, 48, 50

Hezbollah, 120–121

Hochschild, Adam, xii

Hochschild, Arlie Russell, xii, 26, 50

Hochschild, David, 41

Hoodbhoy, Pervez (nephew of Eqbal), 133–136, 153, 157–158, 185n.13

Hooper, Niels, xii

Hoover, J. Edgar, 15–18, 20

hospitality, Arab concept of, 65

Hourani, Cecil, 49, 52

Hovsepian, Amal, xii

Hovsepian, Nubar, xii, 177n.18

al-Hurriya (newspaper; PLO), 58

Hussein, Imdad, 50–51

Hussein, Syad Abid, 38–39

Hussein ibn Talal (king of Jordan), 121–122

Ibn Khaldun, Abd al-Rahman, 95

imperialism: Ahmad's and Said's views on, 68, 69–71, 89, 101–102; Ahmad's critique of U.S., 58–59, 147–148 (see also United States); and beginning of decolonization, 115; and former Yugoslav republics, 57–58; and Israel, 115, 119; strong state structures characteristic of, 111; and U.S.–Iran relationship (pre-revolution), 59, 104, 142, 148

India: Ahmad's family and childhood in, 11–12, 25–32, 105–106; Indian-Pakistani citizen exchanges, 127–133, 135, 140; Indian-Pakistani relations, 65, 127–128, 131–132; nationalist movement and independence of, 77, 107, 115; nuclear weapons of,

133–136; partition of, 8, 32–35, 123–126 (see also Pakistan); right-wing religious movement in, 97–98. See also Gandhi, Mohandas; Kashmir; Tagore, Rabindranath

Institute for Policy Studies (IPS), 55, 56. See also Transnational Institute

Iran: influence of, in Iraq, 2; post-revolutionary power structure in, 5; pre-revolution U.S. relationship with, 59, 104, 142, 148; Reagan's policy toward, 143–144; revolutionaries met by peace activists, 5, 160n.7; revolution in, 103–104

"Iran and the West: A Century of Subjugation" (Ahmad), 103

Iraq: Ahmad on post-Saddam, 1–2; fundamentalist Islamism in, 2; and Gulf War, 3–4, 88, 120; Makiya's books on, 87 (see also Makiya, Kanan); and Operation Desert Storm, 122; under Saddam Hussein, 108; U.S. invasion of, 1–2, 90–91, 147

Islam: Ahmad rooted in culture of, 95, 100, 158, 185n.13; Crone and Cook on, 172n.13; Pakistan as Muslim state, 111–112; progressive, 94–96, 112; as "religion of the oppressed," 97; sectarian differences in, 120–121, 147; used for political ends, 96, 99–100, 124 (see also United States: and mujahideen in Afghanistan); and women, 96. See also Islamist (radical Muslim) movements

Islamist (radical Muslim) movements: characteristics of, shared with other right-wing religious extremist groups, 97–98; free and fair elections as antidote to, 93–94; and madrassas, 96; political agenda of, 95, 100; as response to crisis of modernity and identity, 97; rise of, 2–5, 59–60, 99–100, 145, 146–147. *See also* jihadist movement; al-Qaeda; Taliban

Israel: Arab-Israeli conflict, 53, 69, 113–120 (*see also* Palestinians); Arab media portrayal of, 68; binational single state suggested for, 114, 118–119; creation of, 115, 119; right-wing religious movement in, 97–98; and U.S. Middle East policy, 58–59, 142

Jahangir, Asma, xii, 129–131, 156
Jerusalem, 115–116
jihad, 4, 5, 60, 97, 100
jihadist movement: in Afghanistan, 2–3, 4–5, 99–100 (*see also* Taliban); outside Afghanistan, 59–60. *See also* Islamist (radical Muslim) movements
Jinnah, Muhammad Ali, 95, 111, 124
Jones, Jim, xi
Jordan, 121–122

Karzai, Hamid (president of Afghanistan), 147, 183n.13
Kashmir, 35–37, 101, 129, 131–132
Kazim, Rashida, 157, 185n.13
Kazim, Raza, xii, 58, 103, 107, 137, 157, 181n.32

Khaldunia University (proposed), 65, 75–77, 94–95, 151, 157, 161n.12
Khan, Shamim Alam, 134
Khanum, Sharfa Jahani (sister of Eqbal), xi, 25, 30, 33, 159n.1
Khartoon (mother of Eqbal), figure 5; and Ahmad's childhood, 11, 12, 26, 27; death of, 33; influence of, on Ahmad, 11, 12, 29, 32–33; politics of, 11, 32–33
Khartoon, Halima (wife of Zafar Ahmad), 31
Khomeini, Ayatollah Ruhollah, 98–99, 103, 143
Kissinger, Henry, 12–13, 17, 141–142. *See also* Harrisburg 7
Kosovo, 58, 72, 98, 123
Kothari, Rajni, 127, 129
Krim, Belkacen, 78–79
Kumar, Amitava, 161n.12
Kumar, Radha (partner of Eqbal), xi, 65, 125–126, 156, 157
Kunstler, William, 21
Kurds, 2

Lebanon, 61, 117–118, 120–121
Leninism, 40, 112
Le Tourneau, Roger, 46–47
Lewis, Bernard, 85
Lockwood, Lee, 163n.34, 164n.46
Lown, Bernard, 153–154, 156, 157
Lyautey, Hubert, 84–85
Lydon, Christopher, 90–91
Lynch, William S., 162n.38

MacReynolds, Dave, 54
madrassas, 96

Occidental College, 41

oil, 58–59

Omar, Najeeb (nephew of Eqbal), xi, 76

Organization of Arab Students, Ahmad's talk before, 69, 117–118

Orientalism (Said), 68, 70. *See also* Said, Edward W.

"Osama bin Ladin Is a Sign of Things to Come" (Ahmad), 6–7

Osmani, Nisar, 129–131

Pakistan: Ahmad and government of, 54, 184n.6; Ahmad's criticism of, 138–139; Ahmad's dissatisfaction with, 156; Ahmad's efforts to start a university in, 65, 75–77, 94–95, 151, 157, 161n.12; Ahmad's return to, 65, 137, 151–152; Ahmad's ties to, as an adult, 60–61, 75–76, 126–127; Ahmad's visit to, 51; Ahmad's young adulthood in, 12, 34–41, 101; Ahmad urged to form/lead party in, 137–138; creation of, 8, 32–33, 34–35, 95–96, 111–112, 123–126; democracy in, 111, 138; Indian-Pakistani citizen exchanges, 127–133, 135, 140; Indian-Pakistani relations, 65, 127–128, 131–132; media freedom in, 126; and mujahideen and Taliban, 60, 145; nuclear weapons of, 133–137; state institutions in, 111, 138; violence in Karachi, 139. *See also* Foreman Christian College; Kashmir

Palestine Liberation Organization (PLO), 6, 69, 116–118. *See also* Palestinians

Palestinians: Ahmad's support for cause of, 5–6, 53, 68–69, 114–117, 160n.8; displacement of, by Jewish immigrants, 119–120; and Jerusalem, 115–116, 178n.4; nonviolent resistance by, urged by Ahmed, 6, 9–10; and Oslo Accords, 114, 119; Said on, 68; tactics of, criticized by Ahmad, 116–119; and U.S. foreign policy, 142; and war in Lebanon, 61, 117–118. *See also* Hezbollah; Israel; Palestine Liberation Organization

partition: Ahmad's views on, 123–125, 126; of India, 8, 32–35, 37–38, 114, 123–126 (*see also* Pakistan)

peace movement, 5, 61, 69, 160n.7. *See also* anti–Vietnam War movement

Perle, Richard, 90

Perrin, Constance, 14

"Portrait of an Arab" (Said), 68

postcolonial theory, Fanon on, 83

power: pathology of, 108–109; personal, 110 (*see also* dictators)

Princeton University, 12, 42–47, 52, 167n.27, 28

al-Qaeda, 2–5, 147. *See also* bin Ladin, Osama; Islamist (radical Muslim) movements

Question of Palestine, The (Said), 116

Race & Class (journal), 8, 91, 103, 116, 120

radical Muslim movements. *See* Islamist (radical Muslim) movements radical organizations (1960s–1970s), 18–19

al-Rahman, Atta (father of Eqbal), 11, 12, 25–26, 29–30, 33–34, 160n.1

Ramdas, Kavita (niece of Eqbal), xi

Raskin, Marcus, 55

Reagan, Ronald, 143, 146–147

Rehman, I. A., xii, 140

Republic of Fear, The (Makiya, as al-Khalil), 87. *See also* Makiya, Kanan

revolutionary warfare: Ahmad's theory of, 78–79, 82–83, 105, 142–143; Iranian Revolution, 103–104; and PLO, 118 (*see also* Palestine Liberation Organization); Vietnam War, 104–105 (*see also* Vietnam War). *See also* Algeria: revolution in; Iran: revolution in

right-wing religious movements, 97–98, 100. *See also* Islamist (radical Muslim) movements

Riza, Iqbal, xii, 40, 151, 167n.25, 184n.6

Rouleau, Eric, 121

Rubin, Samuel, 55, 61

Runyon, Marie M., 21–22

Rushdie, Salman, 98–99

Russell, Arlie. *See* Hochschild, Arlie Russell

Rutgers University, 56

Saddam Hussein, 1–2, 56, 108

Saghir, Mahdi, xii

Said, Edward W.: on Ahmad as teacher, 56, 62; attacked by Aijaz Ahmad, 91, 174n.29; in Beirut with Ahmad, 5; on borders and partition, 125, 126; and celebration of Ahmad's life, 149, 152;

detractors criticized by, 81; and Gellner, 83–84, 85–86, 172n.6; and Israeli-Palestinian conflict, 116–117, 119; and Makiya, 87–89; New York salons of, 62; on Oslo Accords, 114; on "outsider" status, 8; and Palestinian cause, 69; rancor between Lewis and, 85; relationship of, with Ahmad, 7, 68–73, 91–92; and Rushdie, 99

Sailer, Randolph Clothier, 37–38

Sarah Lawrence College, 56

Sarwar, Beena, 136

Saudi Arabia, 3–4, 59, 108–109

Schaar, Stuart: with Ahmad in India and Pakistan, x, 137; Ahmad's correspondence with, 47, 52–53; concerns of, over Ahmad's health, 153–154; and Gellner, 84; Hampshire College lectures by, 65; and Harrisburg Defense Committee, ix–x, 14–15 (*see also* Harrisburg Defense Committee); and informal Pakistani delegation to India, 130; in North Africa, x, 47–48; at Princeton with Ahmad, 42–47, figure 3; and Rushdie, 99; works coauthored with Ahmad, 49, 50, 152

Schulman, Jay, 162n.27

segregation, 41

Sethi, Najam, xii

Sharif, Nawaz, 96

Shia Islam, 120–121

Simla Agreement, 126. *See also* India: Indian-Pakistani relations

Simmons, Adele Smith, xii, 61, 64, 76, 151

GPSR Authorized Representative: Easy Access System Europe, Mustamäe tee
50, 10621 Tallinn, Estonia, gpsr.requests@easproject.com

www.ingramcontent.com/pod-product-compliance
Lightning Source LLC
Chambersburg PA
CBHW032131020426
42334CB00016B/1124